# The Justice Factory

## "Show me the judge and I'll tell you the law"

*Ian Mitchell*

# Table of Contents

The photograph on the front cover (Ian Mitchell, 2006) shows the procession of the Senators of the College of Justice from the Parliament House to St Giles's Cathedral for the kirking of the court ceremony, which traditionally marks the start of the legal year in September. In the lead is the late Lord Johnston.

*This book is dedicated to my children, Seanaidh,
William and Romy, whose high-spirited
disputatiousness regularly provoked questions
about the rule of law in a domestic setting,
especially when one of them would ask,
"Dad, why do you break your own rules?"*

# Important Note about the Text

Any legal system is a combination of paperwork and people. Most books are about the paperwork: this one is about the people, in particular those at the top of the system, the judges.

Like judges almost everywhere, the Scottish Bench prefers, for very good reasons, to avoid publicity, especially personal publicity. It was therefore hard to get many sheriffs and judges to

**MEMO TO ALL JUDGES**

**MR. IAN MITCHELL, THE JUSTICE FACTORY**

Some, if not all, of you will have received, as I have, a request from an Ian Mitchell for an interview for his above book.

In December 2004 Mr. Mitchell sought the permission of Lord President Cullen to interview a small selection of judges and clerks in Parliament House. After investigation permission was refused. Investigation included a discussion between Elizabeth Cutting and Mr. Mitchell and an enquiry of Bruce McKain, Faculty Officers also having been approached. Both Elizabeth Cutting and Bruce McKain formed the impression that any interviews with judges would be "high risk". Elizabeth also recalls that Mr. Mitchell was unwilling to give to the judges any sight of text prior to publication.

I have myself declined the request for an interview and have advised Mr. Mitchell that while, as is the case, the terms of any response are a matter for individual judges, I have advised my colleagues against co-operating with him.

*acq.*

LORD PRESIDENT
9 October 2006

talk about themselves and their work: impossible in some cases. Perhaps a third of those I approached for interview while preparing this book flatly refused to co-operate. But a surprising number were happy to do so, in most cases because they were concerned that much of the media was painting an inaccurate picture of the Bench as a whole.

The Lord President who wrote the memorandum reproduced on the previous page was Lord Hamilton, the most senior judge in Scotland at the time. He refused to grant me an interview, as did his predecessor, Lord Cullen. So did Lord Gill, the then Lord Justice-Clerk, and current Lord President. Lord Hamilton went further than the others in circulating this memo to his colleagues advising them that, in his view, they should not speak to me. This document was circulated to both serving and retired judges.

When the text was finished, I lent it to several people I knew who could make informed comment. Some of those were judges. The common consensus was that the book would be opposed by the legal establishment because, as one distinguished judge put it to me, "you have lifted the veil, and they don't like that." I take the view that the business of judging, and the corporate character of the Bench, are matters of legitimate public interest in a democracy. However, I am also sensitive to the awkward position which my questioning put some of those who were happy—in some cases positively keen—to talk to me. Many thought there were important issues which needed to be aired, and that a professional view was better than the more amateur one which generally informs (if that is the right word) the media. Therefore I have thought it right to begin with a short description of the way in which this text has been compiled.

Some retired judges were happy to be quoted openly, but I spoke to all the others on the basis that they could not be individually identified from the printed text. For this reason, I have not reproduced the words of any single judge at length. However, everything printed between inverted commas was said to me by one judge or another. They are genuine quotations, but they are very much composites. All extended passages, most paragraphs and many sentences, are made up of the comments of more than one judge. Occasionally I have added a few linking words of my own for the sake of continuity. No single individual, therefore, can be considered to have conducted any particular conversation. Therefore, I hope no-one will try to tie any statement to any judge. More than one of my contacts was female, and I would be surprised if anyone can guess the gender of the talker, from internal evidence, in all but a couple of paragraphs. If even the gender of the talker is uncertain, then anything more definite about his or her identity must surely be speculative.

I liked every one of the judges I met, and do not want to embarrass any of them by inappropriate revelation of their individual views. But at the same time I want this book to be an accurate reflection, not only of the views, but also of their personalities. This can be brought out only by direct quotation. Hence my unconventional technique. This is the first book published in the English-speaking world (as far as I know, anywhere) about the business of judging for which the main sources are the *judges themselves*. It could not have been written any other way. I therefore trust the reader will accept this necessary convention of discretion.

Finally, this text was, in the main, completed four years ago. For commercial reasons, it was not published then. In preparing it for publication now, I decided not to update it (except in detail) since the argument is not one that depends on time or circumstance in any but the most general sense. I trust the reader will make all due allowances for the fact that some references are to people and events no longer as current as they were then, and try to focus on the underlying question, which is how do our judges in Scotland approach their job, and what is the nature of that job, from the widest, international point of view?

Finally, it is worth noting that today this has a wider than purely juridical significance. The Act of Union reserved powers relating to the Church, to education and the law to Scotland. Of these, the Church has lost much of its former influence and practical importance, and education has been considerably anglicised. The only important Scottish institution which has retained much of its own character and self-government since before the Union is the law. In the light of the widespread doubts about Scotland's ability to govern itself if it were to achieve independence it is relevant to ask how well the legal community has done as a largely self-governing institution over the past three centuries. What can we infer about the possible future of the country from the hitherto untold story of the people who sit in the highest courts in the land?

Whether the verdict is positive or negative, I leave to the reader to decide. But I think it can hardly be said that we do not have a lot to learn about ourselves as an autonomous community from the historical record and current status of our judges.


Ian Mitchell
Khimki
Moscow
October 2013

From *Circuit Journeys* by Lord Cockburn,
the diary of a Justiciary Court judge
while on circuit, 1837-1854

"*Arbroath, Friday Night, 22 April 1844:* We left Aberdeen today at eleven and, in spite of many pauses, were here at six.

"We were in Court most part of Tuesday, Wednesday and Thursday. Nothing particular. Bad thefts, and plenty of transportations, but no glorious murder. No earl's son of worth and irregularity, of great courage and beauty, and abominably used by an old hunks of a father or a vindictive step-mother, driven to forgery by the necessity of protecting a clergyman's daughter, whom he had deceived. No theatrical apprentice despising honesty, and delighting the club by his account of cheating his master. None, in short, of the poetry of crime; all prosaic thefts—aggravated by house-breaking, habit and repute, and previous conviction. The truth is that the suppression of the gallows deprives modern Courts of half their charm."

# Introduction

"Show me the judge and I'll tell you the law."

These startling words, which over time gave this book shape and coherence, were spoken almost causally by one of Scotland's best-known advocates, Ian Hamilton QC, while he and I were having a beer one afternoon in a hotel in central Edinburgh. Ian was running through the names of some judges he had appeared in front of over the years and telling me, in surprisingly respectful tones for a famous iconoclast, what he thought of their performance on the Bench, and what sort of people they were off it. In a career spanning half a century, he had known most of them as advocates long before they were made judges. In some cases, he had been at University with them. Today, Ian tells me he doesn't remember saying these words, but I remember, and I have the notes (contemporaneous of course!) to prove it. But it does not really matter who first enunciated what I have chosen to call Hamilton's Rule, because the point is, I shall argue below, universal.

But just because it is universal, that does not mean it is not controversial. Recently a Russian thinking of emigrating to Scotland asked me where she could discover the "law about marriage in Scotland". What, specifically did she want to know? "Everything. Where can I read the law?" Nowhere I said, at least not comprehensively outside a law library, which needs special skills to use. So how could she find out what the law was? I said she would normally ask a neighbour, or friend, or a Citizen's Advice Bureau, or a solicitor if things were getting tricky. My friend was appalled. She assumed that in "a civilised country" it would be easy to discover what the law was. In Russia, she added, there is a Codex for each area of law in which everything is written down.

Though that is not quite accurate about Russia, the basic point is valid. In a codified (or civil law or Continental) legal system it is, in theory, easy to discover what the law is. Whereas in our system, known as a common law one, it is much harder since the traditional core of it is custom and decisions which have been made in the past. It is not always easy to find out what those are. This is a theme which will crop up repeatedly in the text below, and I do not want to say any more about it now, except that there are different approaches to law in different cultures.

However, since ancient times, mankind has accepted certain basic canons of justice: the law must be applied even-handedly, not selectively; the accused must know the case he or she has to answer and be allowed to speak in his or her own defence; courts must sit in public; law must not be retroactive, and so on. These are the foundations of what is sometimes known as natural law. They inform both the United Nations and the European Conventions on Human Rights. But how these great, universal principles are applied is a matter for judges, who often have to work with imperfectly or vaguely-drafted laws, or laws not designed to cope with recent social developments that drafters years ago could not have envisaged.

Standing above all these issues, from both a common law and a civil law perspective there is the issue which was raised in its best known form by the American War of Independence, namely that society—in its modern form at any rate—should be governed by laws and not by men. This is not the place to go into the innumerable theories about the meaning of the phrase, "the rule of law", but two points are relevant here. The idea of government by laws rather than men was a response to medieval and early modern monarchical rule and represented an effort to have an independent and—hopefully, but not necessarily—a popularly accepted set of rules and conventions of behaviour which the ordinary citizen would find reasonably easy to observe while living a conventionally active and productive life. The main idea is that these rules and conventions do not depend for their practical effect on the shifting views of individual human beings in positions of power, or changes at the very top.

The second point is that this ideal is unattainable. More than that, it is not even in principle desirable. If society is to develop and grow, and respond to the world around it, law has to be flexible. More than that, all law has to be applied sympathetically, making due allowance for the facts of any particular case. Given the infinite variety of human life, this can only be done by people. No code of laws has ever been devised, nor could ever be devised, which takes account of all possible variations of human behaviour in all possible situations. Even the rule in the Ten Commandments that "thou shallt not kill" is thought by most people not to apply to war, extreme self-defence or, in the case of animals, our desire to eat. Who is to judge when the tests for legitimate killing have been passed? The *principles* of judicial decision-making can be written down, and many more less concrete ideas can permeate a legal community, or society at large. But in the end, the day-to-day application of law must come down to the person who is entrusted by society with the decision-making role: show me the judge and I'll tell you the law.

But that is not the whole story either, because for a judge to operate rationally and in a way which is acceptable to society at large, given the trust placed in him or her as arbiter of the set of rules and ideas that make up our body of law, judicial thinking has to take a view on a whole host of matters, right down to the meaning of words like "convenient", "reasonable" or "deliberate". To give an example that will be discussed in detail in Chapter 1, President Richard Nixon was widely seen as threatening to overturn the convention of government by laws not men when he appeared unwilling to comply with court orders for the surrender of allegedly incriminating tapes about the Watergate affair in 1973. He countered by saying he would obey a "definitive" ruling of the federal courts. But he never defined "definitive". What exactly this meant in the context became a crucial issue for the Supreme Court judges. No body of written law, however large, could possibly answer all questions of this sort. In such circumstances, human intervention is not just desirable, it is inevitable if the system is to work.

But what are the principles on which this sort of decision is made? The United States Constitution may be longer than the Ten Commandments, but it still one of the shortest, clearest and most succinct statements of fundamental law which humanity has ever devised. Yet the entire existence of the US Supreme Court depends on the fact that the text needs continual re-interpretation, and considered application to situations which the framers could never possibly have envisaged.

The Court has altered its view of the original document (as will also be discussed in more detail below) to take account of social changes like the abolition of slavery. It has questioned the language of the document at its most fundamental level. What does "we, the people" mean? This raises questions of the status of the set of rules which were originally agreed upon in a way which we would not today consider acceptably democratic. Could the Constitution ever be judged unconstitutional?

Obviously that is an absurd question, but it illustrates the extent to which law, even at the most fundamental level, must always be thought of as contested space, a fluid area of life which is, *and should be,* a matter of perpetual contention and continuing public discussion by the community it is meant to serve.

*The Justice Factory* will look at these issues in a Scottish context, but not from a purely Scottish perspective because the principles of justice are universal. The practice of law is local, and always must be. Each jurisdiction is different, just as every society is different. Though this book's focus will be on the judges, a brief background sketch of the place of Scots law in the international context is important. In Scotland we have what is known as a "hybrid" system, meaning that it is derived from both of the two great European legal traditions, the civil and the common law. Civil law derives from Roman jurisprudence as it was codified by Emperor Justinian in 529. It is the basis of all legal systems in the northern part of the landmass which stretches eastward from the Atlantic to the Bering Strait. The common law, which originated in England in the middle ages, and spread to North America and most of today's cricket-playing countries, is the basis of jurisprudence from the North Sea to the Bering Strait, going in the other direction. Scotland, being between the Atlantic and the North Sea, is in the overlap geographically, and also in the sense that it has a legal system that is part civil law and part common law. It is unique within Europe in that respect.

Other jurisdictions with hybrid legal systems include Sri Lanka, South Africa and the Province of Quebec. The State of Louisiana also has a civilian system of private law which it inherited from its former French colonial overlords. That is not an exhaustive list. Scotland, therefore, is not alone in having a foot in both legal camps. Within the body of hybrid jurisdictions internationally, Scotland's is the best known, being by far the oldest and, arguably, the most distinguished. But this is not the main reason for stressing this point. The fact is that Europe, the most populous jurisdiction in the world after India and China, is quietly developing into something of a hybrid system itself. Some scholars see the Scots Law as providing an important example of how to mesh two very different, and in some ways incompatible, approaches to law.

There are two main courts in Europe: the European Court of Justice, which serves members of the European Union, and the European Court of Human Rights, which directly serves all countries belonging to the Council of Europe and, indirectly, the European Union since no EU country is permitted to ignore the ECHR, as the Human Rights Court is known.[1] Both started life in the 1950s as, essentially, courts within the civil law system in that they took their law from codes rather than from custom.[2] But

---

[1] At the time of writing, the EU is negotiating, as a "sovereign" body, to become the 48th signatory of the ECHR.

[2] Strictly speaking, the common law originated as a body of law which was common to the whole of the King of England's jurisdiction, as opposed to the pre-Norman manorial courts, in which law varied from manor to manor. The common law's main feature, which it took from the manor courts and still retains today, is that decisions are based on previous decisions, which in the beginning, that is before the first court, meant custom. This is the principle which is referred to in the Latin maxim, *stare decisis et non quieta movere*—

both of them, especially the Human Rights Court, have come more and more to include elements of the common law principle of precedent, which means taking into account the way in which similar issues have been decided in previous cases. At the same time, many elements of European law and practice have been grafted onto English law, inevitably so as English courts have to give effect to decisions of both the Court of Justice and the ECHR. A process of convergence is at work. Both systems have something to learn from each other. A vast new hybrid system is slowly emerging to serve a population of nearly 500 million people. If Scottish traditions help shape the way in which that evolves, they will have played an important role in one of the most significant developments in legal history.

In a sense they have already done that, although at one remove. The US Constitution was substantially framed by men steeped in Scots legal thinking, including Thomas Jefferson, whose law tutor came from Aberdeen, and Benjamin Franklin whose close friend was the Enlightenment philosopher and Librarian of the Faculty of Advocates in Edinburgh, David Hume. They embraced the idea of the separation of powers, and envisaged (if not explicitly) a supreme court which would pass judgement on the actions of the new American legislature. Everyone knows that the Court today is very powerful. What is

---

stand by the decision and do not disturb what is settled. Nothing may be changed unless there is a clearly argued reason for it (or a new statute). The original hope behind this was that it would contribute to legal certainty, and therefore social, constitutional and economic stability. In civil law systems, judges are free to arrive at judgements based on principles expressed in a written code and informed by their own view of the justice of the case, without necessarily being bound by previous decisions in similar cases. There are good arguments for both systems. Some lawyers would say that the common law is more predictable and the civil law more flexible. Others would argue the common law's lack of codification means the opposite: that the civil law is more predictable and the common law, which reasons by analogy rather than logic, is more flexible. This debate illustrates the only definite observation that can be made about law in general, which is that there is never universal agreement about anything.

less well appreciated is the extent to which it has a more civilian law approach than a common law one, not least because it operates on the basis of a legal code, namely the US Constitution. Crucially also, it is not bound by precedent. Indeed its main function is to re-interpret existing law in the light of changing circumstances and, where necessary, overturn them. Even the United States has, in some important respects, a hybrid legal system.

It is not just Scottish traditions, and the writings of the Scottish institutional authorities in the past, which are so important. It is also Scottish legal officers today. Almost all judges and advocates have both training in Roman jurisprudence and experience of English law. They are in an advantageous position to act as mediators between the two systems as interpreters of one to the other. That is perhaps why two of the first three judges which the United Kingdom sent to sit on the European Court of Justice were Scots.[3] This is a new experience for English lawyers who have been accustomed throughout the period of the Unions with Scotland and Ireland—Welsh law was abolished by Henry VIII in 1536—to being part of the largest and therefore most influential jurisdiction within their legal ambit. Now they find themselves, for the first time in history, in a minority, a position which Scots lawyers have been familiar with since 1707. But Europe is a fact that will not go away and the English will have to adapt, just as Europe will want to adapt to having a large common law jurisdiction in its midst. Scotland could play an important creative role in the reconciliation of these two systems. This point has been put with particular force by a French scholar, Eric Descheemaeker.

Scots Law is in a position that no other legal system in Europe or

---

[3] The first of these, the judge Lord Mackenzie Stuart, was explicitly appointed by the British government in 1973, when Britain entered the (then) EEC, to help integrate the two, potentially incompatible, legal systems. He was so successful that he was elected President of the Court in 1984. The second Scot was Sir David Edward who was a leading QC and Professor of European Studies at the University of Edinburgh when he was appointed in 1992. He sat until 2004.

elsewhere is. Obviously, Scots lawyers are in a position to communicate with their English colleagues in a way that only a handful of Continental lawyers are. Not only do they share the same language and the same sovereign; English law has had a deep influence on Scots law, meaning that Scots lawyers can understand it with relative ease; English and Scottish judges mingle in the House of Lords... However, possibly because of a typical minoritarian conscience, Scotland has to this day maintained a remarkably strong school of Romanists, whose contribution to European scholarship has historically been and continues to be out of all proportion to the size of their jurisdiction, meaning that they are more apt to foster an understanding of the structure of civil law... The alternative for English law is, therefore, between Scots law and nothing.[4]

The greatest threat to the future of Scots law, ironically, comes from within Scotland itself. The new Scottish parliament is intent on changing many aspects of the way in which Scottish judges and courts operate. The criticism has been made that the people in charge of this process have an inadequate understanding of Scots legal traditions. It is my hope that readers will come to understand more about what makes this system important and unusual. I believe that to live successfully under the rule of law, any society needs to understand its law and the way it is applied by its judges.

This is particularly important today because the reputation of judges is so low. The most cursory research into public attitudes towards the courts in Scotland, even if only conducted in the pub with a copy of that morning's tabloid newspaper on the bar counter, will reveal that the majority of people think that our judges are arrogant, idle, capricious, snobbish, old, elitist, ignorant, male, Tory, toffish, chauvinist, rude and occasionally corrupt, and operate an informal conspiracy to ensure that the law is applied primarily for the benefit of people like themselves.

---

[4] Mapping the Common Law: on a Recent English Attempt and its Links with Scottish Jurisprudence, *Juridical Review* 2003, p. 310

That is a dangerously inaccurate picture of one of the most important parts of our living constitution. Hence this book.

1

# The Law as Guardian

Though all law is local and specific to its own jurisdiction, justice is universal and rooted in the general conscience of mankind. It is not possible to give fair consideration to the former without some idea of the context provided by the latter. For that reason I am going to start by describing in some detail two cases which were fought outside Scotland and which, to my mind, illustrate judging at its best and at its worst.

The first of these cases, *United States v Nixon,* was an emergency hearing in the American Supreme Court in July 1974, right at the end of the great drama of Watergate. The background was that in the summer of 1972, just before the Presidential election that year, when Richard Nixon was standing for a second term, a team of semi-authorised criminals had tried to plant listening devices in the Democratic Party national headquarters, within a building called the Watergate, with the aim of acquiring campaign intelligence. Nixon was the Republican candidate and was expected to beat George McGovern, his Democratic opponent, very easily. But Nixon wanted not just to win, but to win by a landslide. He thought that was the only way he would have the moral authority to carry through a radical programme for rolling back the liberal reforms which had characterised American government over the previous twenty years.

The break-in was carried out in June 1972. It was bungled, and the criminals caught red-handed. In September, they were put on trial, but they kept silent when asked whom they had been working for. In return for failing to tell the whole truth on the witness stand they expected protection. The fear in the White House was that if they didn't get it they might refuse to perjure themselves, and reveal awkward facts about the Nixon campaign's methods just weeks before the election in November. Though Nixon's own involvement with the break-in itself was negligible, he had approved the cover-up plan. He arranged for money to be paid indirectly to the criminals, from campaign funds, in order to help them in court. He also tried to prevent the FBI investigating any possible political dimension to the crimes by suggesting that the break-in had been part of a CIA operation and therefore a foreign affairs matter, where unlawful acts were traditionally tolerated. Crucially for what followed, there was at least one senior officer within the FBI who resented this misuse of public authority.

In November 1972 Nixon won the election by the hoped-for landslide. In January 1973 the burglars were convicted. But instead of reducing public concern, this only seemed to exacerbate it, a process which was helped by the fact that one of the guilty men spoke publicly about the original conspiracy and the perjury committed in trying to cover it up. The Attorney-General and the President's Counsel were both named in evidence before a Senate committee which had been specially convened to investigate the allegations surrounding Watergate.

In April 1973, Nixon was compelled to make a public statement about the whole affair. He lied, saying that he had first heard about the plotting only a month before. Not everyone believed him. The leaks continued. Two weeks later, in a vain attempt to regain trust, he announced in a nation-wide broadcast that he had fired some of his closest advisors. He called the men who, it later transpired, had orchestrated the cover-up "two of the finest public servants it has been my privilege to know."

In May the Senate called for the President to appoint a Special Prosecutor who would try to find out where responsibility for the break-in really lay. The final act in the long drama began in July 1973 when it was suggested in the course of the Senate investigation, by a senior Nixon aide who had played no part in the either the break-in or the cover-up, that further information on higher responsibility, if any, might be obtained from the tapes which the President routinely made of all his conversations and phone calls in the Oval Office. Nixon, it transpired, had set up an elaborate recording system to provide verbatim evidence of confidential discussions for use in writing his memoirs. "Nixon's bugged himself!" one astonished employee of the White House exclaimed when he heard that the country's chief executive had been caught out by his own deviousness.

Naturally, the Special Prosecutor wanted to hear this new evidence. He was Archibald Cox, a patrician Harvard law professor who had worked for the Kennedy administration and whose reputation was such that Nixon could not easily deny him. But, though the Senate made a similar request, Nixon refused to hand over anything, citing "executive privilege". So both the Senate and Cox subpoenaed the tapes. Nixon ignored the subpoenas, citing "executive privilege" and claiming that he was "the sole judge of executive privilege". In other words, he could withhold whatever documents he liked from any court in the land. He would, in practical effect, be above the law.

A federal judge ordered Nixon to hand the material over, if only for an *in camera* hearing. He refused again. The US Court of Appeals in the District of Columbia heard the case on October and upheld the judgement of the lower court, saying that the President could not withhold material that might be relevant to a criminal trial using the claim of "executive privilege", adding, "Support for this kind of mischief simply cannot be spun from the incantation of the doctrine of the separation of powers."[5]

Nixon offered to deliver summaries of the tapes to the Special Prosecutor, who rejected the offer saying that would "defeat the fair administration of justice". So the President fired Cox, even though it had been explicitly written into his commission that he could be dismissed only for "extraordinary

---

[5] The best account of the legal, as opposed to the political and personal, aspects of this case is in *"We Have a Duty"*, by Howard Ball (1990). The quotation in the title is taken from the Supreme Court's justification for its intervention.

improprieties". But before he could do so, Nixon also had to fire the Attorney General who had hired Cox and now refused to fire him precisely because he had not committed any extraordinary improprieties. This unprecedented series of events, which took place on 20 October 1973, became known as the Saturday Night Massacre, and provoked national outrage. Nixon was forced to hand over the six tapes Cox had requested. His counsel said in an accompanying letter to the court, "The President does not defy the law."

Nixon was also forced to appoint a new Special Prosecutor, a man he hoped would be more accommodating than the Harvard Democrat had been, a wealthy Republican lawyer from Texas called Leon Jaworski. But, though deferential to the dignity of the office of the President, Jaworski was no more compliant than Cox had been. One of the impressive aspects of the Watergate story is how few of the legal figures involved (except, of course, the Nixon operatives) were prepared to act in obedience to anything other than their own, conscientiously-considered view of the law.[6]

The six tapes turned out to have gaps in them and other suspicious deficiencies. Some did not arrive at all. The public

---

[6] Jaworski was the son of a Polish immigrant, and had served after World War II as one of the American war crimes prosecutors in Germany. But he refused to participate in the Nuremberg trials because he thought that they would try people for acts which were not crimes in the place and at the time they were committed. It is a cardinal principle of justice that no-one should be punished for acts which were legal when they were carried out. Retroactive legislation was later explicitly forbidden by the United Nations and European Conventions on Human Rights. However justified the trials may have been morally, many people felt they were flawed legally. Winston Churchill was one of them. He suggested instead that the top five hundred Nazis should simply be shot out of hand. Stalin opposed this, thinking that it looked too much like revenge. He supported the American proposal for a public trial, not being worried about legal objections to the indictment. Given that the prosecutions were going ahead anyway, for an ambitious young lawyer like Jaworski to decline the professional honour (and personal satisfaction) which helping to hang Nazi war criminals would have brought him showed unusual independence of character.

mood hardened, and in February 1974 the House of Representatives asked the Judiciary Committee to commence impeachment hearings. In April, Jaworski subpoenaed all of the sixty-four additional tapes which Archibald Cox had asked for nearly a year before, but which had been set aside during the battle to get just the six tapes. Once again, Nixon refused on the basis of "executive privilege". The issue was now clear: could the President invoke rules designed to facilitate state business in order to protect himself personally from charges of common criminality?

Nixon's view was that executive privilege covered anything the President might want to do. "If the President does it, that means that it is not illegal," he said later in a televised interview with David Frost. This essentially monarchical conception of power is precisely what the framers of the Constitution wanted to avoid when they introduced into practical government for the first time in history the concept of the separation of powers. The history of American government is, in part, the story of the rise of the executive branch, as against the legislative and the judicial. In the eighteenth century, no country in the world had much in the way of executive capabilities, beyond those necessary to make war and raise taxes. It was only with the industrialisation and consequent bureaucratisation of society from the late nineteenth onwards that public administration became the gigantic business it is today. Nowadays, the Presidency is much more influential than Congress, the opposite of the situation when the Constitution was drafted.[7]

By 1974, having substantially eclipsed Capitol Hill, the White House seemed on the verge of eclipsing the Supreme

---

[7] Though the Constitution provided for "a supreme Court", it gave no detail. When the court was created, in 1789, it was so insignificant a feature of the administrative landscape that for three years it did not have a single case to try. Over the next two centuries, by fits and starts and with many improvisations and occasional retreats, it developed to the point where it came to be seen as the ultimate referee in the continual struggle for supremacy between the Executive and the Legislative branches of government.

Court too. If Nixon's claim of absolute executive privilege were successful, the Presidency would henceforth be out of control of the judiciary. The judges on the Supreme Court at the time realised that this could lead to catastrophe. If presidents could make law by executive order, and evade judicial scrutiny of their actions on the same ground, what would prevent a relapse into political gangsterism or a form of elective autocracy? Even the traditional weapon of last resort, an impeachment trial in the Senate, would not necessarily be effective if the White House could control the evidence which was available to Congress, as Nixon was seeking to do.

That these concerns seem far-fetched today is partly as a result of what happened in the summer of 1974. But they were very real at the time. When Nixon fired Cox, he ordered the FBI to go into his office and seal all the files. He also handed the disputed tapes over to the Secret Service, so that even the FBI could not get hold of them without his say so. The Court knew that it had no force with which it could oppose the FBI, much less the Secret Service.[8] It depended for its power entirely on its prestige and upon the unspoken convention that the organs of state obeyed the country's courts. But any such convention would be meaningless if Nixon were to feel free to ignore rulings from Supreme Court. That would, to all intents and purposes, have meant the end of the rule of law in the United States.[9] What would have happened to the rest of the free world if America had

---

[8] These fears were real. The Director of the FBI, Patrick Grey, a recent Nixon appointee, had, on White House instructions, taken home an important set of documents taken from one of the burglars, Howard Hunt, and burnt them in his fireplace. For destroying evidence in criminal case, he was forced to resign. But that did not enable recovery of the documents.

[9] It is also worth noting that this is the normal method by which the Russian authorities today open proceedings against important commercial opponents. A police raid is mounted, documents either sealed or seized and the defence from then on has no access to material with which to mount a defence. Court proceedings can then move forward without the inconvenience of equality of arms.

abandoned the rule of law? In the context of the Cold War, it is not hard to imagine ways in which more authoritarian governments might have taken advantage of the West's abrogation of its fundamental civic value.

So the stakes could hardly have been higher when, on 24 May 1974, Jaworski sent his request for adjudication on the matter of the sixty-four withheld tapes over to the great, stone building which has "Equal Justice Under Law" engraved in huge letters above the entrance. Inside, the nine judges of the US Supreme Court arguably stood between law and political gangsterism—and possibly worse. It seemed to them then that the slightest sign of division in their ranks might enable the President to claim that his views had some legal justification, on which basis he could possibly find grounds to ignore a split decision, even if the majority were against him.[10] He had previously said that he would obey a "definitive" decision of the Court, but no-one was sure what that meant. What if Nixon announced that a split decision, which was the norm in the Court, was not "definitive" and that he was not therefore bound to obey it? It would be a disaster for the judicial system as a whole if the most powerful person in the land could ignore the highest court in the land. Would this still be government of law not men? Or would it now be a case of: show me the president and I'll tell you the law?

It seemed to the Justices that, for the prestige of the Court and its continued authority within the Constitution, they had to arrive at a unanimous verdict. But they were deeply split on the issues. All were men of deeply held, but often very different, convictions about law and the meaning of the Constitution. Even Leon Jaworski expected a split decision. And he had no idea how events would move after that. This was going to be a challenge to the rule of law in America like no other before it, certainly not

---

[10] This view has retrospective justification because of what Nixon wrote in the statement he made accepting the pardon which his successor, President Ford, offered him for his Watergate offences shortly after his resignation. Nixon did not accept any blame, saying only that he had made "mistakes and misjudgements" in the way he "tried to deal with Watergate".

since the Civil War. It was a protean moment.

Who were these nine men who were being called upon to tell the President of the United States what the law of the land was?

The first point to make is that only three of the Justices had not been appointed by Republican presidents; and of that six, three had been appointed by Nixon himself. But he had a small set-back when, before considering the Special Prosecutor's writ in any way, the newest member of the Court, William Rehnquist (who was to be Chief Justice from 1986 until his death in 2006), recused himself on the ground of a possible conflict of interest because he had until recently been a law officer in the Nixon administration. So the Republican President's case was going to be considered by eight judges, of whom two were his own appointees. The possibility of a unanimous decision seemed remote.

The Chief Justice was Warren Burger. He had been born on a small farm in Minnesota and had studied law at night-school while selling insurance to support a young family. Later, as a Federal Appeal Court judge, he had become known for his strict "constructionist" legal views, which means that he favoured sticking as closely as was practicable to a literal interpretation of the Constitution. Roughly since the Second World War, this has indicated a conservative judicial stance rather than the more liberal one which had been held by his predecessor as Chief Justice, Earl Warren. He favoured what is known as judicial "activism", meaning using the court to move law forward as circumstances seem to dictate while using the Constitution more as a guide to general principle than a detailed rule-book.[11]

The Warren Court's greatest achievement had been outlawing racial segregation in the 1950s, starting with schools, yet this was done without any explicit authority from the

---

[11] There have been times, for example in the early 1900s and in the 1930s, when judicial activism has been of the conservative sort. Then the Justices have opposed liberal Presidential initiatives, most notably the Roosevelt New Deal which nearly came to grief as a result of the Supreme Court in 1935-6.

Constitution, which is silent on issues of race (this will be discussed in detail in Chapter 7). Judicial activism is based on values which the Justices think might have been endorsed by the framers of the Constitution, but which therefore involves a certain amount of historico-legal guesswork. Many feel such "activism" is not warranted. Richard Nixon was one of those, and that is why he appointed Burger, to the post of Chief Justice when he had the opportunity to do so in 1969.

In their book about the Supreme Court, *The Brethren* (1979), Bob Woodward and Scott Armstrong, describe Burger as "experienced, industrious, middle-class, middle-aged, middle-of-the-road, Middle-Western, Presbyterian, orderly and handsome." But a judge who sat with him on the Court of Appeals, said something which was to become highly relevant to the Nixon hearing: "He is a very emotional guy, who somehow tends to make you take the opposition position on issues. To suggest that he can bring the Court together—as hopefully a Chief Justice should—is simply a dream." A recent author, Edward Lazarus, in *Closed Chambers* (2005), called Burger "an intellectual lightweight whose pomposity, pettiness and outright dissembling alienated his colleagues, even his natural allies." (p. 191) He is widely thought to have been a vain man who wanted to arrange things so that he got the kudos of writing the Court's opinion. The problem with this was that, as a recent author has put it, "He fussed over the placement of ceremonial silverware for private receptions while misunderstanding basic legal arguments."[12] These problems were to come to the surface when dealing with *Nixon*.

Even with perfect judgement, it would have been difficult for Burger to get a unanimous decision from the seven strong-willed and independent-minded men who sat with him on the case. Perhaps the most crustily independent-minded, and intelligent, was William O. Douglas, an aloof, idiosyncratic, 76-year old New Deal Democrat who had been appointed to the Court by Franklin Roosevelt in 1939. In thirty-four years,

---

12 *The Supreme Court*, Jeffrey Rosen (2006), p. 13

Douglas had acquired the reputation of a fierce defender of liberal and democratic causes. He considered law ultimately political. He was a prolific author, as well as being an environmentally-conscious, spare-time backwoodsman. He was well-known for drawing legal inspiration as much from philosophy and art as from the Constitution or judicial precedent.

Partly, it seems, this was to reduce his workload. A ruinous divorce from his second wife meant that most of his salary as a judge was paid in alimony. He compounded his problems by marrying a 23-year old environmental activist, then divorcing her and marrying a 20-year old waitress. He was forced to earn a good part of his living by writing. But he wrote from genuine conviction, convictions which his critics say he occasionally brought into court. In 1972 he held in a major dissent that rivers or trees should be able to sue on their own behalf, just as other "inanimate objects", like ships or corporations, can. Douglas hated Nixon and the one-dimensional approach to life which he thought the President stood for. When, in the 1930s, Nixon had been a law student at Duke University, he once saw Douglas make a speech. Thirty years later, Nixon told Douglas that he had found his words so inspiring that they had persuaded him to embark upon a career of public service. Douglas's reaction to this clumsy attempt at flattery was to say that it was the only time in his entire life when he had felt genuinely suicidal.

The only way a judge can be removed from the Bench is through Congressional impeachment proceedings. Douglas's implacability had led to his being subject to impeachment no fewer than four times. Since the only Supreme Court judge ever to have been successfully impeached was Judge John Pickering, who went mad in the early nineteenth century and was charged with shouting, swearing and being drunk on the Bench, Douglas was obviously the target of some very dedicated enemies. The first was in the 1950s when Nixon was Vice-President and the last was in 1970 when he was President. On that occasion, Douglas had just married his third wife, the environmentalist, and published a book apparently under her inspiration which had been enthusiastically received by the "underground" press. In

Nixon's aggressively narrow-minded White House, that constituted *lèse-majesté* and was enough to provoke impeachment, although the real aim was to get high-profile Democrats off the Supreme Court Bench to make way for Republicans. Douglas fought back, and in the end the President had second thoughts. It would not have been hard though, in May 1974, to predict how Douglas would react to Nixon's claim for absolute executive privilege: show me the judge and I'll tell you the law.

The next oldest member of the Court was a bright but equally unbending character, William Brennan, the only Catholic. He was one of eight children born to immigrants from County Roscommon in Ireland. Without formal education, his father had risen from factory hand to the commissioner of police for New Jersey. Though nominally an Eisenhower Republican, Brennan soon turned into a liberal judicial activist who once wrote that judges should read the Constitution "in the only way we can: as twentieth-century Americans." That meant, not trying to divine what the framers might have wanted two hundred years ago, but what they might have wanted in present circumstances. Though the Constitution might be fixed on paper, interpretations must change with the times.

Brennan's record on the Court was so distinguished that he was talked of at one time as a possible future Chief Justice. After Douglas, he holds the record for the largest number of Supreme Court opinions ever written: 1,360—a mind-numbing amount of work. Perhaps most famously, Brennan drafted the opinion of the Court in *New York Times v Sullivan* (1964), the landmark case which established the rule—still to be introduced in Britain—that public officials cannot sue in defamation on matters related to their work unless they can prove that the author of the defamatory material knew it to be false, which is very rarely the case. "Debate on public issues should be uninhibited, robust, and wide-open," Brennan wrote, "and that may well include vehement, caustic and sometimes unpleasantly sharp attacks on government and public officials."

Though personally well-liked within the Court, Brennan

could be tiresomely, and sometimes self-defeatingly, conspiratorial. Initially, he took the view that Burger was "ideologically reactionary, but not evil". Soon he came to resent Burger's attempts to control a court which is supposed to made up of equals, not a chief with subordinates. More than once, Brennan considered resigning. But he was "political" enough not only to stay on but also to agree with Burger when he thought it tactically productive to do so. Discussing whether or not the Court should hear a particularly complex anti-trust case at about the time the Watergate burglaries were being undertaken, Brennan found himself in a 4-2 majority agreeing to take the case, in opposition, as usual, to Burger. But when he looked at the six shelf-feet of paperwork which he might have to plough through if the Court were to agree to consider the matter, Brennan announced "with a twinkle in his eye" that "on further reflection he was persuaded by the Chief's logic" and would switch his vote. This made it a 3-3 tie, which meant by normal procedure that the case was rejected, thus sparing anyone the task of reading thousands of pages of legal submissions.

Apart from Douglas and Brennan, Burger had a third fairly settled opponent in the Court, Thurgood Marshall, the only black on the Bench. The jovial, pragmatic, unintellectual Marshall was Brennan's closest friend amongst the Justices. He was a veteran of the southern civil rights litigation which culminated in *Brown v Board of Education of Topeka* (1953), which lit the touch-paper of for the civil rights movement of the 1960s (see Chapter 7). Though Marshall won more cases before the Supreme Court than any other Counsel—because there were so many similar race cases—he had been refused entry to the University of Maryland Law School in 1930 because he was black. He was the grandson of a slave, and his father had been a steward at a smart Southern yacht club.

After *Brown v Board of Education,* Marshall became something of a celebrity. Later, he was brought into government by his close friend and bourbon-drinking buddy, Lyndon Johnson, who eventually nominated him for the Supreme Court. In 1965, Johnson appointed him Solicitor General—succeeding

Archibald Cox incidentally. When Marshall hesitated, Johnson told him how badly he needed him from a public relations point of view. "I want folks to walk down the hall in the Justice Department," the President said with a grin, "and look in the door and see a nigger sitting there." After his death, Marshall said of the plain-spoken Texan Democrat, "I loved that man."

Of the other four judges, the most senior was Potter Stewart, a blue-chip Republican law expert, son of a prominent judge in Ohio and an ex-Skull and Bones Club member from Yale. He had been appointed to the Court by Eisenhower. Subsequently, Nixon wanted to make him Chief Justice. But he declined, preferring the relative anonymity of his Associate Judgeship, which left the way open for Burger. Without ambition, Stewart was independent of faction on the Bench. The danger for Nixon was that he was known for his distrust of governmental power. He had written opinions prohibiting the use of illegally obtained evidence in court, including unauthorized wiretaps, and which restricted police from obtaining evidence without a search warrant. In these respects, he was not a natural Burger ally either.

Byron White was an equally independent character. A laconic, modest, pragmatic but tough ex-professional footballer, he had been John F. Kennedy's only appointment to the Court. He had met the future President when he had been a Rhodes Scholar at Oxford in 1939, and later served with him in the Navy during World War II. Known as "Whizzer White" in his footballing youth, it was he who, as assistant attorney general in 1961, personally ordered 600 federal marshals down to Alabama to protect the Freedom Riders during the civil rights bus campaign when neither the state governor, who was a member of the Ku Klux Klan, nor J. Edgar Hoover would do so. Though a staunch anti-racist, White was not a doctrinaire liberal, being opposed to such flagship causes as liberalised abortion, affirmative action in university admissions and gay rights.

The two remaining Justices were both Nixon appointees. Lewis Powell was a personally courteous and modest southerner who at first refused Nixon's offer of a seat on the Court. Though a lifelong Democrat, he was prepared to be tough on crime, which Nixon liked, and also had personal experience of issues of race and discrimination, which was important in those years. Co-incidentally, it was his firm which opposed Marshall in front of the Supreme Court in *Brown v Board of Education.* Powell did not at first believe in compulsory integration, though he later changed his mind. But he never lost his dislike of hypocritical anti-racists who, as he saw it, tried to salve their consciences by demonising the south. Four years after the Nixon case, he was to write the Court's opinion in *The University of California Regents v Bakke,* which upheld affirmative action insofar as a generally race-conscious attitude towards admission was concerned on the part of universities, but which also outlawed rigid racial quotas.

This sort of compromise was typical of Powell, who had the unique distinction amongst the Justices of being almost always "right" about the law. He achieved this apparently difficult feat by the actually very simple method of almost always occupying the centre ground. In a court with a certain amount of political voting, Powell was the "swing Justice". He voted, therefore, most often with the majority. From the point of view of the litigants, he was normally the judge they needed to influence if they were to get the decision they wanted. Powell was, one observer suggested, the most powerful man in America. Ironically, he didn't like the job, preferring the drama of normal trials to the funereal quiet of a constitutional court where, apart from brief oral hearings, everything is decided on paper. He threw light of a different sort onto the workings of the court when he once remarked to a clerk of his, "I find my health is better when I only work a six-and-a-half day week."

The final member of the tribunal which was to settle President Nixon's future was Harry Blackmun, who was then best known for writing the opinion of the Court in *Roe v Wade* (1973), the landmark ruling which changed America's abortion laws fundamentally (with White dissenting). Blackmun had grown up poor in Minnesota, like Warren Burger, with whom he had been close friends. He was best man at the future Chief Justice's wedding. But not even those ties were able to prevent Blackmun taking an independent view of his friend's performance on the Court. Blackmun did not like Burger's egocentric approach. Though an emollient character, who disliked fuss, Blackmun refused to attend the funeral of Burger's wife when she died in 1994.

So deeply felt were the passions aroused by the Nixon case that in a biography of him, called *Becoming Justice Blackmun*, Linda Greenwood wrote, "Years later, Blackmun would identify the tense weeks in the summer of 1974, when the Court confronted the Watergate crisis amid an internal crisis of its own, as a signal event in the dissolution of the friendship."

These eight men—the full court minus Rehnquist—met on 31 May to decide whether they would accept Jaworski's request for an expedited hearing on the issue of the sixty-four tapes Nixon wanted to keep out of court and to withhold from the Senate. By then, the House of Representatives had also started to debate impeaching the President. The Special Prosecutor's request was qualified in that he was not asking for the full contents of all the tapes to be made public. What he wanted was the right to hear them all, to decide what material they contained which was relevant to the criminal prosecutions in progress and then to return everything else to the President under seal. The White House's confidentially of communication was challenged only to the extent that it conflicted with the requirements of the criminal justice system.

The "expedited" hearing would come to the Supreme Court directly from the federal court which had ordered production of the tapes, but whose decision the President had appealed. It would thus by-pass the Court of Appeals. This would only be the seventh time in history of the United States that such a route had been taken. There were two basic arguments in favour: first, it would prevent delay, by an estimated six months, the trial which had been set down for September of Nixon's previous assistants, starting with the former Attorney-General and including what Nixon had called "two of finest public servants it has been my privilege to know." Not all the Justices thought this was important, but most were agreed on the second argument, which was that it was becoming a matter of national importance that the whole mess of Watergate be cleared up so that public business, which had been seriously interrupted by question marks over the presidency, could get back to normal. In formal legal terms, the question was whether this was a matter of "imperative public importance" or not.

Against that was, first, that the Justices disliked—with good reason—being rushed to judgement. It often results in ill-considered outcomes, and there could have been few cases ever to have come before the Court which it had been more important to get right than this one. Secondly, the Court's annual term was soon to end, and the holidays were looming. None liked being in Washington in the middle of summer, and their punishing schedule for the rest of the year necessitated, very fairly, some proper rest before the juggernaut of litigation cranked into life again in the autumn.

On 31 May, the Justices met in conference to decide whether they would take the case on an expedited basis or not. Initially only Brennan and Marshall were in favour. They had an extraordinarily clear and incisive nine-page review of the facts and legal aspects of the case from the clerk of the Court (which is reproduced in facsimile in Ball). This was legal analysis of the highest quality. Brennan argued that "after two years of Watergate, it was time the nation had access to the evidence that would reveal the truth about Watergate." Justices Powell, Douglas an Stewart were persuaded and voted to take the hearing. So it was 5 to 3. The tradition is that the senior Justice (or the Chief Justice) who votes with the majority has the right to assign authorship of the resulting opinion. Burger was so keen to have the opinion in this case attributed to him that he, too, switched votes so that he would be able to assign himself the job of writing the Court's opinion.

The parties were given three weeks to file and exchange briefs, and a further three weeks to file responses. A week after that, on 8 July, there was to be oral argument in Court, with each party allotted one hour only for argument. Unlike in English courts, where counsel can argue for as long as their client's fees

last, in the United States Supreme Court (and many European
courts), submissions are time-limited. Half an hour for each side
is the normal allowance. But whatever the length of time
specified, it is so strictly observed that one Chief Justice is
reputed to have cut off a pleader "in the middle of the word 'if'".

In front of the Justices, the press and the 120 members of the
public who had managed to get seats in the gallery, the special
prosecutor presented his argument which was simply that the
President was wrong when he said that he was the final arbiter of
what the Constitution meant and that he therefore had a duty, like
anyone else in the jurisdiction, to obey the law. He is "decidedly
*not* the sovereign". Perhaps executive privilege was part of the
law, but if so it was not absolute. It must be qualified and
restricted to matters necessarily and honestly relevant to the
conduct of public business. This did not extend to withholding
relevant and admissible evidence from a criminal trial.

The underlying issue was who was the final authority on
what the law said about this, or indeed any other, matter.
Jaworski put this very clearly:

> "The President may be right in how he reads the Constitution, but
> he may also be wrong. And if he is wrong, who is there to tell him
> so? And if there is no-one then the President, of course, is free to
> pursue his course of erroneous interpretations. What then becomes
> of our constitutional form of government?"

The President's counsel, James St Clair, argued that this was
essentially a political case, given the impeachment debate already
in progress. Because it was "political", it was not a matter for the
courts. Only impeachment could warrant forcing the President to
hand over material which he considered covered by executive
privilege, which in all other circumstances was absolute. But he
weakened his case under questioning from Marshall who put it to
him that most conceivable impeachment actions could never be
undertaken, no matter how gross the offences, without the
evidence which ordinary subpoenas might disclose. "If you know
the President is doing something wrong, you can impeach him.
But if the only way you can find out is [by a subpoena with

which he can refuse to comply], you can't impeach him... You lose me some place along there." This so clearly exposed the circularity of St Clair's argument that there was laughter in Court. None of the judges was impressed.

St Clair's went on to say that the freedom of communication necessary between the President and his advisors would be impaired if their conversations could be brought into open court. Finally, he argued that the separation of powers doctrine, on which the American Constitution rests, means that only the Executive can investigate actions of the Executive. This implies absolute privilege, without any judicial oversight. Powell, despite his desire for a finely-balanced outcome, responded by asking the most fundamental and dangerous question of all: "Mr. St. Clair, what public interest is there in preserving secrecy with respect to a criminal conspiracy?"

It was a bruising session. Unlike in the English courts—much less so in Scotland—where the judges try to intervene as rarely as possible, the more "civilian" style of the Supreme Court can get almost conversational. The Justices put well over a hundred questions to the special prosecutor and nearly two hundred to the President's counsel. Douglas asked Jaworski, for example, if it was right that "we start with a Constitution that does not contain the words 'executive privilege'." Of course it was right. Not only that, the fact was that the term had only been in wide currency in any sense related to Nixon's claim since 1953, incidentally in claims made by President Eisenhower, when Nixon was Vice-President.

Next morning the Justices met in conference. They had hardly started discussing the case when White took issue with Powell's suggestion that the President should have a higher standard of evidence applied to him. Nothing in the Constitution stated that presidents should be treated differently from any other citizen, White insisted. Douglas had already submitted a draft opinion saying that "to allow [Nixon] to conceal from a court information which may be critical to the fairness of a trail of named defendants would be a monstrous affront to the rule of law under which we live." Against that Powell had argued that it was up to the President to decide when release of material might be injurious to the public interest.

After oral argument, the Justices were all in agreement that the Special Prosecutor's clear request for specific evidence outweighed any general claim of absolute executive privilege. But it was clear that there were many shades of opinion within that general line. Brennan started to wonder whether Burger was the right person to unify the Court by writing, as he suspected the Chief Justice wanted to do for essentially egotistical reasons, the opinion of the Court. He started lobbying the other Justices with the aim of getting, not just an opinion of the whole Court but a single opinion signed by all the Justices rather than just by Burger, with their concurrence simply noted. Brennan thought that necessary to drive home to Nixon the unity of the Court since if everyone signed, then authorship would be anonymous. That too would have been an unusual event. The last time this had been done was in 1958 when the Court wished to show maximum internal solidarity on a case arising from a particularly contentious desegregation case in Little Rock, Arkansas.

Brennan's first call was on his friend Douglas, who objected to this approach on the ground that it would make the judgement appear political, something the Court was always at pains to avoid. He wanted Nixon to be seen as a simple criminal. Next, Brennan called on White, who suspected another Brennan plot. He said he did not wish to consider the issue until he had heard the arguments of the parties. Marshall, Stewart and Blackmun, however, agreed with the single opinion approach. Burger, smelling a rat, was warily non-committal.

Since authorship of the opinion had not yet been formally assigned, Stewart suggested that in this critical case the author, even if anonymous, should be a Republican nominee to the Court, to forestall allegations of prejudice. But he should be a centre-grounder and preferably not one who had been appointed by Nixon. Brennan soon realised that there was only one person who fitted that description: Stewart himself.

Blackmun, who had voted against taking the expedited hearing, thought the author should be both a Republican *and* a

Nixon appointee, in order to drive the message home to the outside world even harder. There were only two of those: one was Rehnquist, who had recused himself, and the other was Blackmun himself.

Powell's position was different from any of the others. He wanted the President to lose the case, but by the narrowest possible margin so that his defeat would not open the floodgates to criticism of future presidents.[13] A certain amount of confidentiality is necessary in public life, he felt: "Government cannot function in a goldfish bowl." Powell argued that the standard of evidence required when the president was a party should be higher than for ordinary people. In normal circumstances, the ultimate decision on the extent of executive privilege should lie with the executive. Brennan responded by saying that, given the way Nixon was capable of twisting words and using the power of the state for his own ends, a split decision, or any other form of ambiguity, could mean the President effectively winning, in fact if not in law, the case Powell wanted him to lose.

Nobody supported Brennan's idea. Instead, Burger said he would write the opinion of the Court himself, as he had a right to do. But he said he would do it within a week, which would mean working at eight times the speed the experienced Brennan thought the reasonable maximum. For once, Douglas supported Burger—perhaps he had another ecology article to write—though he thought the President's case so weak it would not need much effort to refute.

Recently, the late Chief Justice William Rehnquist threw light on what some might see as Burger's masochistic desire to do all the work on this crucial, and therefore historic, opinion. The decision had been taken to abandon the idea of an anonymous opinion, so Rehnquist's comment in his book, *The Supreme Court,* is directly relevant:

---

[13] There was justice in this approach, as the unsuccessful attempt to impeach Bill Clinton was undoubtedly driven in part by knowledge of what happened to Nixon.

The signed opinions are to a very large extent the only visible record of a Justice's work on the Court, and the office offers no greater reward than the opportunity to author an opinion on an important point of constitutional law.

Since this was to be one of the most important decisions on constitutional law ever to come before the Court, it was perhaps understandable that Burger wanted the glory for himself. To speed up the work, Burger allocated sections of the opinion to each of his clerks.

In the Supreme Court each Justice has either three or four clerks who do the donkey-work of legal research (Burger had five). They draft skeleton arguments, look up the precedents and provide reasoned opposition to proposals from the Justices. There were no clerks before 1882 when the first one was employed privately, and it was not until 1922 that the job was made an official, salaried one. The theory is that the opinion is still primarily the work of the Justice. But the reality is that they are so overwhelmed with work for most of the Term that they rarely have time to do much more than top and tail their clerks' drafts. Many clerks use their superior time resources to research arguments with which they try to persuade the judge they are working for to adopt on a particular case. If the Justice is undecided, the clerk can have considerable influence. Edward Lazarus, who was once a clerk himself, has written about "the guerrilla war that liberal and conservative clerks conduct, largely out of sight of the Justices, to control the course of constitutional law", and said that "the polarising effect of these dynamics cannot be overstated." He witnessed "midnight screaming matches" between Blackmun's clerks, of whom he was one, and those of a more conservative Justice. He saw two slightly drunk clerks at the end-of-term party in one of the courtyards within the Supreme Court building get so angry with each other's approach to constitutional jurisprudence that they started trading "taunts", "epithets", "shoves", then "swings" until the two men wrestled each other into the courtyard fountain. A "vaguely pathetic liberal rage", he wrote, was at war with "the bullyboy swagger of ascendant conservatism".

The significance of this in the Nixon case was that, as the Court's term had nearly ended, many of the clerks had a bit of time on their hands, as did the judges for once. With Burger's chambers hard at work, the others had time to plot and organise. Their approach was typified by Stewart, who considered Burger legally ignorant, politically naive and intellectually dishonest. He thought Nixon had appointed him because of his good looks and lack of substance. He felt the Court needed leadership from a more substantial figure, so he got together with Powell to review the first parts of the opinion which Burger circulated for discussion.

Both men thought the Chief Justice's effort so poor they would embarrass the Court if published as they stood. They knew from experience that if they submitted comments or corrections to Burger he would discard most of them, so they decided the only thing to do was to get the other judges together and produce their own, jointly drafted, alternative opinion, much along the lines Brennan had originally suggested. It would reach a similar conclusion to Burger's, but would be expressed elegantly and concisely, and use legal arguments which would give Nixon no possible ground for ignoring the will of the Court. Naturally, Burger could not be allowed to know of these plans.

Their first call was on Blackmun, once Burger's friend. He was so appalled at the Chief Justice's recitation of the facts, the first and simplest part of any opinion, that he readily agreed to draft an alternative version. Brennan and Douglas were happy to join in, the latter because he felt Burger had either misunderstood the line agreed at the judges' conference, or was wilfully ignoring it. Stewart told his clerks that Burger's first draft would have got a Grade D in law school. White held himself aloof from the cabal, but still thought the Chief Justice's work deeply unsatisfactory. He produced an alternative draft of the section relating to the standard of evidence required to grant the subpoena, which annoyed Powell.

In the middle of the blizzard of memos and counter-memos accompanying all these suggestions, Burger sat bewildered. Was there some conspiracy afoot? Despite the secrecy, rumours were in the air. He smelled sabotage. Brennan, Douglas, Powell, Stewart and now White were against him, and Marshall was sure to follow them. But he still had Blackmun left as an ally—or so he thought. "It's my opinion," Burger complained to his old friend when he went to see him, "and they are trying to take it away from me."

No greater disloyalty could be manifest towards a man who wanted to be remembered by posterity than having his colleagues rob him of the glory of having authored one of the most important legal opinion's in his country's history. Hating conspiracy, Blackmun could do nothing other than show Burger his own draft which was soon to be added to that of the other objectors. The Chief Justice was dumbfounded and walked out of his friend's chambers without saying a word. This became known in the building as the "Et tu Harry?" meeting.

Once the alternative opinion was organised, several of the Justices left Washington for their holiday homes. It was already July and they felt they could leave their clerks to ensure that nothing untoward happened while they embarked upon their hard-earned summer vacation. On Saturday 13 July, with Douglas at his cabin in Goose Prairie, Washington State—the nearest telephone was ten miles away outside a truckers' cafe—and all of the other judges either on holiday or at home, Brennan, White and Stewart met in the Court and decided to go out with their clerks to lunch to discuss the developing counter-opinion.

It was an unusual privilege for clerks to be invited to such a meeting, so on Monday Marshall's clerks, who had also been in the building on the Saturday but not invited to the lunch, complained to their boss, who had not been around on the weekend, having long-since lost any workaholic tendencies he might once have had. The reason they had not been invited was simply that Marshall was staying well clear of the frantic work on the Nixon opinion and so his clerks' opinion would not have been relevant to the meeting. Marshall initially took this as a slight to himself and it required all Brennan's considerable political skills to smooth the ruffled feathers. He managed to convince the old civil rights warrior that this was no more than a trivial case of professional jealousy on the part of the clerks, since it had been a working rather than a social lunch.

But this incident focussed Marshall's attention. He talked to his clerks and sent a memo to Burger aligning himself unequivocally with the objectors. This "went off like a grenade" in the Chief Justice's chambers and appears to have cracked his will to hold out against the rest of the Court. He was now prepared to listen to views that he had previously ignored. Since Marshall's clerks were a more left-wing group than Burger's clerks, it would not be much of an exaggeration to say that the great national struggle to defend the rule of law in America boiled down at its most critical moment to a battle between Burger's clerks and Marshall's clerks, which erupted only after the latter were sent into battle following a misunderstood Saturday lunch-date snub. It was almost a case of: show me the clerk and I'll tell you the law.

Woodward and Armstrong describe Burger's mood at the time:

> He resented the challenge to his authority and competence. It was different in the English legal system he loved so much. Once when he was in England for a judicial meeting, everyone was talking and the senior English judge had just lifted his finger. The others stopped in mid-sentence. The senior judge did not even have to speak to obtain silence. Unfortunately, the Chief Justice of the United States did not command the same respect.[14]

Burger rallied briefly, hitting back with a couple of plainly-worded memos and some lobbying of his own. He was desperate to keep control, and therefore technically-speaking authorship, of this opinion, even if his own personal view of the law was going to be lost in the unified opinion he was drafting. Trying to get

---

[14] I have drawn significantly on these authors in respect of the manoeuvring inside the Court. It is the only full account which has ever been published. Almost all subsequent commentators and researchers have described it as accurate.

Douglas back on side, he went so far as to send a new draft of his text by special courier out to Goose Prairie.

With Brennan now away on holiday in Nantucket, it was left to Marshall, or rather his clerks, to repel the last, wavering counter-attack. This they did with gusto, on one occasion attacking a Burger footnote which, following Douglas's point in oral argument, observed, quite correctly, that the Constitution made no mention of executive privilege. They observed sarcastically that, "there is similarly nothing said in the Constitution authorising the subpoena at issue in this case."

Suddenly Burger caved in completely. He incorporated paragraphs which Stewart, Brennan and Marshall wanted in the opinion, with Brennan completely re-writing the statement of the facts of the case. Burger discarded the section of his draft to which White had objected most strongly and substituted White's wording. He got Douglas down to the phone booth in Goose Prairie and, in the intervals of audibility between trucks roaring past, discussed these amendments. Douglas's memos had been invaluable, Burger shouted into the receiver. He then asked his old friend Blackmun, one of the few still hanging around in the building, to edit his completed draft, correcting the grammar and spelling and removing any stylistic gaffes. There were still many more compromises and corrections to make, but the objectors had won their battle.

At least, they had won *most* of what they wanted. What Burger had achieved, and it was important, was a discussion of executive privilege which for the first time in American constitutional history gave legal backing to a qualified privilege. Most of the Justices would have preferred to have left that out, since, as Douglas argued repeatedly, it was not necessary to take a view for their decision on the case. But Burger had felt so strongly that it was a "core function" of the presidency, that the other Justices, in the interest of their overarching aim of achieving unanimity in their judgement on Nixon had let it pass, though considerably modified.

Burger had been appointed to the Court by Nixon because he hoped he would bring a strict "constructivist" approach to constitutional issues. Since the Constitution is silent on executive privilege, and since the Court had not considered it once in the first century and a half of its life, it was deeply ironic that this was the man who put executive privilege on the country's constitutional map for the first time. In other circumstances, this would have been "judicial activism" of the sort Nixon hated most. "I was gratified," the President said immediately after reading the opinion, "to note that the Court reaffirmed (*sic*) both the validity and the importance of the principle of executive privilege, the principle I had sought to maintain."

So it was that the Supreme Court managed to get an opinion put together which would give President Nixon no room whatsoever to mount any sort of challenge to the Federal District Court's subpoena for the sixty-four tapes at issue in the trial of Nixon's assistants. The result of all the horse-trading, legal argument and ego-assertion inside the great stone building was a unanimous opinion which dashed all Nixon's hopes.

On 24 July, sixteen days after hearing oral argument, Burger formally announced the judgement:

> Neither the doctrine of separation of powers, nor the need for confidentiality of high-level communications, without more, can sustain an absolute, unqualified Presidential privilege of immunity from judicial process under all circumstances.... To read the [Constitutional] powers of the President as providing an absolute privilege as against a subpoena essential to the enforcement of criminal statutes on no more than a generalised claim of the public interest in confidentiality of non-military and non-diplomatic discussions would upset the constitutional balance of a "a workable government" and gravely impair the role of the courts... We conclude that when the ground for asserting privilege as to subpoenaed materials sought for use in a criminal trial is based only on the generalised interest in confidentiality, it cannot prevail over the fundamental demands of due process of law in the fair administration of criminal justice.[15]

---

[15] *United States v Nixon* (1974), 418 US 683

The next day the subpoenaed tapes were delivered to the Federal District Court. On 5 August it became clear that, as a result of what was revealed by the newly-released tapes, the House of Representatives Judicial Committee would vote unanimously for impeachment if the President did not resign with immediate effect. On 10 August, Nixon did just that. The rule of law had been saved.

Soon afterwards, Burger was offended to hear it suggested in the press that the momentous opinion was not, despite having his name at the top, entirely his own work. The Court's public relations officer called a press conference at which he said the Chief Justice had worked "forty-one (*sic*) straight days at the Court drafting the Nixon case", stopping only to sleep and eat. Any rumours to the effect that other judges had been involved in writing the opinion were "lies".

2

# The Law as Theatre

If the best of judging is when judges can apply the law on behalf of the people to call the mightiest in the land to order, the worst of judging is when courts are used as a cloak to deceive the public about the machinations of the mightiest. There is, sadly, a wealth of examples to chose from, but one of the most important and best documented cases, as well as the one which came closest to success in its underlying deception, happened forty years before the United States Supreme Court heard *Nixon.* It took place in the Supreme Court of the USSR, convened in the Hall of Columns in the Central House of the Unions, near the Kremlin.

On trial was a group of Britons and Russians accused of espionage and of "wrecking", by which was meant sabotaging the USSR's industrialisation programme by sabotaging some of its newest and largest power stations. It became known as the Metro-Vickers trial, after the name of the British company, Metropolitan-Vickers, which had supplied the generating machinery, and which employed most of the accused. The story is now largely forgotten. The Soviet Union and the ideals which gave birth to it have vanished. But it made headlines all over the world at the time, not least because it took place in April 1933, three months after Hitler seized power in Germany, and in the middle of the terrible famine created by Stalin's war against his own peasantry.

The trial had a bizarre parallel in England when, a month before the Moscow court sat, an eccentric English Army officer was put on trial in the drill hall of the Duke of York's Barracks in

Chelsea, London, accused of treasonously selling his country's military secrets to the Germans, for "£90 and a fuck". In the context of the Metro-Vickers trial, this case, which was almost as highly publicised at the time, is worth summarizing briefly. It was theatre of a remarkably similar sort.

The prisoner was accused of having passed details of the organisation of armoured formations in the British Army, plus the specifications of a new assault rifle, to Germany. On close examination, the information divulged turned out to be trivial. But this did not affect the approach of the court. The offences carried a maximum penalty of 140 years in jail. Only the fact that his country was not at war saved him for a possible death sentence. The prisoner denied that he had handed over military secrets and that the £90 he had received was payment for "services rendered" to a German lady whom he had met in South Africa and had sex with in a wood at her invitation beside a lake in Berlin.

The President of the Court Martial was a starchy, monocled, huntin'-shootin' Irish Protestant General called Winston Dugan, who treated the prisoner with contempt throughout the trial. "Do you mean to say," he roared when he heard the defence case, "that this Marie Louise paid you 90 pun' for immoral services rendered—for you to be her paramour?"

The prisoner said, "Yes."

His lawyer explained, "He would not say so, but she became infatuated with him. You will hear evidence that the accused always had a particular attraction for women, and a peculiar attitude towards them, which perhaps I may best describe as a lack of chivalry."

*Time,* the American news magazine which covered the trial extensively, commented, "It seemed almost as though the British government were copying the famed Soviet propaganda trials in Moscow."

This was not just because the prisoner's defence seemed to be acting in collusion with the prosecution; nor because of the inflation of relatively trivial acts into charges of possible treason; nor even because of the bluster, aggression and blatant bias of the judge; but also because of the unspoken issue which was at stake: class. The prisoner's name was Norman Wright. He had been born in Portsmouth into an army family, and gone to Sandhurst where he did extremely well. But he soon realised that he would never fulfil his full potential in the British Army unless he glamorised his background a bit. So he changed his surname from Wright to Baillie-Stewart and began hinting at an obscurely romantic Highland pedigree. He was commissioned into the Seaforth Highlanders, which had a majority of English officers. The Prince of Wales was the Colonel-in-Chief. But he came to despise his fellow officers.

> The England I knew in 1933 [he later wrote] and the Army I knew was a world in which a doctor looked down on a dentist and an infantryman looked down on the air force, and so on *ad infinitum*. I myself had the misfortune to join a regiment [whose] officers looked down on everybody, including each other. A man who rode a motorcycle was a 'cad'. An air force officer was a 'shit'. I was badly reported on because I 'did not put my leg across a horse', that is to say I could not afford to go hunting or play polo and chose instead to stay out of debt.

Disenchanted with army life, Baillie-Stewart took three months' leave in Africa. There he went on safari with some German officers, and was so impressed by them that he decided to abandon Britain and become German himself. But MI5 was on his tail. Soon afterwards he found himself standing trial for treason.

Presumably to emphasise the seriousness with which the authorities took his case, Baillie-Stewart was held in the Tower of London. Society ladies paid the entrance fee just to see the tall, mysterious Englishman in the Glengarry and kilt striding round Tower Green every day. The *Daily Express* did its best to sensationalise the already sensational story, while *Time* told its international readership that when the Prime Minister, Ramsay Macdonald, came back from his "peace pilgrimage" to France and Italy the British public largely ignored him and "paid more attention to what was going on in the echoing, draughty drill hall in Chelsea."

The result of the growing publicity storm was that the Crown abandoned its most serious charges. The trial was aborted. Baillie-Stewart given five years, which he served in the Tower— the last Briton ever to be imprisoned there. General Dugan was sent out to govern South Australia.

To understand the authorities' approach to people like Baillie-Stewart, it is necessary to skip forward and tell the rest of his story. Baillie-Stewart was released from prison in 1938, and went to live in Austria. After the Anschluss, he moved to Germany. In 1940 he took German citizenship. He made a few broadcasts to Britain early in the war, though he soon refused to continue because he disagreed with the aggressively triumphalist line he was expected to take on air. Incidentally, it was his drawling, pseudo-upper class voice which suggested the nickname Lord Haw-Haw to the British journalist who coined the phrase. The "real" Lord Haw-Haw, William Joyce, spoke in an ostentatiously suburban accent which was intended to disguise his working-class origins.

In 1945, Baillie-Stewart was arrested by Allied forces in Austria. He was wearing chamois-leather shorts, embroidered braces, white stockings and a green forester's jacket. This obviously comic, lightweight figure was taken back to London and, for the second time, gravely accused of having committed treason. However, the Attorney-General, Sir Hartley Shawcross (of subsequent Nuremberg War Crimes Tribunal fame), decided that such a serious charge might not stick, partly due to technical problems about the exact time the accused had taken German citizenship. But he was not going to allow Baillie-Stewart to go free, so he had him tried for committing "an act likely to assist the enemy".

MI5 was furious. They wanted the "cad" punished severely. With their hands tied in Britain, some officers lobbied for him to be sent to the Russian zone, where the trials of the 1930s had convinced them there would be no "namby-pamby legal hair-splitting", as one of them put it. But they were unsuccessful. For a second time, Baillie-Stewart was given five years. After his release, disgusted with England, he emigrated to Ireland. There he married a "shop girl half his age" (as Fleet Street dismissively called her), by whom he fathered two children. He spent time on the Arran islands, wrote Wild West novels for a living, and died on a Dublin bar-stool in 1966.

It would not have escaped a Soviet observer that Baillie-Stewart was imprisoned while P.G. Wodehouse, who had also broadcast from Germany in war-time, was allowed to go free, even though his "acts" were much better publicised, and he had no conceivable excuse about confusion of nationality. The cases are not entirely congruent, but they are similar enough to raise questions about differential treatment. Likewise William Joyce, the actual Lord Haw-Haw, was sentenced to death by the British state even though he was Irish by birth and American by nationality. Though he did, very briefly, have a British passport in wartime, questions can legitimately be raised here too. His actions were much more aggressive, and prolonged, but his legal position arguably secure.

It would be interesting to know what a William O. Douglas, or a Thurgood Marshall, would have made of the three cases, taken together. Though each was accused of broadcasting from Germany in wartime, the well-known writer of comic novels, who had an honorary Doctorate of Letters from Oxford, was not even put on trial, while the eccentric infantry officer with a history of philandering was sent to jail, and the lower class Irish-American loud-mouth was sentenced to death by hanging. Equal justice under law? It is not hard to imagine a Bolshevik jurist smiling cynically at bourgeois practice and saying, "Show me the prisoner and I'll tell you the law."

The theatre in which the Metro-Vickers trial was to be staged was more stately and less draughty than Baillie-Stewart's Chelsea drill-hall. The House of the Unions, where most of the major show trials of the 1920s and 30s were held, is a palatial building which had once been the Moscow Nobleman's Club. Lenin lay in state there after his death in 1924, as Stalin did in 1953, surrounded by red flowers and weeping mourners. In 1931

George Bernard Shaw, one of the West's most vocal admirers of Communism, was allowed to celebrate his seventy-fifth birthday there.

Used as a court, the building conveyed impressive theatrical overtones. But Soviet justice had not always tried to impress. The background to this approach is both important to a fair understanding of the trial, and also not widely known, unlike the evolution of the Anglo-American legal system which most people have some idea about. So the reader will forgive me if I sketch in some relevant aspects.

When the Bolsheviks seized power, in October 1917, they found the old imperial legal system largely intact, except that all the judges had fled. Lenin, who had a first-class legal training, wanted the new republic to settle its internal disputes without the elaborately organised tribunals, with their labyrinthine rules of procedure and evidence which seemed to critics of "bourgeois justice" designed to exclude workers and peasants. He said, "Anybody can act as a judge basing himself on the revolutionary sense of justice of the working classes."

Within a month of seizing power, the Bolsheviks abolished all the old courts, substituting Revolutionary Tribunals, which had little formal definition and in any case were constantly changing. Likewise law, too, tended to become what the local commissar thought it ought to be. The left-wing intelligentsia welcomed this practical vacuum and some strange but innovative thinkers emerged. One of the odder was Lev Petrazhitsky, who had been well-known before the Revolution for his "intuitive" approach to legal philosophy. He wrote, "Law is only a psychic phenomenon. It exists only as a spiritual experience, emotions, in the psyche of human beings. Legal norms themselves, statutes, etc., have no real existence. They are merely figments of the imagination, fantastic notions, phantasmata." Rights were not just unenforceable in conditions of civil war, as was obvious in practical terms all around, but they were actually, in all circumstances, in principle imaginary. Successful human interaction could only depend upon the benevolence of others.

From then until the mid-1930s a titanic struggle was waged

for control of Soviet law between two powerful, intelligent but very different men: Nikolai Krylenko and Andrei Vyshinsky. They had irreconcilable views about what the Revolution meant for the rule of law, indeed whether the phrase had any meaning in a communist society. In essence, Krylenko wanted the courts to demonstrate the power of an implacable state, thirsting for vengeance over its class enemy. That was Lenin's approach. Stalin's was different, and when Vyshinsky sniffed the wind in the late 1920s he started developing a highly sophisticated view of the courts as placed in which to demonstrate the underlying benevolence of Socialist law. Both wanted what they thought of as justice to be seen to be done, but Krylenko wanted vengeance first and foremost, while Vyshinsky wanted theatre. The outcome largely dictated the fate of the British engineers.

Born in 1885, Krylenko graduated from the history faculty of St Petersburg University and the law faculty of the University of Kiev. He was subsequently forced into political exile, where he became close friends with Lenin. After the Revolution, Krylenko went into law, rising quickly through the hierarchy to become deputy Commissar of Justice and Prosecutor-General of the Russian republic in 1922. His was the public face of the state in most of the big trials of the 1920s. A British observer who met him at this time, Robert Bruce Lockhart described him in his book, *Memoirs of a British Agent*, as "an epileptic degenerate" and "the most repulsive type I came across in all my dealings with the Bolsheviks."

Krylenko was not a "degenerate" in the conventional sense of the word. He was a mountaineer of distinction—he claimed several first ascents in the Pamirs—and was also responsible for the rise of Soviet chess to world mastery. His attitude to the game, which he had played with Lenin while they killed time abroad, was similar to his approach to law. "We must finish once and for all with the neutrality of chess," he wrote. "We must condemn once and for all the formula 'chess for the sake of chess'. We must organise shock-brigades of chess-players, and begin the immediate realisation of a Five Year Plan for chess."

These were not empty words. Russia had not been the preeminent force in world chess which it was later to become until Krylenko turned the game into "a scientific weapon in the battle on the cultural front". He established a country-wide chess development programme, starting in the schools, while at the same time infiltrating the international governing body. The result was that, though the period from the establishment of the classical title in 1886 until the Second World War, Russia and the Soviet Union produced only one of the five world champions, in the period after the War, when the players and administrators who had come through the Krylenko system had matured, eight of the nine world champions came from the Soviet Union, the only exception being Bobby Fischer.

Krylenko's ruthless approach to chess was mirrored in his self-consciously Bolshevik, or "revolutionary", attitude towards law. Like MI5, he had no time for namby-pamby legal hair-splitting. "Execution of the guilty is not enough," he once said. "Execution of a few innocents as well will be even more impressive to the general public."[16]

By the late 1920s he was the Soviet Union's chief Prosecutor. His best-known appearance was at the so-called Shakhty, trial in 1928, when a large number of miners from a village called Shakhty in the Donbas were accused of sabotaging Soviet coal production. *Time* described the impression he made in court:

> Prosecutor Krylenko is stocky and kinetic, with large Asiatic features, and a close-cropped bullet head. His tongue is adept at wooing a prisoner into indiscretion and then lashing him upon the raw. A smile that verges easily into a sneer, a peculiar hypnotic stare, and a panther-like bound are other useful attributes of Comrade Krylenko. On the first day he strode in wearing what US citizens would call hunting costume: khaki coat and breeches, soft roll collar, homespun stockings and hobnail shoes. Within a few

---

[16] Krylenko was not the only person to think this way. In his monograph *Terrorism and Communism*, Trotsky had written scornfully of "Kantian-clerical, vegetarian-Quaker chatter about the 'sanctity of human life'."

hours he had wrung confessions from three small-fry technicians which should set them before a firing squad, and since then his hunting has been good.

Krylenko's practical efforts were backed up at an academic level by another strange figure, Evgeny Pashukanis. He was the leading Soviet legal theorist until Vyshinsky established dominance in the mid-1930s—a dominance which would last until the demise of the Soviet Union fifty years later. Like Krylenko, Pashukanis was an uncompromising Old Bolshevik. A large, dark-haired, bullying Lithuanian, he had read law at Munich University before the First World War. In 1924, he published *The General Theory of Law and Marxism*. Marx had held that the state came into being only after society was divided into mutually antagonistic classes. Friedrich Engels had drawn the logical conclusion that, after the achievement of communism, when class differences had been abolished, the state would "wither away". Extending this idea, Pashukanis's theory dealt with "the withering away of law". It came to be known as the "commodity-exchange" school of legal thought since the only purpose of law, he argued, was to control of the exchange of property. Even that would become unnecessary when a planned economy replaced private with fully communal property.

Krylenko's contribution to the debate was to argue, forcefully and successfully, that in applying a truly Soviet legal code, judges should be given almost complete discretion to dispose of cases in accordance with their "socialist legal conscience". In the early 1920s, there had been some discussion about re-introducing the pre-revolutionary principle of *nullum crimen, nullum poena, sine praevia lege* (no crime, no punishment, without previous law).[17] Krylenko argued vigorously against this. The state, he said, could not anticipate all the crimes that were likely to be committed in the new social conditions

---

[17] This is the generally-accepted principle against retroactive legislation and retrospective justice, which is what Leon Jaworski objected to in the charges at the Nuremberg Tribunals.

called forth by communism. The country was surrounded by enemies. More importantly in view of the trials that were soon to take place, there were innumerable, invisible enemies within. Judges needed flexibility. They should not have to depend on specific formulations of crime in law; rather they should be free to reason by analogy with similar offences and come up with their own conception of crime to fit the circumstances of the case before them.

In fact there was nothing revolutionary about this. It is what judges have always done in Common Law courts. The difference is that the scope for judicial "creativity" is more limited than he wanted. It is also hedged about by procedural constraints, and overshadowed by the right of appeal. But these are distinctions of scale rather than substance. Within the limitations of statute, Krylenko's proposals were challenging more due to the context in which they were made than because there is something inherently shocking in the Hamiltonian idea that you can infer the reality of the law from the character of the judge.

In 1927 Krylenko went further and argued (unsuccessfully, in the event) for an extension of this principle to preventative detention. He drafted an amendment to the Criminal Code which would provide for imprisonment of those "who had not committed any crime at all but, because of their connections with criminal surroundings or because of their past activity, they give reason to expect that they could commit some crime." This was not so revolutionary either. It had been common practice in the eighteenth century, and the same thinking was revisited in 2005 when the British government proposed house-arrest without trial for *suspected* terrorists, that is people who had not been convicted of any offence. They would be incarcerated in their homes without knowing the charges against them or the evidence for those charges. Members of their family would be searched every time they entered or left the house. Echoing Krylenko's justification, the then Home Secretary, Charles Clarke, said, "There are serious people and serious organisations trying to destroy our society."

Lenin would have approved of most of these ideas, and they

suited Stalin in the years when he was engineering a social
revolution. But when, in the early 1930s, the Five Year Plans
started to show results, he discovered that he needed incentives to
motivate workers who were increasingly often trained engineers.
He realised that, while you can incentivise manual workers by
threats of violence or death, you cannot kill all the engineers you
have just spent time and effort training and still retain the
capacity to produce engineering marvels. Law had to allow for
the accumulation of private property. It had to have an element of
certainty. Since Stalin still wanted to be able to murder people
when he felt he needed to, law had be developed as a form of
theatre which disguised reality.[18] That was where Vyshinsky
came in.

Vyshinsky was the son of a well-to-do Polish chemist. He
grew up in southern Russia and studied law at Kiev University.
He learned to dance elegantly and speak French fluently, and he
married happily. He also joined the Mensheviks, a fact which
later came back to haunt him, and in 1907 was sent to jail for his
role in a railway strike. There he met Stalin, a fact which later
enabled him to offset his lapse in revolutionary taste. He was not
to make the same mistake again. Unlike either Krylenko or
Pashukanis, Vyshinsky actually practised law. But he gave it up
after the Bolsheviks took power. Instead he joined the People's
Commissariat for Food. He was put in charge of the Moscow
supply organisation in the midst of catastrophic shortages.
"Nowadays in distribution one does not have to follow the

---

[18] Stalin's private thoughts about justice have recently been revealed in a book
entitled *Stalin's Letters to Molotov, 1925-36* (eds. Lih, Naumov and
Khlevniuk). For example, when there was a shortage of coins in circulation due
to hoarding, problems with the mint, inflation and other practical issues, Stalin
immediately decided this was not due to accident, disorganisation or petty
criminality; it was due to "financial wreckers". The solution was simple:
"Definitely shoot two or three dozen wreckers from these apparati, including
several dozen common cashiers," he wrote to Molotov. No namby-pamby legal
hair-splitting there. Though becoming an outward Vyshinskyite, he stayed
inwardly Krylenkoist.

universal principle of justice," he said. "We give herrings to the workers and leave the herrings' tails for the bourgeoisie."

Vyshinsky soon returned to his real vocation, the law. In 1925 he was "elected" Rector of Moscow University. When the Shakhty technicians were arrested in 1928, he was appointed to judge the trial, despite the fact that he had no judicial experience at all. His Russian biographer, Arkady Vaksberg, explains why:

> The important thing was not so much selecting an eloquent prosecutor [as there were many of those available], but an obedient and devoted judge. A figure was needed who would combine many different qualities: impressiveness and respectability, erudition and repute, ingenuity in the event of unexpected and unforeseen turns in the trial, reliability from the organisers' viewpoint, an ability to influence the accused and the public. There was no suitable candidate from among the official judges who had all been promoted from quite humble working positions, and were mostly without legal education. Vyshinsky was a lucky find. I do not think there was anyone else among the performers Stalin had to choose from at the time who could have competed for the role. There was only one obstacle: officially, in the formal sense of the word, he was not a judge.[19]

Procedural obstacles rarely stood in the way of the Soviet judicial machine, so the trial went ahead with Krylenko prosecuting and Vyshinsky on the Bench. It appears that this was the last time they co-operated.

Whereas Krylenko was aggressive, insensitive and sneering, as *Time* noted, Vyshinsky was polite, dignified and responsive.

---

[19] *Stalin's Prosecutor* Arkady Vaksberg p.43. Two extraordinary facts supporting the view that the Soviet legal profession took a long time to recover from the Revolution are contained in an article by Eugene Huskey entitled "Vyshinksy, Krylenko and the Shaping of the Soviet Legal Order" (*Slavic Review* 46, 1987, p. 414). In 1935, 85% of People's Court judges had no more than a primary education; and the Procuracy was so short of resources that the journal *Soviet Justice* carried an article about a campaign headlined: "A Bicycle for Every Investigator!".

By normal Soviet procedure, no evidence was led, only confessions produced and discussed, mainly by the Prosecutor as there was only a token Defence. Sometimes confessions were retracted. But the next day, after the retractor had spent a night in the basement cells, they were unretracted. Muscovites queued every night round the block for tickets to a public gallery which could hold three hundred.[20] After two months, eleven of the 52 defendants were sentenced to death, thirty-seven jailed and four acquitted. Within a couple weeks, the judge had published a book about the trial he had just presided over. There is no question that public relations were at the heart of the whole exercise. The big question was: had it worked?

The *New York Times* correspondent in Moscow, Walter Duranty, wrote, "The prosecution has shown by the testimony of the accused themselves that an organised conspiracy existed. It has been shown how the money came and how it was spent. But serious flaws remain. For there is but little proof, really valid proof, of any actual instances of sabotage. Also the whole story dovetails together too perfectly. It is felt that things may happen so in books or in the theatre, but not in real life."

Had Vyshinsky and his trial management team over-egged the pudding?

The evidence from the swarm of European and American well-wishers who holidayed in, or emigrated to, the Soviet Union in those years was that they had not. The Great Crash, with its resulting mass unemployment, naturally helped to change Western perceptions of the USSR. Over the next two years, the number of Americans visiting the country quadrupled. Eugene Lyons, the veteran American correspondent in Moscow,

---

[20] The average British court has a public gallery with space for a couple of dozen spectators. In civil cases, other than libel or those involving celebrities, it is usually empty. In criminal cases, it is rare for anyone to be present other than relatives of the accused. However, in the days before the abolition of the death penalty and the introduction of television, the situation was completely different. People queued, sometimes all night, for seats in well-publicised murder trials. Court was cheaper than the cinema and often more dramatic.

originally a committed communist but who later repented, described them as "amateur sociologists, bubbly school teachers, liberal ministers, earnest probers, socialite thrill seekers and miscellaneous neurotics". They wanted "statistics, not scenery; the economic not the exotic."[21]

British visitors were more likely to be middle-class celebrities wanting first-hand experience of socialism with which to fortify the moral authoritarianism common in left-wing circles. Apart from Bernard Shaw and H.G. Wells, the best known were the fashionable socialists, Sidney and Beatrice Webb. Their nephew was the wealthy, ascetic, sanctimonious, dogmatic, vegetarian scientist, lawyer, politician and communist, Sir Stafford Cripps, who was to be British Ambassador in Moscow 1940-42.[22] The Webbs toured collective farms and were shown round model factories before returning to Britain and proclaiming the Soviet Union "the hope of the world". They particularly admired "communist self-criticism", which justified the use in court of confessions rather than evidence. They knew that some people by-passed the court system altogether, disappearing without trace, but they accepted injustice as part of the necessary crusade against their own class.

---

[21] *Assignment in Utopia* Eugene Lyons, London 1937, p. 226. The reaction of nervous, hidebound Soviet officialdom unintentionally fed the visitors' sense of importance. "Two or more foreigners arriving anywhere, even a lavatory, were a 'delegation' in Russian eyes," wrote Lyons.

[22] It was Cripps who was responsible for Britain's refusal to sign the European Convention on Human Rights in its original form. As Chancellor of the Exchequer under Clement Attlee in the late 1940s, he objected to the security of property clauses (which is why today they are in Article 1 of the First Protocol, signed later). The relevant Cabinet minute states: "The Chancellor of the Exchequer said that a government committed to the policy of a planned economy could not ratify this Convention on Human Rights. He drew attention to the various articles in the draft Convention which were inconsistent with the powers of economic control which were essential to the operation of a planned economy... The draft Convention would be acceptable only to those who believed in a free economy and a minimum amount of State interference in economic affairs."

The Webbs toured the Ukraine during the early stages of what turned out to be the most serious famine in Russian history and were given facts and figures which they used in their book, *Soviet Communism: a New Civilisation*. They would brook no alternative view. They threatened at least one other authority, better-informed than themselves, when the truth about the famine seemed likely to be published.[23] Millions of people were taken in by the Webbs, one of the most celebrated being John Maynard Keynes. He said in a radio broadcast that "the Webbs have enabled us to see the direction in which things appear to be moving [in the Soviet Union]. The results are impressive. The Russian innovators have passed not only from the revolutionary stage, but also from the doctrinaire stage… The largest scale empiricism and experimentation which has ever been attempted by *disinterested administrators* is in operation." (emphasis added)

The opinion of the world was becoming increasingly important to Stalin. By 1932 it was clear that the first Five Year Plan, which started in 1928, was seriously under-performing. The Soviet Union needed more machinery which could only be produced in the West, at a time when his ability to pay for it was declining. The Great Crash had reduced commodity prices world-wide and commodities like wheat and lumber were almost all that the Soviet Union had to offer by way of payment. Consequently, Stalin needed credits. But capitalists do not lend money to countries that have a chaotic, Krylenko-style legal system. That was one more reason why Vyshinsky's start began to rise.

The courts were a vital part of Stalin's public relations drive, which is why, five years after the Shakhty trial, Vyshinsky was promoted from judge to Public Prosecutor of the Russian republic, displacing Krylenko. Soon he had engineered the eclipse of Pashukanis too. Vyshinsky was at least as cunning and vicious as his opponents. He later justified his shift by claiming he had come to realise that the two men were legal "wreckers" who had developed "a nihilist attitude to Soviet law."

---

[23] See *Stalin's Apologist: Walter Duranty* S.J. Taylor, p. 196

One of their crimes was to have advocated a system of criminal judging which "did not bind judges, only orientate them"—which of course is exactly what judicial discretion is supposed to do. But this was no longer acceptable. Stalin now wanted judges who did exactly as he required, without referring to their socialist consciences (or, of course, the law). This later became known as "telephone justice", since they had to phone the Great Leader and Teacher to find out what verdicts and sentences to hand down. In effect, the only judge in the country who had independent tenure was Stalin himself.

To jump forward briefly: the end of the two lions of the twenties was almost pathetic. The once-bullying Pashukanis was denounced in *Pravda* in January 1937 as an "enemy of the people" who had been responsible for "judicial cretinism of Herculean proportions". Soon afterwards he was arrested. In the cells, he soon confessed to having been a "terrorist" for years, "working in the sphere of the theory of Soviet criminal law."

Sensing the new chill wind, Krylenko realised his only hope was to denounce his former mentor. Soon after Pashukanis's arrest, he publicly called him a "double-dealer", a "spiteful critic" and a "slanderer". But that turned out not to be enough, so he went further and denounced himself. "My defective idea," Krylenko said, "was that it was possible to pass judgement without proven guilt. I permitted myself the blasphemy of applying Lenin's system of punishment, in which every tenth member of a regiment in whose ranks a theft has occurred is put to death. But I forgot that Lenin permitted these special forms of repression only under certain conditions of time and place and that they were not applied through the courts."

Pashukanis was given a five-minute trial *in camera* in August 1937, and shot half an hour later. Krylenko was arrested the following January. After three days of torture, the man who had made the highest-ever single-handed ascent by a Soviet mountaineer broke down. The bullet-headed Bolshevik with the sneering smile and the panther-like bound signed a confession saying he had been an anti-Soviet conspirator since before the Revolution. In subsequent interrogations he named thirty other "wreckers" with whom he had conspired to assassinate Stalin and take power. After a few more months of imprisonment, Krylenko was tried as quickly and secretly as Pashukanis had been. He put up no defence, saying he was tired and was thinking now only of his family. Twenty minutes later he was shot.

The man who tried both Pashukanis and Krylenko, and who was to try the Metro-Vickers engineers, was Citizen Judge Vassily Vassilich Ulrikh. Over the course of the 1930s, he was to become the archetypal Stalinist judge.

Ulrikh was an over-weight, unbecoming Latvian whose father had been a German revolutionary and mother a Russian aristocrat. Though his family had been exiled to Siberia on account of his father's subversive activities, the young Ulrikh was commissioned into the Tsarist army in 1914. In 1918, Trotsky got him into the Cheka, and in 1926 he was appointed Chairman of the Military Collegium of the Supreme Court of the USSR.

Ulrikh's appearance in court was intimidating. He had a bald, spherical head, set above an almost spherical body. Beneath beady, bulging, compulsively blinking eyes, he sported a small, square, Hitler-style moustache. One Russian historian called him "a uniformed toad with watery eyes". Eugene Lyons, wrote of Ulrikh:

> In his round podgy face the gods had modelled a mask of impish, gloating cruelty. His flushed, over-stuffed features were twisted continually into a grimace of brutal sarcasm. The muscles of his mouth seemed incapable of anything suggesting a judicial expression: that melon-face hovering above the court, sneering and jeering, was a caricature of the very idea of justice.[24]

Ulrikh never owned any property. Instead he lived in a modest room in the Metropol Hotel where, in his later years, Vyshinsky's biographer says he used to take "representatives of the oldest profession, trembling with fear. After getting drunk, he

---

[24] *Assignment in Utopia, op. cit.*, p. 568

used to regale them with stories of the executions he had attended." Apparently his enthusiasm for executions was such that he had occasionally carried them out himself.

Today Ulrikh's remains lie beneath an unkempt grave, with weeds and brambles growing over it, in the Novodevichi Cemetery in suburban Moscow. The plain, lichen-covered headstone carries a little oval photograph which shows him wearing a line of medals on his chest and a sneering half-smile. It is perhaps relevant to the hierarchy in a prosecutorial system that Vyshinsky is buried below the Kremlin wall, the gardens around which are kept immaculate by state employees to this day.

Ulrikh often paid nocturnal visits to Stalin to discuss sentencing in a then-current trial. In other cases, he would receive lists of prisoners before the proceedings opened. Some of the names had a "1" marked against them. These people were to be found guilty and sentenced to death. Those with a "2" were to be found guilty and given ten years in the labour camps. If there was no mark, then the judge was free to do as he liked, even follow the evidence, though there was not much point in that as it had usually been obtained by either torture, trickery or threat. Retractions in the safety of the court-room were ignored. In one case, a famous Old Bolshevik told Ulrikh that he had signed the confession which was being used against him only after "torture, terrible torture". Ulrikh replied, "I see you are now going to slander the NKVD." The prisoner started to say, "I categorically deny…" But he was cut off by the judge who said, "Have you nothing else to add?" Without waiting for a reply, he pronounced sentence.

In the Metro-Vickers trial, many of the defendants confessed, though all who spoke to the world's press said they had been treated well by their interrogators. So why did they surrender their will to others? Many observers assumed they did so because they, too, were tortured. But Vyshinsky made a public statement denying this before the trial started. A.J. Cummings, of the London *News Chronicle,* was the only eye-witness to write a book about the case. In it he comments wryly:

There is no reason to doubt that M. Vyshinsky was correct in his assertion that what he calls "the presiding magistracy" had not deviated "from the established rules of procedure". But unfortunately the established rules of OGPU[25] procedure, while they do not comprise such brutal and clumsy practices as the thumbscrew, the rack, the bastinado, feet-tickling or starvation, undoubtedly include delicate psychological methods of persuasion... The whole question offers a wide and profoundly interesting field of psychological study; and it is to be hoped that in time to come, when the new Russia has evolved a stage further, M. Vyshinsky and some of his able associates (if they are still alive) will be willing to supply medical experts, psycho-analysts and the appropriate departments of scientific research in the principle universities of the world with the valuable data they must have collected in the course of their patriotic labours.[26]

This is the sinister world into which six British subjects— three Englishmen, a Welshman, a New Zealander and a South African—were catapulted (along with twelve Soviet citizens) by the OGPU on the evening of 11 March 1933 when two of them were arrested during dinner at a comfortable company house in the forest north-east of Moscow. The arrests made headlines around the world. In Britain, the right-wing press suddenly took an intense interest in the Soviet Union and its justice system, something which it had studiously ignored for years, despite the almost continuous news about sabotage, spies and executions. Indeed on the same day, the Soviets announced the execution without trial by the OGPU of thirty-five "wreckers" in the agricultural industry.

The lack of interest hitherto was because no previous trial had involved any British subjects. With the exception of the Shakhty case five years earlier, in which three Germans were amongst the accused, none had involved any non-Soviets. In

---

[25] Объединённое Государственное Политическое Управление (ОГПУ, or OGPU), the Unified State Political Administration. It was the successor to the Cheka, part of the NKVD, and predecessor of the KGB.

[26] *The Moscow Trial* A.J. Cumming, London 1933, p. 46

America, *Time* noted the existence of the twelve Russians also standing trial, but said "neither the Soviet nor the world press took much interest in them". With their six British co-accused it was quite different. Long before details of the charges were known, *The Times* was writing about the "horrible methods" of a "ruthless and unscrupulous tyranny". The *Morning Post* called the Soviet government "ruffians". The *Daily Telegraph* said the charges were "trumped up". The *Daily Mail* wrote of "Soviet bandits", and the *Evening News* said that the British government should "notify the Soviet government that its antics are intolerable and its judicial methods uncivilised". One of the more level-headed reporters described the upcoming trial as the most significant since the Dreyfus case in 1894. Rather clumsily, the *Daily Express,* deprecating the use of diplomatic channels, called on the British government to condemn Moscow "through the mouth of its head."

The left-wing press had the opposite affliction: everything in the Soviet Union was admirable, possibly even civilised. The trial was of purely local significance because the Soviet Union was a place where fundamental social justice was being done now that the exploitation of labour by capital had been abolished. If there was occasionally an excess of proletarian zeal, that was regrettable, but it did not affect the underlying fact of a fair and progressive society.

One of the few insiders to object to this view was the British journalist Malcolm Muggeridge. Married to a niece of the Webbs, Muggeridge had emigrated from Manchester to Moscow six months earlier, intending to change class and stay for life in the paradise of the workers. But by early spring of 1933 he had been completely disillusioned, partly by the famine which was by then enveloping much of southern Russia and the Ukraine. After defying Soviet orders not to visit the stricken areas, Muggeridge sent three coruscating reports about the tragedy to his newspaper, the *Manchester Guardian*. But his articles were cut, and they were not placed prominently enough within the paper, he thought. Now we know that Muggeridge was right: eight million people died from starvation in these years, maybe more.  In the last of his articles, Muggeridge prophesied that the Kremlin would deal with internal opposition created by the famine by "employing its familiar tactics—speeches, slogans, enthusiastic conferences in Moscow—in the villages, ruthless, organised force." This was published in the *Manchester Guardian* on 28 March 1933, three weeks after Roosevelt's inauguration, and two weeks before the trial opened.

The *Manchester Guardian* maintained its complacent attitude after the British engineers were arrested, even though there was a local angle to the story since Metropolitan Vickers was based in Manchester and most of the "wrecked" turbines had been built at Trafford Park. Muggeridge wrote to his editor accusing him of wilful blindness:

> You don't want to know what is going on in Russia, and you don't want your readers to know either. If the Metro-Vickers people had been Jews or Negroes, your righteous indignation would have been unbounded. You'd have published photographs of their lacerated backsides. They being just Englishmen, you refuse to publish the truth about their treatment or the general facts which make that truth significant—and this when the *Manchester Guardian* is packed with stories of what the Nazis are doing to the Jews, and the Poles to their Ukrainian and Silesian minorities.

The British official reaction was different. The day after the arrests, when nothing whatsoever was known of the details, the ambassador in Moscow, Sir Esmond Ovey, telegraphed London saying he recommended warning the Soviet government that diplomatic relations would be broken off if it did not "refrain from being drawn by an excessive zeal on the part of the police into permitting the trumping up of frivolous and fantastic accusations against a friendly and reputable British company." The next day Stanley Baldwin, deputising for the Prime Minister, told the House of Commons that "his Majesty's government are convinced that there can be no justification for the charge on which the arrests were made."

Making what A.J. Cummings called "pontifical claims to incorruptible rectitude", the British ambassador met "the

Commissar for Foreign Affairs, Monsieur Litvinov" and demanded that his government order the Soviet judicial authorities to abandon the trial. This was in itself a surprise since Sir Esmond had arrived in Moscow determined to try to understand the Bolshevik experiment. His previous post had been in Mexico, where he had watched Dwight Morrow, the American banker, act as "good-will ambassador". He seemed determined to adopt a similar approach in the land of the Soviets. Eugene Lyons wrote that, to begin with, Ovey was "the lone 'Bolshevik' in the diplomatic corps, apologising and explaining everything Soviet as stoutly as a *Manchester Guardian* emissary. Then he turned— and in his apostasy grew as sharply critical as any *Manchester Guardian* emissary in reverse."[27] He surely had Muggeridge in mind.

Litvinov replied to the Ambassador's démarche with an uncharacteristic personal insult, probably dictated by Stalin: "Permit me, Sir Esmond, to tell you that even if such methods of diplomacy might perhaps be successful, let us say, with Mexico, they are doomed in advance to complete failure in the USSR."[28] After this, Sir Esmond asked to be recalled to London "for consultations", and the British Embassy was, for the duration of the trial, in the hands of his more stable deputy, William Strang.

The first to be released, after just forty-eight hours in custody, was the most senior of the Metro-Vickers executives, Allan Monkhouse, the New Zealander. He is the only one who

---

[27] *Assignment in Utopia, op.cit.,* p.563

[28] Litvinov, who was born Meir Wallach-Finkelstein, came from a family of wealthy bankers in Poland. He was an early convert to Bolshevism and spent many years in Britain before the First World War, some of them living off the Shankill Road in north Belfast. As Ambassador to Britain in the 1920s, he was responsible for engineering the end of Britain's economic blockade of the Soviet Union. He was later described by *Time* as being "a daring moderate in a land of humdrum radicals". Married to the daughter of a prominent English Jewish family, his last deathbed utterance was: "Englishwoman, go home." She did. His adversary, Sir Esmond Ovey, was a widely-travelled Old Etonian who was the uncle of Michael Palin, the Monty Python actor and television travel presenter.

published a detailed account of his ordeal. Monkhouse had first travelled to Russia in 1911 as a junior engineer. Like all others in similar positions, he was asked by the British government to stay on after the First World War broke out to help accelerate Russian armament production. After the Revolution in October 1917, Monkhouse and others were ordered to help destroy Allied arms dumps which the retreating Russians were abandoning to the advancing Germans. Though he was not in fact able to commit any destruction, he was nevertheless arrested on Christmas Day 1917 by the Bolsheviks, who wanted to get hold of the British supplies, and accused of provocation and sabotage.

The account Monkhouse gave of his trial in his memoirs throws a sharp light on his experiences in 1933. It is also one of the only first-hand accounts we have of a westerner in the clutches of the early post-Revolution judicial system:

> This Court had nothing of the ceremonial and theatrical setting which sabotage trials now have in Moscow. It consisted of one Jewish lawyer, a political agitator and two workmen, one of whom I recognised as an illiterate plumber who had formerly been in my employ. Prisoner, judges and witnesses sat round a rough table with a torn, green-baize cover. The room was full of tobacco smoke. The president, a glass of tea in one hand, and a thick slice of black bread spread with red caviar in the other hand, addressed me with his mouth so full that I could hardly distinguish his words. My case dragged on until the late evening. In those days punishment for crimes of this nature was immediate execution and, though I was entirely innocent of the charges against me, nevertheless my case went badly, and I shall always remember watching the sun set over the Kremlin Towers and thinking to myself that in all probability it was the last time I should see it... [This was] infinitely more trying than waiting for Judge Ulrikh's verdict in the Moscow Court on April 19th 1933.[29]

Monkhouse was saved only when proof was found that he had not actually managed to do what he intended to do. After

---

[29] *Moscow 1911-1933* Allan Monkhouse, London 1933, pp. 71-2

being acquitted, he fled in very dramatic circumstances, via Vladivostok, to Britain. There he joined the British Army and returned to Russia, in July 1918, as a translator and later junior officer with the Anglo-American force which had been sent to Archangel, ostensibly also to protect Allied arms dumps falling into unauthorised hands.

Monkhouse soon formed an unflattering, almost Baillie-Stewart-ish, view of the British officer class abroad. Co-operating with pro-Allied Russians, rather than simply giving them orders, he wrote,

> brought me into some disrepute with my superiors as being a Russophile... Unfortunately many of our Allied officers had evidently been accustomed to dealing with Asiatic and dark races, and were inclined to treat our Russian allies in the manner which they had previously adopted towards less enlightened peoples.[30]

In 1924 Monkhouse returned to the USSR on behalf of Metropolitan Vickers. Lenin had defined communism as "Soviet power plus electrification of the whole country", and Metro-Vickers was the largest foreign firm involved with the electrification. Monkhouse loved his work and respected most of the Russians with whom he worked. By 1933, he was in charge of all Metro-Vickers' operations within the Soviet Union. He cut a commanding figure in court. Cummings described him as a "tall, dark, wiry, athletic-looking man, with level piercing eyes, and a cool command of himself". He said he thought he was the sort of person who could be depended on, "with equal steadfastness and efficiency" to "repair a defective turbine, lead a platoon in a forlorn hope and stand up unflinchingly to a few hours of heavy questioning by the OGPU."

Immediately after his release from the Lubyanka on 13 March, Monkhouse drove to the British Embassy. "I was treated with extraordinary courtesy and consideration," he told the press when asked the inevitable question about the horrible methods of the Soviet bandits. "Although I was under prison regime, the

---

[30] *Ibid.*, p. 101

conditions seemed to me better than those I witnessed once on a visit to Dartmoor. Everywhere, the last word in efficiency was manifest. My questioners knew what they were doing. That is, amongst other things, they knew engineering. At intervals food was brought in, and in abundance. Among other things there was caviar."

In his book, written in Britain after his trial, he told a different story. For four hours the OGPU searched his house, then took him to the Lubyanka where he was strip-searched in a room that was "approximately the temperature of a Turkish bath", then finally given a bed in a cell at about 4 a.m. At 6.30 a.m. he was woken, told to clean his cell, and given some liquid which the guard "described as tea". After that he was taken downstairs for examination by a man who was "obviously capable of making his strong personality felt" but was "nevertheless not a man of any education".

> The method of cross-examination employed never included physical torture. Hypnotism and drugs were not used on me, but my examination was continued uninterruptedly from breakfast-time until approximately 2 a.m. the following morning... Towards the late evening I began to get very tired. [My interrogator] obviously knew this, and endeavoured to persuade me to write a statement regarding the behaviour of certain machines which the Metropolitan Vickers company had supplied... Finally he dictated a statement to me, which I wrote in English. Almost every phrase he dictated I disputed, altered and finally wrote in a form which I thought would satisfy him and yet not harm my employers' high reputation. After midnight, I felt that my nerve was going. I was dead tired after the previous night's search and arrest, and a very long day's intensive examination I felt my tongue and mouth so dry that they gave me considerable discomfort. My lips twitched in a way I never knew before. It was a hard mental effort to resist writing exactly what my interrogator dictated... [After this experience] I understand and realise how it is that victims can be induced to make all manner of confessions, even without recourse to the practices—hypnotism, drugs and physical torture—which

the OGPU are accredited with employing.[31]

The next day Monkhouse went through the same thing again. At no stage was he told what the charges against him were. The only clue he had was information that colleagues had testified that he had been involved in spying and wrecking. He was warned that if he did not co-operate with the examination procedure he would be treated as a criminal by the OGPU. His interrogator said, "If the OGPU act, they will act in such a way that you will cease to be of any use either to the Soviet Union or to Great Britain."

The next morning Monkhouse was released. He was free to go to his office and work normally, which he did, until he was recalled ten days later for an examination by Vyshinksy, of whom he wrote, "Outside the Moscow Court, I imagine that he would prove to be a well-informed and cultured man of the old intelligentsia."

It was not until two days before the trial was due to start that Monkhouse and the other defendants were handed copies of the indictment, in Russian. Though he had given nothing away to Vyshinksy, Monkhouse said, "I bit my lip until it bled when I once again realised the temporary weakness I had shown on that awful Sunday in the Lubyanka."

What of the others? The stoutest resistance to the OGPU was put up by John Cushny, the South African. A tall, burly, ebullient man from Johannesburg, he was described by Cummings as "devil-may-care". He gave his interrogators nothing at all. When asked during his interrogation if he pled guilty to collecting economic and political information, he said, "I do not wish to reply."

"What are the reasons for refusing to tell about your spying operations in the USSR?" he was then asked.

"I do not with to reply to that question."

"Why do you not wish to reply to the questions put to you

---

[31] *Ibid.,* pp. 295, 299

previously?"

"I do not wish to reply to that question."[32]

Towards the end of the trial, Vyshinsky commented on this exchange. "This is the classic conduct of an exposed spy under examination, of a spy who is a little worm-eaten for all that."[33]

The Welshman, William Gregory, was the only one who was actually acquitted. He appears to have borne up well under interrogation too, at least if his conduct in court is any indication. There he spoke extremely forcefully in his own defence. At one stage, during cross-examination of one of the Russians, he shouted out from the dock, "This man is fouling my reputation and you are taking his statement without any proof. Is this fair? Is this justice?" Ulrikh was so taken aback that he allowed Gregory to come to the witness stand and make a statement of rebuttal.

However two of the three Englishmen on trial made confessions of such gravity that they sent themselves to jail and nearly did the same for all the others. The first of these, in terms of importance to the trial, was the rather pathetic figure of William Macdonald, a 29-year old, partly-crippled Londoner with a drink problem and a particular fondness for his Russian house-keeper. She had been arrested in January 1933, the time when, it now seems, the OGPU had begun assembling the case against the Metro-Vickers staff. Macdonald was the only Briton who was not released before the trial.

The British press was outraged. The Soviets hit back with

---

[32] An almost complete transcript of the trial was published in Moscow by the State Law Publishing House, and in Britain by George Allen & Unwin, under the title *Wrecking Activities at Power Stations in the Soviet Union* (1933). (This quote is from p. 657.)

[33] Cushny behaved exactly as Kim Philby recommended Soviet spies caught by Western intelligence should do. In July 1977 Philby gave a lecture to KGB operatives in which he argued that spies should never confess. "We must always remember," he said, "that bourgeois law is designed primarily to safeguard the possession and acquisition of property. It therefore involves elaborate safeguards for all sorts of individual skulduggery. It is up to us to take advantage of every opportunity of using bourgeois law, and turning it against itself." *Private Life of Kim Philby*, Rufina Philby, London 1999, p. 257.

the fact that Baillie-Stewart had been, in equally sensational circumstances, held for longer in the Tower of London before his trial opened. A.J. Cummings noticed that when Macdonald came into court on the first day he looked "pinched and haggard". He kept his "downward glance fixed on the bench in front of him. Throughout the trial his British colleagues rarely looked at him; and I did not see him glance more than once in their direction." Eugene Lyons described Macdonald as "a thin, nervous man" with "weak, pallid features" who "made an unpleasant impression."

The trial started with the reading of the indictment. This was really a statement for the prosecution as it contained much of the evidence against the accused. The evidence turned out to be nothing more than a series of inter-related confessions. The accused were then asked how they pleaded. Four said, "Not guilty". Of the other two, Macdonald said, "Guilty", and Cushy said, "Emphatically not guilty on any count."

For all his apparent plasticity, Macdonald did make a show of defiance when, on the second day, he retracted some of what he had said while in custody.

"Then why did you depose to this effect at the preliminary investigation?" Vyshinsky asked.

"Because I considered it convenient to do so in the circumstances," Macdonald replied, lackadaisically.

After a brief pause while the Court digested this potentially disastrous turn of events, Vyshinksy said, "When you signed your deposition, were any special methods of examination applied to you?"

"No," said Macdonald.

"Were you forced to write it?"

"No, but I signed it because it was not the open court. In the beginning I refused to sign."

"Where?"

"Before the investigator. When the investigator said, 'Sign!' I said, 'No'. But he did not allow me to do otherwise."

"He forced you to?"

Macdonald looked down at his feet and said nothing.

Vyshinksy then asked why he did not dispute the deposition at his final interrogation,

"I do not want to discuss this point," Macdonald said.

Vyshinsky reminded him of his guilty plea, and asked him if he still considered himself guilty or not.

"According to the testimony given by myself, I plead guilty," Macdonald said. "In actual fact, not guilty."

"I am not asking about that," Vyshinksy replied. "Yesterday, did you say that you considered yourself guilty, or didn't you? Perhaps I dreamed it all."

"Yesterday I pleaded guilty."

"And today?"

"Today, in accordance with what I have just said not guilty."

"It follows that we may expect that perhaps tomorrow you will do the opposite."

"No."

Later in the same session, Vyshinsky confronted Macdonald with the fact that he had confessed to gathering political, military and economic intelligence about the Soviet Union.

"I wish it to be understood this way," Macdonald said. "I saw the deposition of Mr Thornton, and I also saw a large book which was said to contain other depositions and so decided that it was no use on my part to deny the charges."

When, later in the proceedings, it became plain that Macdonald was going to persist in his refutation of the evidence the OGPU thought it had secured, the approach changed. According to the statement he made to the Foreign Office two months after the trial, Macdonald was taken aside during a court recess and told that if he did not stick to his confession, his beloved housekeeper would be shot. From then on Macdonald co-operated with Vyshinsky, and was rewarded with a sentence of two years' jail.

But Macdonald's confession was not so damaging as that of the other Englishman to be sent to jail, Leslie Thornton. Thornton had been born in St Petersburg, where his father had been a factory-owner. Apart from his school years, he had spent much of his life in Russia, and met Monkhouse in Moscow during the war. By the time of the trial, he was Monkhouse's deputy and rumoured to be having an affair with his boss's secretary, Miss Kutuzova, another of the accused. Thornton's wife had left for England and he had fallen into depression, it was said.

Monkhouse, in his memoirs, described Kutuzova as "a bright, clever and extraordinarily efficient woman". One afternoon in late January, at about the same time as Macdonald's housekeeper was arrested, Kutuzova was tricked into leaving the Metro-Vickers office by the OGPU. She was dragged into a waiting car and driven to the Lubyanka. Monkhouse phoned London and reported her disappearance. Due, Monkhouse subsequently thought, to the tapping of his phone, Kutuzova was released next morning. "The exhausted and terrified woman who collapsed into my office was a spectre of the girl who had been dragged to OGPU headquarter eighteen hours before. What had occurred she would not, and probably dare not, say. That she had written much was evidence from the ink-marks which I noticed on her fingers."

Monkhouse was convinced that threats against her relatives had forced her to start helping the OGPU build up the case against the Metro-Vickers defendants. In his memoirs, he gallantly forgave her, saying, "After my own short experience at the Lubyanka, I shall never bear Miss Kutuzova the slightest ill will for whatever she was forced into saying or writing."

In court, Kutuzova was the only Russian to make any attempt to bandy words with Vyshinsky, though only about personal rather than substantive matters. All the others, according to Monkhouse gave "false testimony" in a "parrot-like manner." Eugene Lyons said of them that, "with one or two negligible exceptions, they were panic-stricken, half-hysterical penitents collaborating with the OGPU and the prosecution. All of them watched for the flick of Vyshinsky's whip and obeyed with the frightened alacrity of trained animals."

Thornton's confession was introduced without warning into the trial on the third day. Vyshinsky played his trump card in the interests of theatre rather than justice. Coming from one of the

British accused, it carried special weight. In minute detail, Thornton described who had done what by way of espionage in the Soviet Union by all the accused on behalf of Metropolitan Vickers and the British Secret Service. It was devastating material. But it was all fantasy.

After his words had been read to the court, Thornton, looking sheepish and embarrassed, said, "I wish to repudiate this document entirely."

Ulrikh was so astonished that he was almost lost for words. He could only counter by saying, "Your wish alone is not enough."

Vyshinksy asked him why he wrote it.

"At the time," Thornton replied, "it was a matter of indifference to me what I wrote."

"But why was it a matter of indifference?"

"I was in such a frame of mind."

Soon afterwards, when asked why he gave so many names of his colleagues to the investigators (with potentially very serious consequences for them), he said, "I simply don't know. I was asked to confess."

The only explanation came when he was asked about his statements implicating Macdonald.

"Why did you make an untrue statement?" Vyshinsky asked.

"Because I was very excited and I lost my courage."

"Why did you lose your courage?"

"Under the influence of events."

"What events?"

"My arrest."

At that, Ulrikh commented contemptuously, "You were kept under arrest for one day and you lost your nerve."

Later Vyshinsky asked, "Do you confirm you made your confession voluntarily without being influenced, without pressure?"

"Yes," said Thornton.

"Then you signed it?"

"Yes, and now the Court will examine it."

"But why did you give such information?" Ulrikh asked.

"Was it only to take up everybody's time, the Court's and the Public Prosecutor's time. What you are saying is absurd. You have been making depositions for three weeks so as to deny them now."

"I merely—"

"Decided to make more work for the Court," Ulrikh interrupted.

"I did it because, as I said, I was frightened."

"How were you frightened?" Ulrikh said, taking over the examination himself. "By whom were you frightened? Where and when were you frightened?"

"I was not frightened by arrest and by the consequences, but simply this way—"

"No. You give a straight reply so that it will be clear and plain to everybody. Who frightened you? When did they frighten you? In what room?"

Thornton gave no answer, but it was as a result of this series of exchanges that the legend of Tibetan powders first gained currency as an explanation for the way in which apparently sane men could be induced by the OGPU to incriminate themselves. The next day the *Daily Mail* carried a story about a White Russian general who had been kidnapped by the OGPU in 1930 and taken to Moscow, where he made confessions which resulted in "wholesale executions". The *Mail*'s story was that "these drugs, unknown in the West, are prepared by Tibetans in the employ of the OGPU from herbs and are administered in the food of prisoners without their knowledge. The effect of such concoctions is totally to destroy the will-power of those being questioned, and to place them entirely in the psychic power of their gaolers."

A.J. Cummings commented: "Of all the witless trash published in the course of the trial, nothing was quite so witless as this maudlin acceptance of the malicious fable of a handful of Russian refugees."

So why did the accused confess? In the case of the Russians, it is likely that threats against family and loved-ones played a large, perhaps decisive, part. Perhaps the same applied to the two

Englishmen: Thornton seeking to protect Miss Kutuzova and Macdonald his housekeeper. Monkhouse viewed Kutuzova's betrayal indulgently. Lyons was not so generous. He pointed out that the confessions went beyond even the claims of the prosecution. He wrote:

> Even the theory that they were guilty does not suffice to explain their confessions... It was not as though they had been confronted by incontrovertible proofs of guilt and obliged to accept the inevitable. Not one scrap of independent evidence to support their admissions was offered by the government, though all foreigners are under constant surveillance and a thorough search had been made of the Britishers' homes and offices.... To this day, though all the Britishers are free and have small reason to protect the reputation of the OGPU, no tenable explanation for these confessions has been forthcoming. Both Macdonald and Thornton have remained in the employ of the Metropolitan-Vickers Electrical company despite their "betrayal", thus adding another element of mystery to the whole business.[34]

William Strang was exasperated by the weakness displayed by Macdonald and Thornton. A Soviet official told one journalist that, whatever the truth about their confessions, if they had been Communists who had behaved like that in a capitalist court he would have had them shot, simply for cowardice.

Ulrikh's outburst at Thornton's repudiation of his confession briefly threatened to destroy the impression of legality that the court proceedings were designed to convey. For the rest of the time, Cummings felt Ulrikh was trying to please, to put on a show, though ultimately unsuccessfully:

> I have never seen a judge who smiled so much on the slightest provocation, or on none. But I did not like Judge Ulrikh's smile. The more I saw of it the less I liked it. There was a malign element in its oily quality. And at times it became transfixed into something that resembled too closely a diabolic sneer. My first

---

[34] *Assignment in Utopia, op. cit.*, p. 564-5

impression of him was that, despite his unimpeachable Communist antecedents, he might be mistaken in England for a middle-class stock-broker with a genial outlook on the world at large.... He was nevertheless a good presiding judge. He preserved strict order; he kept himself well in hand, rarely attempting to be dogmatic, clever or funny, after the manner of some of my favourites on the English Bench.[35]

Vyshinsky also laughed, occasionally at himself. For a man of his vanity and ambition, there had, in the context of Stalinist Moscow, to be a reason for that. The bonhomie of both men was clearly put for the benefit of the foreign journalists. Monkhouse also noted the lack of the normal red communist decoration in the court-room, saying that "the trial had obviously been arranged in order to give the Court that air of west-European solemnity which the authorities wished it to have in view of the world-wide attention which had been focussed on it."

Monkhouse thought that "Vyshinsky was the authority who directed every move of the Court. Judge Ulrikh referred to him for guidance on procedure on every occasion when such matters were raised." Since Vyshinsky was intimate with Stalin, it was clearly the Great Leader and Teacher who was orchestrating this trial.

The international attention focussed on the Moscow court in April 1933 was unique in Soviet history. Few cases anywhere in modern times have attracted so much attention. Yet, in the end, a strange air of mystery still surrounds these proceedings, not only because of the apparently unforced confessions to acts which were almost certainly never committed. Eugene Lyons wrote more explicitly than others about this. He was one of the few journalists able to follow the proceedings without the aid of an interpreter. He sat through every minute of the trial and read everything published about it. But, in the end, he admitted that he was still "as much at sea as any casual newspaper customer." Writing four years after the event, he expressed his puzzlement in

---

[35] *The Moscow Trial, op. cit.* p. 114

this way:

> Of this I feel sure: that the real story, the real compulsions, were located far behind the scenes. What transpired at the former Nobles Club seemed to me little more than a shadow play on a screen... The conviction grew in my mind at the time, and has been deepened since, that immense unseen forces were at work. The OGPU and the prosecution had a club over the heads of some of the Britishers. British guilt (whether of the British Intelligence Service or of individual Britishers, I dare not surmise) was involved, but that guilt referred to matters which were not even mentioned at the trial. If that theory has any validity, it was not the first time that men and governments have accepted responsibility for lesser crimes to conceal larger ones.[36]

Even if the method of obtaining the confessions was personal blackmail, that explains only how the evidence was collected, not why the project was undertaken in the first place. Lyons' suggestion of a sort of international, unpublicised plea-bargain going on behind the trial is one explanation for the events of spring 1933 in Moscow, but not the only one. There was also a political angle, perhaps two of them, in this case. So where does the truth lie behind this Potemkin trial, which was arguably, given the international dimension that was largely absent from the later show trials, the most extreme example of the use of legal proceedings as a theatrical device in modern times?

It seems to me that there are three possible explanations, a political, a diplomatic and a legal one. They are not mutually exclusive, and it is quite likely that the Kremlin had more than one aim in mind when it launched the investigations that led eventually to the indictments, probably towards the end of 1932. It is entirely possible that *all* the explanations are valid. Stalin was never a man to kill one bird with a stone which could be used to kill two, or better still three.

The simplest explanation is the internal, political one,

---

[36] *Assignment in Utopia, op. cit.*, pp. 565-6

namely that the case was initiated as a way of concealing the famine. The importance of this can hardly be overstated. In 1932 the harvest failed dramatically due to the stubborn resistance of kulaks and other peasants to Stalin's plan for collectivising agriculture. This was the final battle in a war which had begun in 1928 when peasants responded to the beginning of the first Five Year Plan by withholding produce from a market which would not give them a price they thought reasonable for it. Stalin's response to opposition was to abrogate all law and revert to the tactics of war communism, including a policy of confiscation. This provoked attacks on the confiscators, which brought military-backed reprisals, and so in an escalating spiral of violence. The winter of 1932-3 was the climax of this desperate conflict, one which Stalin later told Churchill was, at its worst, more threatening for him than the Nazi invasion in 1941. Millions of people died, and millions more were reduced to beggary. The survivors were to understand that henceforth there was no law but conformity to the will of the Great Leader and Teacher.[37]

To prevent tens of millions of hungry peasants converging on the big cities in search of food, and thereby also alerting the rest of the world to the famine, a system of internal passports was introduced in December 1932. In January 1933, Eugene Lyons tipped off two American reporters about rumours he had heard of famine developing in the north Caucasus and Kuban districts. The resulting report of a trip to the affected areas, which made horrifying reading—roads choked with corpses; outbreaks of cannibalism—was smuggled out of the country by "an obliging German Jewish fur trader". The Soviet Press Office was so alarmed by the response to its publication, in the United States particularly, that in February it placed a ban on journalists

---

[37] Though it is outside the scope of this chapter, it is worth noting that it was the near disintegration of society during the war against the peasants that appears to have convinced Stalin that Vyshinsky's idea for the legal cloak of due process and a Constitution was necessary to keep the system of lawless violence muddling along.

travelling outside Moscow.

Three weeks after the imposition of the travel ban, the Metro-Vickers engineers were arrested. From what he learned of the OGPU investigation, Monkhouse thought that the original idea was to try a far larger number of people, in a vastly more complex case, which would take months to prepare. But the exigencies of the moment forced haste and therefore a change of plan. Journalists confined to Moscow had to be given something to write about. What better than a trial of foreigners as wreckers and spies? That would create a sensation. It was not until the middle of the summer, when Macdonald and Thornton were sent back to England, that press interest in the case abated. By then, a new harvest was being reaped. Partly due to favourable weather, it was one of the best on record. Stalin had so arranged things that he had largely concealed what has been called one of the greatest man-made disasters of modern times. The Metro-Vickers trial played a major part in that.

Though the guilt or innocence of the accused was not relevant to the Kremlin's purposes, guilty verdicts were required to justify the whole show. Lenient sentences for the Britons in court were expedient in order not to antagonise a major trading partner. Britain imposed an embargo on imports from the Soviet Union towards the end of the trial. Despite the famine, these imports had included food. Eugene Lyons noted a sharp increase in the availability of butter in Moscow during May. The embargo was lifted when Macdonald and Thornton arrived home three months later—whereupon the butter glut evaporated. As far as the British government was concerned, the matter was now closed. Metro-Vickers continued to do business with the Soviet Union throughout the 1930s, even though its convicted Russian employees stayed in jail, unnoticed and unlamented.

The second likely explanation for the trial, the diplomatic one, was even more important for Stalin, namely the need to conciliate American opinion in the hope of reversing President Wilson's decision, taken immediately after the Revolution, not to afford diplomatic recognition to the new Soviet state. During the

Depression, this policy came under increasing attack. It was one of the main issues in the 1932 Presidential election. The United States was the last major power to abandon a policy of trying to influence the Soviet Union by putting it in "quarantine", force having been abandoned when the last American troops left Soviet soil in 1920. Due to the Great Crash and the misery unplanned capitalism caused, moderate American opinion began to look more sympathetically on state intervention in economic affairs. America had fifteen million unemployed, and many influential people believed that the Soviet Union, whatever its other faults might be, had "abolished" unemployment.

Stalin desperately needed American economic co-operation. He understood that the Roosevelt's victory in 1932 was a major opportunity for breaking the diplomatic log-jam. He already had one important ally in this endeavour, the best-known western journalist in Moscow in those years, Walter Duranty. Duranty subsequently became a controversial figure because of the way in which he made light of the 1932-3 famine. "There is no actual starvation or deaths from starvation but there is widespread mortality from diseases due to malnutrition," he wrote, on 30 March 1933. He was awarded the Pulitzer Prize for his famine reporting.

Duranty came from a Quaker family in Liverpool, and had been educated at Harrow and Cambridge, but he spent most of his journalistic life working for the *New York Times*. He had been so upset by the horrors of the trenches while covering the western front during the First World War, that he was driven to bohemian pacifism in Paris while he covered the Armistice negotiations. He was a regular attender at opium parties presided over by Aleister Crowley, the notorious occultist and orgiast. Duranty went to the Soviet Union in 1921 to investigate reports of starvation in the Volga regions, apparently due to the food confiscations carried out under war communism. Millions died, but Duranty later said of his venture into Russia: "Luck broke my way in the shape of the great Russian famine, which probably cost 5 or 6 million lives, including deaths from disease."

Duranty chafed under Soviet press censorship, loathed

communism, and did not much like ordinary Russians. But he quickly came to admire Stalin, seeing him as "one of the most remarkable men in Russia today". He was wont to justify the excesses of Stalinism by saying, "You can't make an omelette without breaking eggs." In the summer of 1932, while still Governor of New York, Roosevelt summoned him for a briefing on the advisability of recognising the Soviet Union. (The main question Roosevelt seemed concerned about was Moscow's ability to pay in gold for the goods it might want to buy from order-starved American manufacturers.) Just over a year later, with Roosevelt now President, Duranty accompanied Litvinov across the Atlantic to make arrangements for the final diplomatic negotiations. Both sides credited Duranty with a pivotal role in the making each side acceptable to the other. In New York, he was the star guest at a grand dinner at the Waldorf-Astoria in Litvinov's honour. In Moscow, Stalin gave him one of his rare interviews. According to Duranty, the Father of the People told him, "You have done a good job in reporting the USSR, though you are not a Marxist... I might say you bet on our horse to win when others thought it had no chance."

Stalin attached great importance to avoiding giving offence to American public opinion throughout 1933. He also wanted American diplomatic support against Japan, which had invaded Manchuria, on the Soviet Far Eastern border, the year before. If there needed to be a trial in early 1933 to conceal the famine, it had to be conducted in a way which people like Duranty could say was, though perhaps different from trials in capitalist countries, nonetheless essentially fair. But in the end, Duranty was not as impressed as many of the other observers who felt some sort of justice had been done.[38] He summarised his view in his memoirs:

---

[38] The veteran anti-Bolshevik, Sir Robert Bruce Lockhart, reflected this opinion. "On the whole," he wrote in his diary immediately after the trial, "intelligent opinion [in London] holds: that (1) the sentences are lighter than expected; (2) there was some foundation for the Bolshevist case; and (3) that we mishandled the case from the beginning."

[The trial] caused more ink to flow abroad than anything which had happened in Russia since the case of the Roman Catholic priests ten years before. [The charges of sabotaging] were ridiculous on the face of it, although supported by a mass of verbal testimony from their Russian fellow-accused, and of espionage for which no scrap of documentary evidence was produced, save a fantastic confession by one of them named Thornton, who was born in Russian and appears to have yielded to panic. Nevertheless the trial created an unpleasant impression on all foreigners who attended it... The prevailing impression in foreign circles in Moscow was that voiced to me by a prominent diplomat, 'I don't believe they are guilty as charged, although their defence was supine, mais'—he sniffed significantly—'mais, ça sent mauvais quelque part'."[39]

Cummings heard views similar to those which the diplomat expressed to Duranty. He explained his unpopularity in his book by saying that, though a fluent Russian speaker and "easily the ablest journalist in Eastern Europe", Duranty "refuses to rant in the proper anti-Bolshevik fashion" and so "I have heard him described foolishly and meanly behind his back as 'a renegade Englishman'." On the other hand, a Briton who had lived in Moscow for ten years told Cummings at the end of the trial that he had never previously believed in the existence of saboteurs, but now he did. Cummings, himself, felt compelled to agree.

Even Eugene Lyons, for all his other reservations, was not critical of the procedure: "The trial itself, at least as far as it applied to the accused foreigners, seemed to me a closer approximation of justice than any previous demonstration trial."

The impression that the Soviet government was putting on a show for the outside world is reinforced by a sentence which was left out of the official English-language transcript of the trial. Vyshinsky, who found it hard to conceal his contempt for Thornton, said in his closing statement, "Your only use would be to manure the soil of our Soviet fields." Both Monkhouse and

---

[39] *I Write as I Please* Walter Duranty, p. 307

Cummings record this in their books, but it is absent from the voluminous, published Soviet record. Monkhouse also says that Ulrikh "to me, personally, made two deprecatory remarks, neither of which was included in the verbatim report of the trial."

In Britain, Sir Stafford Cripps said a fortnight after the trial finished that, "it was impossible to say through reading the notes that the men were not guilty." The pro-Soviet Anglo-Russian Parliamentary Committee published a full account of the trial, which was prefaced by a description of Soviet court procedure, written by one of the few London barristers who had made a study of the relevant law, Denis Pritt, KC. Pritt wrote,

> The method of investigation and trial of criminal charges in Soviet Russia, in sober truth, bears an unexpectedly close resemblance in its main features to that prevailing in many non-Communist countries; indeed the distinctions between the methods of Russia and those of, say, Denmark are perhaps smaller than the distinction between those of Denmark and England....
>
> The hearing itself is remarkable for its ease and simplicity, the court does not dominate either the accused or the advocates; accused who prefer not to be represented are not confused either by technical rules of evidence... The foreign observer gets the impression of an informal friendly and even easy-going trial, conducted without heat and with the real co-operation of all concerned, and with a real desire to arrive at the truth.
>
> The only true standard by which to form an estimate of the Russian, as of any other, legal system is the homely one as to whether it gives what the ordinary citizen regards as a fair trial... On all these points, it is not in human nature that any country should be perfect, but in my considered judgement Soviet Russia is better than most countries, and not far short of the best.[40]

What Pritt, of course, omits to mention is what went on out

---

[40] *The Moscow Trial (April 1933)* compiled by W.P. Coates, London 1933, pp. 9-11. Pritt was a Winchester-educated, left-wing Labour MP, who represented Hammersmith from 1935-50.

of court, in the OGPU cells. But what goes on in the basement of the Lubyanka and elsewhere is not part of the small proportion of the iceberg of justice that is seen in court. The OGPU could continue to operate, in secret always, without affecting what Stalin wanted to achieve by having Vyshinsky manage this trial.

It should also be remembered that the years when Ulrikh sat on the Bench in Moscow and Vyshinsky prosecuted were not years in which every aspect of justice in the West excited universal admiration. I have already quoted the Baillie-Stewart case in England, but courts in America were just as bad when anything to do with Bolshevism was at issue. Eugene Lyons made this point when he compared the Metro-Vickers trial with another one he witnessed in Tulsa, Oklahoma in 1919 when the Red Scare—America's obverse of Stalin's "wreckers and spies" campaign—was at its height.

The case concerned a Dutch labour activist from Pennsylvania called Krieger who was accused of dynamiting the porch of the house of an employee of Standard Oil—genuine wrecking. The person concerned was away from home, and the damage done was negligible. But that did not stop the prosecution. Lyons says that the case was "so palpably a frame-up that no one even pretended it was anything else." Krieger's lawyer left for court taking "his hat and his revolver" since the town was "ruled" by vigilantes Though the accused had, it turned out, not been in Tulsa when the explosion had taken place, this "did not checkmate the police's patriotic ardour." They simply altered the charges to *organising* the crime.

The trial became the longest in Oklahoma's history, forcing the court to recess every so often "for a few hours to dispose of some minor matters like murder cases." In echoes of Vyshinsky, Standard Oil hired an assistant to the public prosecutor who, Lyons says, was in complete control of the case. Even the court stenographer was "also stenographer for the vigilantes", who one evening threatened "to run the defence lawyer and other Reds out of town". Luckily they had protection in the shape of "the picturesque three-hundred-pound dictator of a nearby town". He happened to be the last independent oil operator in the vicinity, and therefore "hated Standard Oil as much as Standard Oil hated the Reds". This man gave Lyons and the defence team "the sharp-eyed protection of a little army of private gunmen who sat in court, under orders to shoot down the first man who touched us." The oilman recruited his gang "from the prisons of the Southwest under laws permitting the parole of prisoners who could show respectable jobs waiting for them." He gave automatic support to anyone "accused of an attempt to erase a Standard Oil official." His only regret, expressed after the trial, was that Krieger had pleaded innocent because that implied that "private terror was not part of [his] code".

As in the Moscow trial, whenever the defence demolished a state witness, "the prosecution got a brief adjournment and the court opened up again with brand-new witnesses to bolster the blasted sector." Two "rat-faced yeggs" (thieves) testified how Krieger had recruited them to his conspiracy. They spoke in "low voices" and with "down-cast eyes", in much the same way as the Russians who testified against the Metro-Vickers accused did. The Defence's burdens included "perjured witnesses, murderous public hostility, a frankly unfriendly jury, and financial distress." The Tulsa courtroom presented a negative contrast to Ulrikh's decorously-conducted proceedings.

> The judge puffed a big cigar under the No Smoking sign. Spectators with revolvers in their holsters threw 'Howdy!' to their friends in the jury box... and clergymen who sat in court preached sermons to the jury on Sundays, since jurors could not be denied the solace of spiritual uplift, on themes as remote from the case as patriotism and foreign agitators.

At the end of the case, Lyons wrote,

> The jury reported eleven to one for conviction. The only recalcitrant juror emerged with visible proofs that the arguments used on him were the kind that left marks on the body. We learned later that he had a personal grudge against Standard Oil in some matter connected with a pipeline on his farm. His insistence on Krieger's innocence apparently had no more to do with the

evidence than the others' insistence on his guilt.

That was Oklahoma in 1919, but even at the summit of the American judicial system, and when Bolshevism was not at issue, justice could be equally offensive to modern notions of fairness. *Buck v Bell* (1927) is a Supreme Court case which should give the self-righteous critic of Soviet justice pause for thought. Carrie Buck was one of more than six thousand citizens of Virginia—there were even more victims in California—who were forcibly sterilized on the grounds of "hereditary insanity or imbecility." In fact, she was not feeble-minded, but she had given birth to an illegitimate child at the age of seventeen. The authorities deemed this evidence of promiscuity, and considered promiscuity evidence of feeble-mindedness. They therefore had lawful grounds for enforced sterilisation under a law passed in 1924.

Miss Buck objected. Her case reached the Supreme Court in 1927. Judgement was delivered by Oliver Wendell Holmes, one of the best-known and most distinguished Justices in the Court's history. Holmes was known as "the Yankee from Olympus" because of his deep learning, dignified bearing and length of service to the law—he was eighty-six when he pronounced on Miss Buck's case. One legal writer said of him that "no other man of comparable intellect and spirit has been a judge in the United States, or for that matter in the English-speaking world." Another went even further, calling him "the summit of hundreds of years of civilisation, the inspiration of ages to come."

Holmes's judgement ran to a mere five paragraphs. Shorn of its contemptuously brief statement of the law, this is what he wrote:

> Carrie Buck is a feeble-minded white woman who... is the daughter of a feeble-minded mother... and the mother of an illegitimate feeble-minded child... It is better for all the world, if instead of waiting to execute degenerate offspring for crime, or to let them starve for their imbecility, society can prevent those who are manifestly unfit from continuing their kind... Three generations of imbeciles is enough.[41]

Seven of the eight other Justices adopted Holmes's view, including the famous liberals, Louis Brandeis and Harlan Fiske Stone. Ironically, Holmes himself was a man of fierce liberal convictions. He had been almost the first student from his year at Harvard to volunteer for the Union Army when the Civil War broke out. So strong were his feelings against slavery that he returned to the Army on three separate occasions after having been shot through, respectively, the leg, the chest and the neck. After his death in 1935, his blood-stained Union Army uniform was found carefully preserved in a cupboard in his house in Washington. On the court, his biggest contribution was to argue for freedom of speech and behaviour. He wanted civil rights for everyone but "imbeciles", and that the Supreme Court lend its authority to his view. Stalin, despite his very much broader definition of imbecility, would surely have understood.

Finally, the legal reason for mounting the trial. Though many commentators have emphasised the cynicism behind the Soviet leader's decision to stage the Metro-Vickers trial when he did, few have taken up Lyons's suggestions that the OGPU "had a club over the Britishers' heads", and that the trial concealed some larger goings-on which were never discussed in court. Recently a Canadian academic, Gordon Morrell, has published a book about the diplomacy surrounding the case, *Britain Confronts the Stalin Revolution,* which argues persuasively that not only were the British government's angry protestations of innocence on the part of the engineers unfounded, but that the government knew they were unfounded. In other words, the British position was almost as hypocritical as the Soviet one.[42]

---

[41] *Buck v Bell,* 274 US 200 (1927)

[42] By far the most interesting account of the background to this case, from internal political struggles within the Politburo to the financial aspects (without British export credits, the Five Year Plan would have failed completely) is by G.L. Owen, "The Metro-Vickers Crisis: Anglo-Soviet Relations between Trade Agreements 1932-1934" in the *Slavonic and East European Review* (1971) p. 92

In 1931, Britain had created a new department of the Committee of Imperial Defence, known as the Industrial Intelligence Centre (IIC). This embodied a novel concept, which was to be copied all over the world within a couple of decades. It collected and collated information on the military-industrial capabilities of likely enemy countries. It was the fore-runner of bodies like the CIA and the KGB. It was based on the premiss that, in an industrial age, success in all forms of conflict, whether armed, ideological or both, depends in the long run on economic strength. The collapse of the Soviet Union in 1991 illustrated that point well.

The two countries which the IIC targeted were Germany and the Soviet Union, but up until 1933, when Hitler came to power in Germany, the prime target was the USSR, which was considered the greater danger, and also was engaged in extensive industrial espionage in Britain. Twelve substantial reports were prepared in the first year of the IIC's operation. An internal memo of the time explained the reasoning behind all this activity:

> A country can only launch and maintain in the field that number of ships, military divisions or aircraft squadrons, which it can equip with machines and explosives. It is, therefore, accepted fact that an extensive study of a country's industry and industrial development must be carried out, in order to ascertain, not only how many armed force units it can maintain in war, but how long it can maintain them... It is the duty of the "Industrial Mobilisation" expert to show in what manner and to what extent the requirements of the armed forces in explosives, weapons, equipment, supplies and transport, can be met and are likely to be met by industry.[43]

The IIC used businessmen working abroad to collect information. It seems clear that Thornton, Monkhouse and the

---

[43] Quoted in *Churchill's Man of Mystery* Gill Bennett, p. 153 The subject of this biography is Major Desmond Morton, who was the first Director of the IIC, and who later became Churchill's secret source for information he used in public about the growing might of the German armed forces.

others working for Metro-Vickers in the USSR were doing this, though the information they collected would not, in a democratic society, have been regarded as state secrets. But they were not in a democratic society, and Soviet law at the time laid down that economic "intelligence gathering" was a counter-revolutionary crime.

In his closing speech, Vyshinsky read out the following definition of espionage:

> "If any sketch, plan, model, article, note, document or information relating to or used in any prohibited place... is made, obtained or communicated by any person other than a person acting under lawful authority, it shall be deemed to have been made, obtained or communicated for a purpose prejudicial to the safety or interests of the state unless the contrary is proved."

This of course, means that the onus of proof is on the accused. Vyshinksy continued reading:

> "On a prosecution under this section, it shall not be necessary to show that the accused person was guilty of any particular act tending to show a purpose prejudicial to the safety or interests of the State, and, notwithstanding that no such act is proved against him, he may be convicted if, from the circumstances of the case, or his conduct, or *his known character* as proved, it appears that his purpose was a purpose prejudicial to the safety of interests of the State." (emphasis added)

Vyshinsky looked up and said, with a twinkle in his eye, "That is how the bourgeoisie protects its interests in this sphere." He was quoting from Section 2 of the British Official Secrets Act, 1911.

Leaving aside the issue of the way the evidence was obtained, there cannot be much question that Thornton and Macdonald would have been found guilty on the evidence as it stood before Ulrikh's court for what they did if they had been Russians tried in England under British law. At one point Monkhouse more or less admitted to intelligence-gathering of the "soft" sort which the IIC specialised in. He said he did not consider it spying, but added, well if that is spying, then I was spying. Macdonald had told the court that Thornton had asked him to collect economic and political information about the situation within the Soviet Union. Cushny accepted that he had discussed the price of bread with Russian colleagues from a "political" point of view. And so on.

It was well known that Metro-Vickers was one of the best-connected foreign firms in the USSR at that time, and also that it was channelling information to the IIC. To all intents and purposes, the spying charge was, to put it at its weakest, not unfounded. The fact that the wrecking charges could not be substantiated—they were presumably included for domestic policy reasons, and were part of the "theatre" aspect of the proceedings—does not take away from the espionage ones. So the third reason why Stalin might have decided to proceed with this case was simply that he thought the accused had broken the law of the land, as they probably had done.

Doubtless he was not too worried about the legal niceties, but he might very plausibly have thought that a trial would curtail such activities in the future. There is no doubt that Stalin would have agreed wholeheartedly with the IIC memo quoted above, justifying its function. Preventing military-industrial espionage would certainly have been a high priority for him. But where foreigners were involved, at a time when he desperately needed international recognition and credits—a need which was much reduced in the later 1930s, and which disappeared after he made his deal with Hitler in August 1939—he had to conduct the trial with the appearance of procedural fairness.

Whatever the outrage which was expressed in the West— and I have tried to suggest that the trial was not uniquely unjust— the fact remains that there was no reason *in law* to take the attitude of the British government, press and public, namely that all the accused were entirely innocent, and that the trial was a frame-up of the sort which could happen only in the Soviet Union. Though Stalin's diplomacy played a large part in bringing the engineers to trial, it was ironically also that diplomacy which gave the foreign accused some protection—the Russians, of course, were not so lucky.

Stalin managed all three aspects of the case, the political, the diplomatic and the legal himself. It appears that he took all the main decisions, including those relating to guilt and to sentencing. In effect, it was he who was in charge of the Court proceedings, not Ulrikh. This case illustrates, at the reciprocal bearing on the legal compass from *United States v Nixon,* that even in Moscow in the dark days of the 1930s, Hamilton's Rule still holds: show me the judge and I'll tell you the law.[44]

---

[44] Writing in 1990, a year before the Communist system collapsed, Professor Mark Beissinger made a similar point in an article entitled The Party and the Rule of Law: "If judicial independence is implemented in earnest, the Party will be effectively ejected from the judge's bench." *Columbia Journal of Transantional Law* vol. 28, p. 41, 51

3

# The Law as Codified Custom

Christ expressed what we would call the brotherhood of man when he said: "Inasmuch as you do it unto one of the least of these my brethren, you do it unto me." Equal justice under law implies not only equality of parties, but also equality of concerns. Thus it is not absurd to examine, alongside the issue of executive privilege for the President of the United States, and allegations of spying and wrecking of the industrial installations of Stalinist Russia, the small flower garden at Fladdabister in Shetland which was the focus of *Christie v Adamson,* a hard-fought Scottish Land Court case in 2002. Law is just as important, and interesting, at a micro level as it is at the macro scale.

The Land Court was established in 1911 after passage of the Small Landholders (Scotland) Act which extended the Crofters Holdings (Scotland) Act of 1886 that gave security of tenure and certain other rights to smallholders classified as crofters in the Highlands and Islands.[45] Today, despite many legislative changes, the Land Court still deals with such matters as succession to crofts, grazing rights, and disputes between

---

[45] I have described in more detail the origins of crofting, the genesis of the Land Court, and a particularly striking modern case which relates to a dispute on the Isle of Colonsay in my book *Isles of the West* (1999, 2012) pp. 3-7. Essentially, crofting is a formalised version of agricultural homesteading in the remoter areas of Scotland. A croft is a heritable but not saleable land holding on which the crofter may build a house that is both heritable and saleable.

landlords and tenants.

The Chairman of the Court is a lawyer with the status of a judge in the Court of Session, which is the senior civil court in Scotland. He is assisted by four non-legally-trained members, each of whom has access to legal expertise, but who acts as a judge with the full official independence which the British state guarantees to all judges. At least one of these members must speak Gaelic, since originally many of the crofters whose cases had to be heard were native, occasionally monoglot, Gaelic-speakers. This is still the case, even though almost all the Court's proceedings are in English.

On a misty day in March 2006 I drove out to Skye to interview the most recently-retired Gaelic-speaking member of the Land Court. I was greeted by a tall, open-faced man in his 60s, Donald MacDonald, who introduced me to his wife, offered me tea and shortbread, and sat me down in a deep armchair next to the fire. A large picture window looked out over the oily calm of the Sound of Sleat. The hills of Knoydart on the opposite shore were invisible in the mist.

Donald told me that his father was born on Hyskeir in the now uninhabited Monach Isles, off the Uists and that he grew up speaking Gaelic only. I asked him whether, in an Anglophone world, there was really any need for people like him on the Land Court.

"I think there is," he said quietly and cautiously. "Because there is a social affiliation with another person who speaks your language, and they seem to accept more readily what's said by somebody who's of their own background. For that purpose I think it is important that the Court always should have somebody who's from a Gaelic-speaking, crofting background. I think a lot of the crofters look to the Court for that."

"But the language itself is hardly ever used in Court," I said.

"That may change, actually, because there is a sheriff who is acting as Deputy Chairman for a year, seconded from Kirkaldy Sheriff Court. He was an advocate, Roddy John Macleod: a very amiable fellow, very capable. He's got a background in the media too, but he's a Skye man. All the people appointed to the court in

recent years have been Skye men. Ronnie Macdonald—I
succeeded him—he's a Skye man, same sort of background as
myself. He was in the civil service, but was a part-time crofter for
most of his life. He is a very capable fellow too. He is a good
Gaelic speaker, and a very strong pursuer of the Gaelic cause. He
lives in Edinburgh. He was about ten years on the Court after he
retired from the Department of Agriculture in a senior position in
Edinburgh. He had previously been with the Highland
Development Board, like myself, as their senior agricultural
expert there. I retired after ten years and was succeeded by
another Skye man, Angus MacDonald. He's the current Gaelic-
speaking member. Prior to that it was Archie Gillespie, who was
a very well-known Islay man, from the Rinns of Islay. He was
very well-regarded, a very keen Gaelic man. In fact he did a
television series on the work of the Court in Gaelic. I'd better not
expose the person who was the biggest opponent of having the
Gaelic-speaker on the Court when I was there, but he'd say,
'Why do you have such a strong leaning towards Gaelic? Would
they not be as well getting a Shetland man, who's just as capable,
and knows as much about crofting?' He had a point I suppose.
There's a lot of crofting in Shetland. It was one of the areas I
really liked to work in was Shetland. They have a very different
outlook on life: they are more Norse."

"How does that manifest itself?" I asked.

"They seem to be a more active people, more inclined to get
going. Having said that, it is not very good to generalise because
I knew some people who were just as active in the Western Isles
crofting, but in general, they have a different attitude to life. Yes,
I had a great affinity with the Shetlanders, and their style.
They're a different people."

I asked about the Chairman of the Land Court, Lord
McGhie. But, out of respect for the hierarchy, Donald would not
comment about a serving judge beyond saying, "He's a
Perthshire man, from Dunning. He's a very nice man. I think his
father was a sanitary inspector."

But he was happy to reminisce about retired Chairmen.
McGhie's predecessor, Lord Philip, he thought of as being very

sympathetic to the Gaelic world and its view of life and the law.

"He was a listener," Donald said. "He'd listen to both sides of the story."

"Was he a Gaelic speaker?"

"No, but he had more affinity with the culture and the social aspects of the Highland area than, say, Lord Elliot, who came before him. He was very much of the old brigade school, a gentleman in every respect, but he had no grip of agriculture whatsoever."

"That's something of a handicap, surely?"

"Not in the Land Court because the Chairmen depend on the lay members to keep them right on that."

"And the lay members have legal advisors to keep them right on the law?"

"That's right. But it's always useful to have a Chairman who has an interest in the land. Having said that, Lord Elliot was a very fine man, a very nice man in every respect. One of my predecessors, Archie Gillespie, fell out with him in a big way, which was a great pity. He had made an assumption, right or wrong I don't know, that Lord Elliot was anti-Gaelic, and Archie was so much for Gaelic that that was anathema to him. Archie was a great fellow in every way, but he took things very seriously. Lord Birsay, who was Chairman before Lord Elliot, was a very different man, a very practical man. He was highly regarded. He was a kenspeckle figure. He usually wore his kilt, irrespective of the weather. He had a very distinctive voice, it was semi-Orkney.[46] Everybody would have respected his judgements in every way, both practical and legal. Lord Philip: the same, I think. He would have been held in very high regard in that way too. Lord Elliot was very much a legal man, but there is no problem with that so long as they take cognisance of what those around them say."

The language issue may seem a small one, and perhaps today it is. But it is very important, as anyone who has ever had to deal with European law, some of which is originally drafted in

---

[46] Birsay is a parish on the mainland of Orkney.

French, will be aware. It is oppressive to try a person in a language he or she does not understand. One of the best non-colonial British examples of this took place in Ireland in 1884 and was written up in a short but gruesomely clear factual account by James Joyce in 1907. It concerned what was known as the Maamtrasna murders, as a result of which three members of the Joyce clan were put on trial in Galway. Much has been written about the case since, and it seems the men were almost certainly innocent. But that is beside the language point, which is that none of them could speak any English, yet their trial was conducted purely in English. Joyce described the questioning of the seventy-year old Myles Joyce:

> On one side of the courtroom was the excessively ceremonious interpreter, while on the other stood the patriarch of a miserable tribe unused to civilised customs, who seemed stupefied by all the judicial ceremony.
>
> At one point, the magistrate said to the interpreter, "Ask the accused if he saw the lady that night?"
>
> The question was referred to him in Irish, and the old man broke out into an involved explanation, gesticulating, appealing to the others accused, and to heaven. Then he quietened down, worn out by his effort.
>
> At this the interpreter turned to the magistrate and said, "He says, 'No, your worship'."
>
> "Ask him if he was in that neighbourhood at that hour?" the magistrate went on.
>
> The old man again began to talk, to protest, to shout, almost beside himself with the anguish of being unable to understand or to make himself understood, weeping in anger and terror. At last he fell silent once more.
>
> And again the interpreter said, "He says, 'No, your worship.'"

Joyce ends his account, after the men had all been condemned to death, by noting: "The story was told that the executioner, also unable to make the victim understand him, kicked at the miserable man's head in anger to shove it into the noose."[47]

Scotland's legal abuses have more often been comic than tragic and one of the most comic was a man called Lord Gibson, who was Chairman of the Land Court for nearly twenty years. Born Robert Gibson in Lanarkshire in 1884, he trained as an advocate and in his forties, stood as parliamentary candidate in numerous constituencies for the Scottish Labour Party, eventually being elected for Greenock, which he served as MP until his appointment to head the Land Court in 1941. Now he was the Honourable Lord Gibson, with the courtesy title which all Session Court judges have in Scotland. Socialist or no socialist, he was delighted with his new status, and sat until his death twenty-four years later, acquiring a reputation for progressively increasing vanity, conceit, pomposity and, in the end, absurdity, all of which did great damage to the reputation of the Court.

The circumstances of Gibson's appointment are interesting. When Winston Churchill's coalition government took office in May 1940, Gibson, being the senior Labour member of the House of Commons who was also a member of the Scots Bar, was by virtue of his seniority next in line for the job of Solicitor-General for Scotland. Gibson's reputation had already got around and such a prospect horrified the Lord Advocate, the senior legal civil servant in the Crown Office in Scotland, and the Solicitor-General's immediate superior. The only way of preventing this was to appoint Gibson to the bench. But he could not possibly be made a Court of Session judge, so he was sent to the Land Court

---

[47] It is worth mentioning in passing that a comparable problem is arising in Britain as a result of the large number of recent immigrants whose native language is Hindi, Polish or Swahili—for example. It is obviously unpractical to consider making judges available fluent in all of the world's languages. Perhaps the difference is that Irish in Ireland, and Gaelic in the west of Scotland (and Welsh in Wales) are native languages and therefore qualify for special treatment. But in a truly globalised world, there will doubtless be many who argue that this is a form of discrimination by birth.

where they thought he would be safely out of the way. The Chairman of the Land Court at the time, David King Murray, later Lord Birnam, had to be persuaded to step down so that Gibson could be appointed in his place.

This only increased Gibson's vanity. According to Lord Brand, his Lordship's pomposity was such that even when he accompanied agricultural members of the court on their inspection of crofts, he wore his red judicial robe. He even wore it for hearings in black-houses, the most primitive type of dwelling which was disappearing even in the 1930s.

A colleague of Donald's on the Land Court for many years, Duncan McDiarmid of Aberfeldy, said to me on another occasion, "Gibson was a disgrace. He was well known for sleeping on the Bench. Also, he would always take the side of one or other party, usually the crofter, on cut-of-the-jib-type grounds. He was quite a cunning and clever guy but he was a total misfit, to put it politely. But you have this problem in the law that in order to have genuinely independent judges you have got to let them be genuinely independent, and if they go off the rails once they've been appointed it can be difficult to bring them back into line. If it's easy to control their behaviour then they're not independent."

McDiarmid's father had been a member of the Court before him and had sat with Gibson. He had told him about Gibson's desire for money.

"The Chairman of the Land Court's salary is less than that of an Outer House judge in the Court of Session," McDiarmid said, "though they have equal judicial status. Lord Gibson felt that as he had the same rank and tenure as a Court of Session judge, he should have the same salary. But this was not a private grievance which he kept to himself, or quietly lobbied the Lord President to have remedied. That was not his style. He used to go touting, quite unashamedly, people whom he thought could help him, like the Minister on Skye. There was a time when the court was sitting in Portree and Gibson actually asked the Minister to announce from the pulpit on Sunday morning that he thought the Chairman of Land Court's salary should be raised. Can you imagine! It was ludicrous. But he got his come-uppance from old 'Squeaky' Robertson, the MacBrayne's skipper, on the ferry back from Portree to the mainland. Swanking around the ship as if he owned it, Gibson went up to the bridge deck, which was not, strictly-speaking, allowed. Old Squeaky humoured him for a while, but eventually it got too much, and he ordered him off the bridge. Gibson turned to him said, 'Are you aware who I am, my man? I'm Lord Gibson.' 'Ha!' says old Squeaky, '*Lord* Gibson are you? Bah! If you were a *real* Lord you wouldnae be on my ship, you'd have a yat of your own.'"

In telling me about Gibson, McDiarmid emphasised how different the judges are in modern times. He served for twenty-one years on the Court and was impressed with all three Chairmen he served under. Perhaps the sharpest contrast to Gibson in his lack of pomposity was Lord Birsay, the Orcadian who started life as Harold Leslie.

"Lord Birsay knew everybody," McDiarmid said, "He'd been High Commissioner of the Church of Scotland for two years, hosted National Trust cruises, given lectures everywhere. He couldn't cross the street without being stopped. He'd go out for his newspaper and be back in an hour. He was that sort of fellow. Partly it was because he had a great sense of humour. Harold had two adopted children. The boy went with Ally Macleod's so-called Tartan Army to the World Cup in Argentina. It appeared in the press that he'd been arrested after Scotland had been beaten by Peru or something. A couple of them had marched down a street with a banner denigrating the SFA. This was the Scottish Football Association, which they thought had let the team down. But the Argentineans stopped them because they thought it was something about Stop the F-ing Argentineans. He was actually locked up for half a game by police with machine-guns. It was in all the papers in Scotland: judge's son arrested and all that. So we were doing a case in Stirling and there was this guy who had lost a previous case in front of Lord Birsay over a tenancy. He got a letter saying that his judgement was rubbish, but that he wouldn't expect much more from the father of a football hooligan. Gibson would have been outraged and probably reported the matter to the police, but Harold just roared with laughter. He thought it a big joke."

"Was Gibson also unusual in being a both a judge and a member of the Labour Party?"

"Not really," he said. "Lord Birsay, stood as a Labour candidate, for Orkney and Shetland I think. He lived in a very modest bungalow in Queensferry Road. Archie Elliott, though he was Eton or Harrow or Cambridge or something, was a great friend of John Smith, the Labour leader, pretty left-wing. Sandy Philip was more middle of the road. But most people's impressions of judges is of absolutely right-wing folk, probably because of BBC television showing only English judges, who I think are much more Tory. If you looked closely at our Bench, you'd find, I think, that the majority of them were left of centre."

The case I had come to talk to Donald about concerned a holding in Fladdabister, a fertile spot on the east coast of the Shetland mainland, nine miles south of Lerwick. It stands above an open bay, with a sandy beach at its most sheltered part, providing a "naast", or "noost", where boats can be drawn up above the high-water mark in winter or during periods of bad weather.

Much of Shetland is still crofted ground, which is what gave rise to *Christie v Adamson* (2002). The Land Court usually sits in Edinburgh, in a stately building in the West End but if need be it will sit anywhere that is necessary for the fair administration of justice. This can mean the Sheriff Court in Lochmaddy, the village hall on Colonsay, where there is no court, or the front room of an infirm crofter's house on an island with neither court nor village hall, as Lord Gibson often did. In this case, Donald conducted a judicial inspection of ground in dispute then heard argument in the Cunningsburgh village hall, two miles away.

The pursuer (plaintiff) was an elderly lady, Mrs Joann Christie, who lived on Burra Isle, which lies immediately to the west of the Shetland mainland, but who "belonged to Fladdabister" and had inherited her mother's croft there. In 1951 the Land Court had been petitioned by the eight landholders in Fladdabister to apportion the ground held runrig, which was a custom of regular reallocation of fertile land in the interests of equitable access to scarce resources that went back to Viking times. The apportionment left the land containing the houses, peat stacks, kale yards and associated access untouched, though it brought the land beyond that within the purview of crofting legislation. Mrs Christie's mother died in 1980 and her house fell into ruin. The pursuer, who had bought her croft in the meantime, placed a caravan next to the ruin so that she had some shelter when she came over from Burra to tend her sheep or lift peats.

In 1988 the respondent, Mrs Fiona Adamson, formerly Miss McCafferty, had bought the East House, or Est Hus as the Shetlanders called it, and some land round about. Five years later, she had a child and acquired a dog. She decided to establish a garden for the child to play in and so fenced off an area round her house and planted flowers in it. Aware that the issue of access was contentious in crofting townships, Mrs Adamson put five gates in the fence round her garden, all with latches on the outside to make it easy for others to walk through.

But when Mrs Christie became aware of the garden and its fence, she objected strongly that it impeded her access from the public road to her property. For three years Mrs Adamson prevaricated, not taking Mrs Christie's threats of litigation seriously. Mrs Christie did not claim exclusive possession of the ground which the garden occupied, only free use of it for access. It had been the custom of her family for generations to lead their horses, carts and livestock through there. While she could still take access on foot she felt that Mrs Adamson had "by erecting gates and a stockade made the disputed land part of her garden". She did not feel comfortable walking through it as "it was full of flowers and like someone's garden". By her actions, Mrs Adamson had taken ground that she may or may not have owned—that was disputed too—but which even if she did own, was subject to communal rights. She could not "privatise" it. What if Mrs Christie wanted to build a road to her holding so that she could come and go by car or tractor, like any other crofter?

What were these communal rights? To simplify an extraordinarily complicated, and imperfectly known, system of individual and communal rights, which not only varied from place to place but which often overlapped in any given place, it would be broadly true to say that the Norse, both in Scandinavia and in the northern isles of Scotland, divided land into hill ground, home-fields and townland. The hill ground was everything beyond a dyke which surrounded a township, and was uncultivated. The home-fields were where crops were grown and domesticated animals grazed. It was this that had been subject for so long to runrig allocation, but, having been individually allocated in 1951, it was not now in dispute. The townland was the land on which the houses stood, with all their associated out-buildings, peat-stacks, milking areas for cows and so on, plus related green-yards or, more recently, kail-yards for individual kitchen-garden-type cultivation. The Shetland/Norse word for this was toonmals. Such areas all belonged to one household or another, but all could be crossed freely on foot by anyone. It was by right of this custom that Mrs Christie claimed Mrs Adamson had overstepped the local mark when she had arrived in Fladdabister and fenced her flower garden.

The question then resolved itself into what general rights attach to toonmals, and what individual freedoms normally associated with property ownership do those rights extinguish?

It is important to stress, first, that none of this has ever been legislated on by a British parliament: the law is purely customary. Secondly, the customary law is not feudal, which is well-known to Scots lawyers, but odal, or udal, a form of tenure unique to the northern isles which derives from the ancient Norse concept of landholding whose essence is that land is held outright, without a superior as was universal in the feudal system. Donald was unable to discover from either side's lawyers what rights and duties attach to land under toonmals, notwithstanding that Mrs Christie was represented by Derek Flyn from Inverness, the best-known expert on crofting law, and author of the standard legal text on the subject.[48]

---

[48] *Crofting Law* (Edinburgh 1992). I once attended a talk by Mr Flyn on his subject. He illustrated its obscurity by saying, "When I studied law at Edinburgh

When the law is uncertain but central to a case, the task of the judge becomes extraordinarily delicate. Mrs Adamson accepted that her garden was subject to rights and duties attached to toonmals, but that resolved nothing if the extent of those rights and duties was not precisely known. Not only was there no statutory authority, there was no case law.[49] Indeed, so far as Donald knew, this is the only case ever to have turned on the rights attached to toonmals. But nonetheless, under common law a right is a right, so long as custom hallows it and no more explicit authority over-rules it. With no legal training, and no legal authority to guide him, and without agreement between the parties about the law relevant to the case, Donald had to do justice as he saw it, and hope that he did so in such a way that both parties accepted his judgement. That they did so illustrates the quality of his work on this case and the care which he took to balance the legal interests of each side.

Donald's judgement runs to forty-eight closely-typed pages and is a model of judicial restraint. He first held that the land in question was subject to crofting tenure only in part, as some of it had been de-crofted by Mrs Adamson, and other parts by Mrs Christie. On the crofted land, Donald held that rights of toonmal, whatever they amounted to, applied even though they derived from udal law. As he put it formally, they "readily translated onto

---

University, we were told only three words about crofting law: 'Don't touch it!'"

[49] The court's attention was drawn to only one reference to the subject. This was from a 1914 application to the Land Court in which toonmals were described as "effeiring" to a croft. Effeiring is a rarely-used Scots law term of art meaning something between "attaching to" and "acting upon". The extremely erudite archivist to the Shetland Islands Council, Brian Smith, briefed the court on the word, but with the result only that Derek Flyn concluded that it "had no exact technical meaning". He further pointed out that Mrs Adamson had bought her house, and he could not see the right attaching to heritable property. But it could attach to the croft land tenanted by neighbours. Perhaps this was irrelevant anyway as Mrs Adamson's solicitor argued that, as toonmals was an ancient Norse right, and therefore not derived from crofting law, the Land Court had no jurisdiction: the right may exist, but it could not be litigated on in Donald's court. This is law at the super-micro limit.

the purview of crofting tenure on the enactment of crofting legislation, whether pertaining to the tenancy of an individual or in common right as might be in the case of an access."

He then came to the main point: did Mrs Adamson's garden obstruct Mrs Christie's legitimate rights of access? Clearly she could not drive beasts, carts or tractors—the successors of carts in respect of the right to bring peats off the hill—through a fenced garden which was planted with flowers and was gated, with openings wide enough only for pedestrian access. But he rejected Mrs Christie's submission that her mother had taken access with a horse and cart, preferring the submission of witnesses without an interest in the case, who had lived in Fladdabister all their lives, which Mrs Christie had not, to the effect that peats were brought home in very small carts pulled by Shetland ponies. This still established a right of access, but not one as substantial as Mrs Christie craved, namely one wide enough for the eventual construction of a road through Mrs Adamson's garden. Since that was the specific terms of Mrs Christie's application, Donald was able to write, "We have of necessity confined our findings to the terms of the crave... We therefore make no determination as to whether the gates and associated vertical boarding erected by Mrs Adamson amount in effect to exclusion of the crofting rights of others over the area."[50]

Finally, Donald turned to the question of costs. Normally these are apportioned on the basis that the loser pays both sides' expenses. Strictly-speaking, neither Mrs Adamson nor Mrs Christie had won, so Donald decided that he should apportion costs on the basis of responsibility for the litigation. Throughout the eight years which passed since Mrs Christie first complained to Mrs Adamson about her garden, the latter denied that the dispute was subject to crofting law. But she admitted this on the first day in court. That aspect of the litigation was therefore wholly unnecessary. However Mrs Anderson had conceded, right

---

[50] If Chief Justice Burger had exercised comparable judicial restraint in *Nixon*, and confined himself to the "crave", as Scots law calls it, he would not have created executive privilege in the unpopular way as he did.

from the start, that she had no right to occupy her garden to the exclusion of others, so Mrs Christie's attempt to litigate on the wider issue of possible road-building, which had been defeated, balanced the first aspect. The result was that Mrs Christie had won one point and the other had been a draw, to use sporting terms. So Donald ended with this judgement of Solomon:

> Given the unnecessary time spent on matters irrelevant to the crave, the respondent's [Mrs Adamson] admission from the beginning that she had no right to occupy the land to the exclusion of others and the applicant's [Mrs Christie] qualified success in obtaining a determination in relation to the disputed area as against the fact that it was necessary for her to bring the action to obtain determination on the matter, we take the view that the interests of justice would be met by Mrs Anderson paying one half of Mrs Christie's judicial expenses.[51]

The density of Donald's reasoning and the care which he took to ensure that neither side could leave court with any sense of injustice were clearly more important than elucidation of the mysterious law of toonmals. In that sense, he was overlaying half-understood legal custom by well-understood social custom, and using his Court as the sanctifier of both—another long-established custom.

Later, driving back past the mountains of Kintail, I passed almost the exact spot which gave rise to one of the most famous land-related cases in Scottish history, the so-called Pet Lamb case, in 1885. Custom was decisive then too, but the case is particularly worth recalling because it represented a clash between law at the macro level and at the micro level. It went was almost as far as it was possible to go in the clash between wealth and poverty. The dispute started in the same year that Myles Joyce was hanged.

The Pet Lamb case concerned one Murdoch Macrae, a cottar who lived at Carn Gorm, on the farm of Morvich, on the huge

---

[51] *Christie v Adamson* (2002) SLC Application 76/99

Kintail Estate. Before the Clearances, some of the Macraes had been tacksmen (land managers) to the Mackenzie Earls of Seaforth, others had been simple clansmen. Two at least had distinguished themselves at the battle of Sheriffmuir during the Jacobite rising in 1715. After the Highlands were commercialised in the late eighteenth century, the Macraes either emigrated to north America or fell down the socio-economic ladder until, by 1884, most of those still living in Kintail were described as cottars, the only status lower than that of a crofter. A crofter has—or did after 1886 when the first Act was passed—a secure and heritable tenancy of ground: poor ground, and not much of it in most cases, but land nevertheless. A cottar simply had his "cot", or house, and potato ground plus, in some cases, the grazing of a cow, though that was usually no more than a tolerance on the part of the laird.

That exactly described Murdoch Macrae's situation in the early 1880s. He earned a small but respectable living as a shoemaker. He and his wife occupied a house he had built himself. Though he spoke Gaelic and "lived quiet", he was still prepared, as many weren't, to speak out publicly by giving evidence to the Napier Commission, which inquired into crofting in the early 1880s preparatory to the passage of the Crofters Holdings Act in 1886.

Macrae's opponent in the Pet Lamb case could hardly have been more different. He was William Louis Winans, from Baltimore, Maryland, a multi-millionaire engineer whose father had built many of the earliest railroads in the United States. His fame was such that he was subsequently asked by Tsar Nicholas I of Russia to provide the rolling stock for the railway connecting Moscow with St Petersburg, the first important line in the country. Winans sent his son, who spent many years in Russia, where he also designed tubular, half-submersible vessels for the Russian Navy that became known as "cigar boats". The family had been Confederates in the American Civil War—they were of Flemish extraction—and William Louis did not like Reconstruction America. So when he left Russia, he did not go back home, but moved instead to England. He did as many rich people did in those days and bought some land and houses in Scotland. (He died in 1897 leaving $12 million, a vast fortune in those days.)

On Whitsunday 1882, Winans took a twenty-one year lease of the Kintail Estate from one of the Seaforth Mackenzies. The estate covered about 200,000 acres, or 350 square miles. It stretched from the high-water mark on Loch Duich, near where Donald MacDonald lives, right over to the east coast of the country. Winans wanted to convert most of the land from sheep ground into deer forest. Unusually, he had no interest in stalking. He preferred to leave his ground alone for years—he rarely visited Scotland anyway—and then drive all the deer onto guns where a massive, undifferentiated slaughter was carried out. Because of this, Winans had a head gamekeeper rather than a head stalker. This man, William Ross, was really the cause of the trouble which led to the litigation.

Ross was a stranger to Kintail. It is not known where he came from, but Winans preferred to employ outsiders on his Highland estates. At any event, Ross noticed that Macrae kept two sheep near his cot and decided that he should not. If Macrae allowed his sheep to nibble the laird's grass, Winans' deer would be disadvantaged. Worse still, if this trespass were condoned, Macrae's neighbours might feel they had a right to permit similar trespasses by their own sheep. Soon they would have cows too, and grazing might be so reduced that the deer would be driven for feed onto the land of Lord Tweedsmouth, Winans's neighbour on the Guisachan Estate. For reasons unknown, Winans hated Tweedsmouth so much that, according to one account, he built "an all-metal deer fence along the march of Affric with Guisachan, thereby preventing the deer from Affric, Glenshiel and Kintail moving onto Guisachan. The ruins of this extensive fence can yet be seen and are a monument to his spite."[52] Macrae

---

[52] The Pet Lamb Case by I.R. Mackay in *Transactions of the Gaelic Society of Inverness* Vol. 48 (1973). Another, equally erudite but more amusing, essay on this case is contained in *Scot Easy: Travels of a Roads Scholar* by the Edinburgh journalist, Wilfred Taylor (London 1955). Of course, the definitive

was therefore told to put off his two sheep.

He objected, saying that it had been the custom for long enough that the tenant of the estate permitted the cottars to use patches of ground to grow potatoes and to graze a sheep or two, or a cow, on estate land. Indeed he had himself once had a house cow. Ross was not interested. He warned Macrae several times over the next few months that his two sheep were trespassing on the laird's ground. Eventually, Macrae got rid of them. But soon afterwards he found a lamb in a ditch when he was out cutting peats. It had obviously lost its mother and was so near death that he decided to take it home. Macrae's wife nursed it back to health by giving it milk "when we had it", Macrae said, and at other times eggs beaten up with sugar.

The lamb became a pet in the household, following Macrae and his children around wherever they went. The eagle-eyed Ross soon spotted the little creature which, at the time he sighted it, was twenty yards from Macrae's house and therefore within his master's deer forest. He reported this fact to Winans, who told him to order Macrae to get rid of the lamb.

This Ross did, though Macrae said, first, that the lamb was only grazing the roadside. It might have wandered away from the road but that could hardly be controlled. Unmoved, Ross said that unless the lamb were put away within three days, Winans would go to court for an interdict against trespassing.

Goaded beyond endurance, Macrae at last responded defiantly, saying, "Devil of a hair of the lamb will I put away for Winans. Instead of putting away this lamb, I am only thinking of getting more sheep, or a cow. Let Winans go his length, and I will meet him."

Winans wrote to Macrae, who was illiterate, formalising his threat of litigation. An interdict—it is called an injunction in England and Wales—is a command of court. To disobey it is contempt of court, which is punishable in a variety of ways,

---

account is in the law report. See: *Winans v Macrae* (1885) 12 R 1051. It was Lord Tweedsmouth who, on Guisachan in these years, first bred the now famous Golden Retriever.

including imprisonment. It is a serious matter.

When Mackenzie, the owner of Kintail, heard about this overbearing approach on the part of his tenant, he was so appalled that he wrote to Winans offering to cancel his lease. Winans refused the offer with contempt. As he later told the court, "What I desire is to get rid of the cottages and their inhabitants. I shan't leave a stone unturned until I get rid of them." Winans was a litigious man, and was as determined to "meet" Macrae as Macrae was now prepared to "meet" him.

That they never physically met in court was due to the fact that Sheriff-substitute Hill, sitting in Dingwall, permitted Winans and Mackenzie to give their evidence in London—an extraordinary concession to privilege.[53] Nonetheless, Hill found for Macrae. He did so because he took the view that "the pursuer [Winans] failed to prove that the defender [Macrae] trespassed on said lands [Morvich farm, part of Kintail estate] by putting a lamb to graze thereon." He accepted that Macrae had failed to prevent the lamb straying onto Winans' ground, but that was a different thing from deliberately setting the lamb to graze there. The former is accident, the second, because *mens rea* or deliberate intention is involved, could be trespass.

Winans immediately appealed to the Sheriff of Ross-shire.[54] Sheriff Mackintosh reversed Sheriff-substitute Hill finding that, though cottars had "by some arrangement with the previous

---

[53] A modern example of this is in the case of *Cherney v Deripaska* which is to come on in London in 2013 (it is thought), despite the fact that the plaintiff, Michael Cherney, a billionaire Russian refugee living in Israel, cannot travel to London because there is a European arrest warrant outstanding against him for alleged money-laundering. The London court has allowed him to give evidence by video link. The difference in Winans's case is that he simply could not be bothered to travel to Inverness, a reason no modern court would be likely to accept.

[54] Whereas today, within each sheriffdom, a Bench of sheriffs is overseen by a sheriff-principal, in the nineteenth century there was a sheriff for each county supported by a Bench of sheriffs-substitute. The distinction is mainly one of terminology (and size of area covered, since today's sheriffdoms cover several counties).

tenants" been allowed to graze cattle and sheep on the lands of Morvich but that Macrae had been told "that privilege was to be discontinued". He had been asked to remove his sheep. He had done so. But after that, the Sheriff said, "the defender [Macrae] turned out the said lamb to graze on the said lands of Morvich", which action, as part of a pattern of conduct which, crucially, included threats to graze more sheep, made him liable to interdict by Winans.

The order which Winans had craved was "to interdict the defender from putting any lamb, lambs, sheep, cattle or other bestial upon the lands of Morvich, in the parish of Glenshiel in the county of Ross, or any part of said lands, for the purpose of grazing, and from grazing any lamb, lambs, sheep, cattle or other bestial upon the lands of Morvich aforesaid or any part thereof, and to find the defender liable in expenses." This was now granted.

In normal circumstances that would have been the end of the matter. Winans had taken action in the first instance. He had lost, but won on appeal. The illiterate shoe-maker had been forced to respond in both cases. The only further action now possible was for an appeal to be lodged against the Sheriff's interdict. But this would involve Macrae in making application to the Court of Session in Edinburgh. For a man in his position, especially given the wealth and evident determination of his opponent, this was hazardous undertaking, to say the least of it. But Macrae clearly had gumption, because appeal he did.

It is not known how he paid for this, but there have been suggestions that the local Minister helped organise a fund. These were the days of agitation for the rights of crofters and cottars, which is what the Napier Commission had been investigating. It is possible that some "land reform" activists took a hand, perhaps at the Minister's instigation. As regards his losses to date, Macrae would probably have been advised that he had already incurred liabilities to Winans in respect of the costs of the two hearings so far which were more than he could conceivably earn in the rest of his life. He would be no worse off if he lost again. Financially-speaking, he might as well be hung for a threatened sheep as for an actual pet lamb. At any event, Macrae found lawyers, an appeal was lodged and the case moved from the Sheriff Court in Dingwall to the Parliament House in Edinburgh.

In their submissions to the court, Macrae's advocate argued that no damage had been done to the Kintail deer forest by the lamb, which had anyway now already been sold (it is said to Mackenzie the proprietor, who had it stuffed). Importantly, Macrae had not asserted any right to graze animals on Kintail, only failed to prevent one animal straying there from the verge of the road outside his house. His threat to graze more sheep was mere vituperation. "If a proprietor whose lands were contiguous to a public road," Macrae's lawyers argued, "wished to prevent animals from straying onto his lands, his only remedy was to fence them." These were days in which large numbers of animals were driven along public roads to market. Recent law gave force to this contention, saying that owners were liable only if their animals wandered onto arable ground, not "common or waste ground" which is what the Kintail deer forest was.

Winans' lawyers concentrated on the pattern of conduct, which implied that Macrae was deliberately flouting the tenant of Kintail's rights to grazing for his deer, that "his conduct amounted to active connivance" in the reduction of the animal food reserves on the estate. They claimed it was necessary to have the Court's sanction to prevent these trespasses being repeated, possibly on a larger scale if others followed Macrae' example.

The case was heard by the Lord Justice-Clerk, the second most senior judge in Scotland, and three other Senators of the College of Justice. They constituted the Second Division of the Inner House of the Court of Session, one of the two appeal courts, the other being the First Division which, then as now, was presided over by the Lord President. There is no hierarchy as between these two courts, they are merely names of convenience. Like Donald Macdonald, they took custom as being part of the essence of law. They seem to have considered this an important case, even though it concerned a very trivial matter. This was probably because of the mounting unrest in the crofting counties, which included Ross-shire. Violence had already broken out in Skye and other places. The example of Ireland, where murders like those the Joyce family had been convicted in connection with were becoming commonplace, was in the forefront of everyone's mind. Justice William Douglas had a point when he said that law is politics.

Of the four judges who sat, the longest and fullest opinion was given by Lord Young, with each of the other three concurring. This is part of what he said:

> I cannot help sympathising with the landlord, Mr Mackenzie of Kintail, who says that when he heard or saw in the papers that Mr Winans, who had 200,000 acres of shootings, was going to bring an action for the trespass of a pet lamb, it seemed so ridiculous that he did not believe it....
>
> Now, I am of the opinion that there was no trespass by the pet lamb of which a man could complain in a Court of justice. I think a trespass—that is, an invasion of a man's right—may be committed by means of a pet lamb, for it may be put where it can do harm. But if you have 200,000 acres of rough grass, with a public road running through it and a cot at the side of the road, the land being unfenced, to fence that land against children or a pet lamb by an interdict of a Court of justice would, I think, be an outrageous proceeding. It is impossible to keep children confined to the high road, as it is in like manner impossible to confine a cat or a dog. Life in that part of the country would not be possible if these unenclosed lands were fenced by interdicts of this Court against trespass of this description....
>
> I decline, by any interdict, to protect unenclosed lands against trespass of this kind. To talk about the lamb growing into flocks of sheep and herds of cattle is really to talk in a way which makes no impression on my mind whatsoever. If a man wants to protect his lands from being invaded in this way—against children toddling on the grass at the roadside, or a lamb going on to it, or a cat, or a kitten—I say, if he wants to exclude that he must do so by

other means—by fencing the lands, for example—but not by applying to Her Majesty's Judges for interdict.

It is important to note the core of Lord Young's reasoning, which was that life on places like Kintail would be impossible if Winans' litigiousness were tolerated by the courts. This was not even customary law: it was pure custom. There was no law involved in Lord Young's vision of ordinary Highland life. No evidence was led on the matter of general standards obtaining at the time for reasonableness in litigation about trespass in the crofting counties. And there was certainly no Impossible Life in the Highlands (Prevention of) (Scotland) Act on the British statute book. The case turned entirely on Lord Young and his colleagues' view of how daily life should go on in late nineteenth century Ross-shire. It was a purely personal view, and not just of what custom was, but what custom *ought to be*, as their Lordships thought. Nonetheless it was a view which carried exceptional force, given the personalities involved and the forum in which they stated it. Show me the judge and I'll tell you the law.

Winans, having lost, was now liable for all of Macrae's costs, as well as his own. According to one authority, the sum involved was £3,000—perhaps £300,000 in today's money. Apparently, he approached Macrae and said, "Well, you have won, and it would have been cheaper for me to have presented you with an effigy of your wretched lamb made of solid gold."

Driving to Dingwall for the first appeal, Winans's coach had been stoned by an angry crowd. Thereafter he feared for his safety if he visited his estate. After he lost in the Court of Session, he is said to have asked Ross, the keeper whose lack of tact did as much to inflame the matter as Winans's contempt for his cottars, whether if he give everyone on Kintail £5 he could go back there. Ross said he should not pay any money as they would only use it to buy rifles with which to kill his deer. Winans never visited Kintail again.

4

## Judging as it Has Been

Having looked at the best of judging and the worst of judging, and considered judging at the macro and the micro levels, it is perhaps appropriate to give some brief historical context to Scottish judging, from both the points of view of personality and approach to the law. I have selected four judges: one from the eighteenth century, one from the nineteenth and two from the twentieth. The first is Lord Braxfield, the man who has been called Scotland's "hanging judge".

Braxfield was born Robert McQueen, the son of a lawyer and later sheriff, in Lanarkshire in 1722. He was educated at Edinburgh University, and was admitted to the Faculty of Advocates in 1744. Soon afterwards, he was, like many new intrants, appointed an advocate for the poor. What was known as the Poor's Roll was a peculiarly Scottish institution, dating back to 1424, which provided professional representation for anyone arraigned before the Justiciary Court who could not afford to hire a defence advocate. The system lasted until the introduction of legal aid in 1950.[55] McQueen was also employed by the Forfeited Estates Commission which had taken over the properties of many of the Jacobite chiefs who had supported Bonnie Prince Charlie

---

[55] It was not the provision of voluntary legal assistance for impecunious people accused of crimes that was peculiarly Scottish. Most European countries had something similar in the middle ages. The unusual aspect in Scotland was that the system lasted in full vigour right up to the time when the state made formal arrangements to shoulder the burden.

during the rebellion in 1745-6. He acquired a reputation as an expert on both the civil (i.e. Roman) law, which predominated in Scotland with respect to movable property, and feudal law, which applied to heritable property. Fifteen years later, he was one of the highest-earning advocates in the country, with an income estimated at over £1,600 per annum, or nearly double that of a Court of Session judge. So when he was appointed to the Bench, as Lord Braxfield, in 1776, he had to take a sharp drop in salary. James Boswell commented in his diary, "Macqueen liked not honour which took so much money from him. But if he should refuse it, he could not expect to have it afterwards."

Boswell's comment about McQueen/Braxfield's approach to money echoed one of his most notable character traits, the unembarrassed Scottishness of his manner, outlook and, especially, speech. These were days when the first strong currents of anglicisation were beginning to flow through Scotland. Fifteen years earlier, an Edinburgh club calling itself the Select Society had founded a Society for Promoting the Reading and Speaking of the English Language in Scotland with the aim, as the *Scots Magazine* reported, of helping "gentlemen educated in Scotland to acquire such knowledge of the English Tongue as to write it with some tolerable purity [and to] avoid many gross improprieties, in quantity, accent, the manner of sounding vowels etc. which, at present, render the Scotch dialect so offensive."

On the Bench and off it, Braxfield spoke the broad Scotch of his native Lanarkshire (though he wrote a more standard English). Forty years later, when Anglicisation had triumphed, he was described by the most literate judge ever to sit in Scotland, Lord Cockburn (who will be described next), in unflattering terms:

> Strong built and dark with rough eyebrows, powerful eyes, threatening lips, and a low growling voice, he was like a formidable blacksmith. His accent and his dialect were exaggerated Scotch; his language, like this thoughts, short, strong, and conclusive.[56]

Cockburn, it must be stressed, knew Braxfield mainly by repute, only being admitted to the Faculty of Advocates a year after Braxfield's death. But by this and many other disparaging statements, he handed down to the twentieth century a view of Braxfield as Scotland's equivalent of the blood-thirsty Judge Jeffreys, who was Lord Chancellor of England under James II (or VII), and dealt with the Monmouth rebellion in 1685 so harshly that his name has become a by-word in the English language for judicial cruelty and excess.[57] Cockburn went on from the passage quoted above to describe Braxfield as "illiterate and without any taste for refined enjoyment or understanding." He had "power without cultivation, which only encouraged him to a more contemptuous disdain of all natures less coarse than his own." Finally, he damned him as a judge in the most offensive terms possible. He wrote that Braxfield said once to his friend and patron, the Lord Advocate, who was the Crown prosecutor, "Let them bring me prisoners, and I'll find them law."

Largely as a result of Cockburn's elegant prose, the image of Braxfield as an uncouth echo of Judge Jeffreys was embedded in the nineteenth century mind. Even Sir Walter Scott contributed to the clamour by—so his first biographer reported—telling a story which implied that Braxfield also took a contemptuously frivolous view of some of the prisoners whose cases he tried. Apparently he used to play chess with a man called Donald, who regularly beat him. Then, on circuit at Dumfries, Donald came before him on a charge of forgery. This was a capital offence in the late eighteenth century. The jury found Donald guilty. Braxfield duly pronounced the death penalty then said to the

---

[56] *Memorials of His Time* Henry Cockburn, Edinburgh 1856, p. 115

[57] Jeffreys's language and approach to justice had many similarities to that of Andrey Vyshinsky. He said of a Presbyterian witness for the defence of a woman charged with sheltering rebels, "I hope, gentlemen of the jury, that you take notice of the horrible carriage of this fellow. How can one help abhorring both these men and their religion? A Turk is a saint to such a fellow as this. A Pagan would be ashamed of such villainy. Oh Blessed Jesus! What a generation of vipers do we live among!"

condemned man, "And now, Donald my man, I think I've checkmated you for once."

Other attributed remarks are reported in the vernacular which so offended Lord Cockburn. "Ye're a vera clever chiel, man, but ye wad be nane the waur o' a hanging," he is supposed to have said to one criminal. On another occasion he justified the death penalty for a juvenile offender by saying, "Hang a thief when he's young, and he'll no steal when he's auld." Perhaps the most outrageous attribution of all, at least to Victorian ears, stemmed from one of the sedition trials which Braxfield presided over in the late 1790s when he was the Lord Justice-Clerk. Believing in the near perfection of the British Constitution in the face of the threat from Revolutionary France, Braxfield gave none of the accused credit for purity of motive, at least when they were shown to have agitated amongst the common people. According to Cockburn, one of them tried to justify his attempts to provoke social change by saying that all great men had been reformers, including "our Saviour himself". Braxfield's response was to say, "And muckle he made o' that, he was hanget."

The obvious conclusion from Cockburn's account is how much better off society was now that the unregenerate Tories like Braxfield had been replaced by enlightened Whigs like himself. This has become received wisdom, long after most of Cockburn's defamatory statements have been shown to be false. The "checkmate" story, for example, actually concerns a quite different judge, Henry Home, Lord Kames. But Chamber's *Scottish Biographical Dictionary*,[58] for example, still says that Braxfield was a "hanging judge" who was "notorious for his harshness".

Though nothing good is said about him, Braxfield, though a stern judge when he needed to be, was in fact a man of warm humanity, great learning and a lot of wit. He was known on some occasions to express profound sympathy for condemned men, and so far from mocking, cajoling and railroading Counsel in court, he was often much more patient than he needed to be. His

[58] Ed. Rosemary Goring, Edinburgh 1992

faults seem to have been that he took whist too seriously for some tastes; he spoke in a blunt, profane and unsophisticated manner; and he preferred traditional Scottish music to the newly fashionable baroque chamber music. But his recent biographer concludes: "Much of his coarseness and broad Scots was, in part, a stand for an older world against the mim-mouthed, perjink, anglicising trends of the Select Society and their followers."[59]

Braxfield was happily married, had four children and was a widely popular man, perfectly acceptable in polite society, despite his old-fashioned ribaldry, high spirits and love of claret. His wife died eight years before he did (in 1799). Fifteen months after his bereavement, at the age of seventy, Braxfield proposed marriage to a Miss Ord in a letter whose brevity sums up his character better than any quote from court:

> Lizzy, I am looking out for a wife, and I thought you just the person that would suit me. Let me have your answer, off or on, the morn, and nae mair aboot it.

What motivated the more decorous Lord Cockburn, and others like him, to disdain Braxfield and his rougher, more colourful world was a political feeling that the old order neither could nor should last into the new century. Edinburgh was changing from a city in which the huge, crowded, often unsanitary tenements of the Old Town, painted in bright, primary colours, were being replaced by the spacious, calm and ordered world of the New Town, which was built uniformly from grey stone. Pillars of the old establishment, like the judges who had dealt severely with supporters of reform during the wars with France, were felt to be obstacles which needed to be removed if a more enlightened and democratic society were to be brought about. To put it in American terms, it was like the change from the frontier world of the original settlements to the calm, Jeffersonian atmosphere of a society that could contemplate life under an impersonal Constitution with a Supreme Court available to settle all high-level disputes.

---

[59] *Braxfield – the hanging judge?* Brian Osborne, Glendaruel 1997. p.104

Cockburn was Solicitor General for Scotland during Lord Grey's Whig Ministry, which came to power in 1830 and passed the first Reform Act two years later. He was made a judge in 1834, and performed creditably on the Bench, though with no special distinction. He married happily, had eleven children, and died in 1854 at his self-consciously rustic home at Bonaly, just outside Edinburgh in the foothills of the Pentlands. Ironically, the old reactionary, Braxfield, had lived in a modern townhouse in George Square, and on his substantial estate at Braxfield in Lanarkshire, which he successfully modernised. The legal moderniser, by contrast, preferred bucolic romance, and wrote poetry in the style of Wordsworth about nature and his own emotions. Reconciling his enthusiasm for political reform with his love of atavistic sentiment, Cockburn said he reasoned with the modern world but dreamt about the past. For all his strictures about Braxfield's adherence to the ways of the old, as yet unanglicised Scotland, Cockburn was unapologetically nostalgic for many aspects of Scottish life—except filthy inns and dirty, untidy villages. He devoted much energy to improving the architecture and layout of Edinburgh. To this day, the Cockburn Society honours this aspect of his outlook in its efforts to preserve the city from insensitive modern development.

Cockburn's book, *Circuit Journeys,* describes his progress round Scotland trying criminal cases in country towns. It is the best account of the judicial mind which has ever been written by a Scottish judge. What the book reveals, perhaps supremely, is the extent to which a balanced and humane judge sees judging as only one component of a full life.

Cockburn's prose, like many of his observations, has a modern feel. He grew up consciously rejecting the Scotticisms of Braxfield and his ilk, and the older tolerance for strong drink and strongly expressed views. Cockburn was a gently anti-industrial romantic, except when he encountered the prejudices of old. He had no time for Bonnie Prince Charlie and his cause, writing of the Jacobites that they were "as paltry, foolish, and selfish fellows as ever dishonoured a cause, which nothing but disinterested heroism could have dignified."

He was equally unsympathetic to the contemporary fashion for Sabbatarianism noting with disgust that even in 1842, Sundays in Perth were disfigured by a "Calvinistic grimness". Very few people ventured out on the North Inch, the great park where they could otherwise have enjoyed the "silver Tay" with its "beautiful bridge" and the sight of sunlight on the "distant blue mountains, some snow still lingering on their loftier summits." He wondered about "the sourness of mind that can think such sullenness against nature a duty." Worse still, was the associated hypocrisy: "Fanatical masters and mistresses are very apt to excuse their hatred of a smile upon the Sunday by ascribing their intolerance to consideration for their servants."

This attitude was not confined to Perth. "I had always heard that a smile upon the Lord's day was a sin in Rothesay," he wrote six months later. "Now I have found it to be so. The people have been literally dead today. Not a foot has been heard on the pavement, no working man's dusty skin has been refreshed in the pure sea, no boat has skimmed from the shore, no eye has performed the pious homage of raising itself to observe glories which God does not veil upon Sunday."

If the Enlightenment philosophy which Cockburn admired could be reduced to a single maxim, it would be the one on which the rule of law is designed to serve: live and let live. In Arbroath, he saw the opposite:

> In addition to its former Catholic and Establishment temples, there is now a Free kirk. I am told that, with true religious spirit, according as religion is too often practised, each sect lives in orthodox hatred of its brother. One would think that the sight of these peaceful and seemingly eternal mountains—gilded as at this moment they are by a cloudless morning sun, diffusing its blessings equally on them all—might teach them the insignificance of many of their follies.

Cockburn preferred nature. He saw a lot of it on his long journeys round the country, from one circuit town to another:

> If any man wants to be happy, I advise him to get a public

allowance for travelling, to cast out any devil by which he may be possessed, and then to get into the dickie of an open carriage, with a suitable assortment of books and cloaks; an amiable, affectionate, sensible, and very quiet niece beside him, and a wife, daughter, and son, with whom he is on good terms, behind; and to drive sixty miles through new and beautiful country, on a sweet and bright autumn day.

But there was a worm in the rose: the march of the railways. "The country is an asylum of railway lunatics," Cockburn wrote in 1845. "One symptom of their malady consists in their being possessed of the idea that all seclusion is a grievance." A year later he remarked, "I never see a scene of Scotch beauty without being thankful that I have beheld it before it has been breathed over by the angel of mechanical destruction." In Aviemore, just four years before his death, Cockburn wrote, "I shall probably never see this noble tract again. They talk of continuing the Aberdeen railway to Inverness. This will destroy the posting inns on what has hitherto been called the Highland road, and will compel us to be conveyed like parcels—speed alone is considered."

But Cockburn was no Luddite. Except on Sundays when no trains ran, he did not avoid railways, as his friend Lord Moncrieff did, though he always preferred to have a "coupé" to himself. "This," he explained, "is a private carriage, and secures the learned Lord from contamination with witnesses, parties, jurors, and the world."

For all his dislike of the effects of railways on the previously peaceful countryside, Cockburn was alive to their benefits for travellers. He described the difficulties of travelling round Scotland in what he referred to as "the age of Braxfield", of which he had caught a glimpse while riding circuit—literally—as a junior Advocate Depute shortly after having been called to the bar nearly half a century earlier.

> Those who were born to railroads, or even to modern mail-coaches, can scarcely understand how we, of the previous age, got on. There was no bridge over the Tay at Dunkeld, or over the Spey

at Fochabers, or over the Findhorn at Forres, nothing but wretched, pierless ferries, let to poor cottars who rowed, or hauled, or pushed, a crazy boat across—or more commonly got their wives to do it. There used to be no mail coach north of Aberdeen until, I think, after the battle of Waterloo. To reach Inverness by the mail took about nine hours short of the time required to get to London.

The court papers and paraphernalia were carried in a wagon, while the judges rode on horseback. Braxfield himself was once forced to go twenty-eight miles up the Findhorn to the Bridge of Dulcie because the river was in spate and the usual crossing impassable. But even in the 1840s Cockburn had the experience of being in a mail-coach when it over-turned in a swollen Morayshire river. As the soaked passengers scrambled to the bank, the court papers floated away downstream, chased by the Clerk.

Travel on the West Circuit could be even more hazardous. As late as 1848, Cockburn and his family were nearly drowned on the ferry at Shean, between Ballachulish and Oban.

> Like an idiot, I let us be put into the same open boat with the carriage, though the sea was as rough as a violent headwind could make it in a space one and a quarter mile wide, and we only had two oars, each with two rowers. It took them above an hour to get us, inch by inch, across; the carriage heavily laden swung; the nine Celts who had charge of us jabbered and roared, all gesticulating in opposite directions... These are disgraceful ferries, having too few boats, and none of them good; no landing places; no planks or gangways or cranes. Passengers, cattle, and carriages are just lifted and thrown into clumsy, crazy boats, and jerked by bad rowers, with unsafe oars, amidst a disorderly tumult of loud, discordant, half-naked, and very hairy Celts who, however, expecting whisky, are at least civil, hearty and strong.

Cockburn was ahead of his time, for a judge, in finding fault not only with the "Celts" but most of the lairds too. The village of Luss, on Loch Lomondside, for example, was so squalid and dirty that "no public infamy is too great for it... God has planted a garden there, and man a hog-stye." But the fault lay not with the inhabitants. "The lairds who permit it are the chief brutes." He felt the same about the ruins on Iona. Not only are the people half-naked, diseased and dirty, but the state of the Abbey was "worse than most pig-styes". The Dukes of Argyll were the owners. "All the waters of Loch Fyne will not cleanse them from the shame of these neglected ruins," Cockburn wrote. "No foul beast ever trod a pearl in the dirt so unconsciously as these titled men have."

Sporting landowners were just as bad, having "become slaves of their own vermin". One who, "grovelling in his own tastes, sacrifices everything to the creation of game", with the result that his woods are allowed to grow into impenetrable jungles. "It is impossible to forgive the selfishness which bequeaths the beautiful scenery which has the misfortune to call him master in a state of decay to the next generation."

But his greatest scorn is reserved for the people like Duke of Leeds who, at Glen Tilt near Braemar, claimed he had the right, in order to protect his deer from disturbance, to prohibit all public access to his property. Pre-dating the modern consensus in Scotland on the right to roam, Cockburn disagreed with the Duke's claim, even though he acknowledged that *de facto* he could make it good in law at the time. "The public says he has no such right; but as there is no town at hand with its contemptuous citizens, of course the steady perseverance and the long purse of the single nobleman will soon get the better of the poor Celtic slave, the irritated tourist, the sulky drover, and even the London newspapers which in this slack season have taken up the case."

Trespass was a new crime in the Highlands, coming in with the partial Anglicisation of land-use law in the early nineteenth century. As will be seen later in this chapter, it became more contentious the more the Highlands came to be owned by outsiders who did not understand, or accept, the local traditions. Cockburn noted with mischievous glee how the Duke of Leeds's neighbour, a General Robertson, responded to attempts by the "Graf", as Cockburn contemptuously referred to him, to "exercise so offensive a privilege". The Duke staged a grand, ostentatious day's deer shooting over the lands of Lude. But the General out-manoeuvred him by a move which everybody admired. His lawn was ornamented by eight or ten cannons. These were distributed conveniently, and whenever the great man and his tail appeared, off went the guns, startling every hill and glen by their echoes, of course off went the deer, and his Grace had nothing for it but to retire, cursing, with every ball in his rifles.

But the most modern of all Cockburn's observations was another one with which Braxfield would probably have agreed: the problem of increasing crime in the industrialising areas of the country. Cockburn makes observations like this one about the more rural parts: "And so ends the South Circuit of autumn 1851. Twenty-four cases in all, out of a population of nearly half a million." In July 1843 on the West Circuit he tried all the indictable crimes committed during the last six months in mid-Argyll in seven hours: "The business at Inverary began on Saturday at ten, and was over that day by five. No case worth mentioning."

At the other end of the scale was Dundee, which Cockburn condemned "for its trade: that is for its steam-engines, its precarious wealth, its starving, turbulent population, its vulgar blackguardism." On circuit in Perth, most of the cases arose from crimes committed in Dundee, which did not yet have its own court. He described the town as "a sink of atrocity which no moral flushing seems capable of cleansing... For many years past it has been the most blackguard place in Scotland. Perth and its shires are always remarkably innocent."

On the West Circuit, Glasgow regularly recorded the highest number of cases ever heard on a single circuit. Even on the largely peaceful South Circuit, the villages round about Ayr were becoming a problem. "I grieve for Dalmellington," Cockburn wrote. "The Devil has disclosed his iron, and speculation has begun to work it. There seem to be about half a dozen of pits sinking within half a mile of the village, and before another year is out these now solitary and peaceful hills will be blazing with furnaces, and blighted by the presence and the vices of a new population of black scoundrels. They are already lying snoring and, I presume, drunk on many indignant knolls."

By the end of his life, Cockburn had begun to sound almost like the Braxfield he disdained. For all his liberal principles, there were many occasions when he wished to hang people whom juries wished to see leniently treated. Perhaps it is the fate of all judges to seem reactionary in old age, when in fact all they are doing is reflecting the desire of the more conservative strata of society for stability. This is as true today as it was a century and a half ago.

Sheriff Bill Hook—sadly now deceased—lived alone in a spacious flat in one of the more elegant parts of the New Town in Edinburgh. I went to see him because, ten years ago, I wrote a book about a celebrated English libel case and, when introduced to him by a mutual friend, he had told me that not only had he read my book, but also he was close friends with the judge who had taken the trial.[60] Since the conduct of the judge was controversial—the case concerned the illegal handover of Cossack prisoners of war to the Soviets by the British Army in 1945—I was naturally very interested to learn more. I was glad when Sheriff Hook—or Bill as he wished to be called—invited me up from Leith for a drink one evening to discuss the case. In the event, we had more than one drink and the conversation wandered far from his old friend, Mr Justice Michael Davies.[61]

---

[60] *The Cost of a Reputation*, Edinburgh 1996

[61] Almost all Scottish legal business is done either in the Court of Session, if it is serious and civil, the High Court of Justiciary, if it is serious and criminal, or in the Sheriff Court if it is less serious, whether criminal or civil. Sheriffs Courts are courts of first instance and are approximately equivalent to both Magistrates and Crown Courts in England. All appeals from them go to either the Session Court or the High Court. Together they constitute the Supreme Court of Scotland, from which there is no criminal appeal anywhere (except on Human Rights issues), while civil appeals can be made to the Supreme Court of the United Kingdom in London. The Court of Session sits exclusively in Edinburgh, while the High Court, though headquarterd there, goes on circuit. Sheriffs are appointed to particular sheriffdoms, in Bill's case, the Sheriffdom of North

"Do you take water in your whisky?" Bill barked cheerfully across the homely clutter in his basement kitchen as he poured a very full measure into a large tumbler.

Almost before I had time to reply, he said, "I have a friend who, whenever I ask that question, always replies, 'Only if there's room.'"

Suitably equipped for conversation, we settled down in Bill's drawing room upstairs where broad bay windows look out to the west and north. It was early spring and a gusty, fresh wind threshed through the high silver birches outside. Bright sunlight slanted in under the dark clouds which we could see moving over the Forth and the hills of Fife.

"I enjoyed your book," he said. "I thought it was a *magnum opus*, scrupulously researched. But I am not as critical of Michael Davies's interventions as you are. Speaking as a judge, I did not find anything to say, hey! a judge can't do that! But I knew him quite well, for a long time, though we've rather fallen out now."

"How did you get to know him?" I asked.

"Only by chance. It was due to George Emslie, my buddy round the corner who became the Lord Justice-General.[62] He

Strathclyde, which includes Greenock, and later West Lothian. They sit only there.

[62] The Lord Justice General has been the senior criminal judge in Scotland since the twelfth century, if not earlier. This office is now held by the same person who is Lord President of the Court of Session, the senior civil judge. The second most senior in both civil and criminal courts is a person who is known in both places as the Lord Justice Clerk. All the High Court judges are Session Court judges, and *vice versa*. Unlike in England, all take criminal as well as civil cases (or almost all, a small amount of specialisation has begun to appear, not supported by everybody). The full body of judges is known as the College of Justice, and it is important to note that Senators of the College of Justice (created in 1532), as they are known, are colleagues and therefore equals in a professional (though not ceremonial) sense. The only rank is that the whole body of judges is divided into those in the Inner House, which is a court of appeal, and the Outer House, which is the court of first instance. The most senior judge has no power at all to direct the opinions of the most junior. Each has complete judicial independence.

brought me back into the Bar-Bench golfing team when I came back to Edinburgh. I had dropped out while I was in Greenock. We play every year against a team of English barristers and judges. I used to stay with that marvellous, acceptable man, Hugh Griffiths, who went to the House of Lords eventually. But he dropped out and I was transferred to Michael Davies, by chance, while we were playing at Woking. Next year, we played at Muirfield, so he came up to stay with me. The following year I went to stay with him, and so it went on, year after year for twenty years. He was an appalling golfer. He didn't like whisky. His wife couldn't keep house. But they were charming, and great fun. They laughed all the time and made you feel at home. It was a most entertaining association, so I was the more bemused when we fell out, because it is not in the pattern I have followed in my life, to take issue with a friend. Anyway, it was the military part of your book that most interested me. I was a prisoner of war myself, some of the time in Colditz. I was captured alongside the Highland Division, though I was not part of it, at St Valery in June 1940. I was virtually locked up as the Germans didn't trust me—I presume because I escaped twice."

"Not from Colditz?"

"No, from hutted camps. I was never able to get out of the fortresses. I spoke German fluently, but I made the mistake of speaking Prussian German when I shouldn't have. I escaped masquerading as a Dutch labourer going on leave from Germany back to Holland. They caught up with me and they said, 'What are you doing?' They became suspicious when I claimed to be Dutch while speaking fluent Prussian. I never thought of that. I was always a bit stupid. They were ruthlessly observant of everything that moved inside Germany. There were so many foreign workers and so many of their own men deserting, people trying to get out of the towns and cities because of the bombing. A lot of the Hitler Jugend were employed scouting for bomber crews and so on. This was 1943. The War Office had told prisoners in Germany that they were no longer obliged to try to escape because the Germans were beginning to shoot prisoners, particularly prisoners dressed out of uniform. I don't know why I wasn't shot. But I do know what it is like to be a prisoner of war.

"The Germans were not nice. We had a very attractive, aristocratic officer, whose family built ships on the Tyne. He had been taken prisoner, although not beside me, in a surprise attack. He was tall, he was 6' 6" and they put him in a column of prisoners, mostly French, and he stuck out above them as most of them were about 5' 6". Two German officers came along the line of prisoners and spotted him. They stopped their vehicle and got out and started to torment him. He responded: that was his nature. He took off his hat and swung it at them, as it was all he had to protect himself with, so they shot him. He wasn't married, but he had a sister who was quite devoted to him and probably kept house for him. I never had the heart to go to her and say, 'I know all about your brother.' Until we went home five years later she still believed he might turn up. Nothing was known about prisoners, really. Is this a drinkable drink? Perhaps we should have another one?"

Settled once more in the bay window, with full glasses glowing in the evening sunlight, I asked about Sir Michael Davies's background.

"He came from Birmingham and took up practice in London. He was a good jury man. He was quite a telling Counsel, I gather."

"I have heard it suggested that he had Welsh antecedents?"

"I suspect he might have done, from his strong voice, loud manner and his rather over-bearing attitude. It is not much of a thing we go in for in Scotland. I think he probably has got Welsh blood in him. That would be my guess. I don't think he has got any Irish blood, and I don't think he is Roman. I think, if he's anything, he's Protestant. His wife was Roman. They say Roman Catholic, but of course they're not Catholic, they're just Roman—so says a true Presbyterian!"

"He certainly came across in the trial transcript as over-bearing," I said. "He was extremely dismissive of all the foreign witnesses, except the one German, even though some of them had been through horrific experiences and were very lucky to be alive. From my own experience of watching trials in Scotland, I find it hard to imagine a judge up here being quite so rude to witnesses."

"I agree with you," Bill said. "I think the English Bench is very much more authoritarian than our judges. Also from watching in the Old Bailey and places like that, their Counsel are much more deferential. Ours are polite but not deferent. And the judges in Scotland are polite, though also emphatic. They don't yield, but at the same time they don't use the heavy hammer."

"What do you think explains the difference?" I asked.

"Of course, I am going back a few years—I am rather out of date, you know—but I think it is partly because a lot of our clever QCs and judges were sons of the Manse."[63]

"What difference did that make?"

"Traditionally in Scotland, in the provinces, public schooling run until fourteen years of age, until public schools on the English pattern came in when boys and girls stayed on until sixteen: that was a novelty. School-masters in the provinces in Scotland, detecting an unusually able boy—I don't think they bothered to promote the girls—did their level best to give him a run to the universities, like Aberdeen or Glasgow. The boy went on his way with a bag of meal, in the traditional Scots fashion, and survived on a little porridge. Somebody would help him with the fees. These boys would do well at Universities and teachers and professors would promote them because they were diligent, and they would perhaps decide to go to the Bar. Those who ended up as judges had a much deeper experience of life than the Oxbridge-educated English."

"But Michael Davies did not go to Oxford or Cambridge."

"No, but he was the sort of man who wanted to be seen in a

---

[63] A "QC" is a Queen's Counsel, which indicates a senior advocate (or barrister in England). It is a term which came to Scotland from England at the end of the nineteenth century. In both Braxfield's and Cockburn's day, all advocates were of equal rank, unlike in England where there had been a hierarchy since at least Chaucer's day (the senior rank then called Serjeants). Today about a tenth the members of the Faculty of Advocates, to which all advocates have to belong if they are to practice, are QCs (or KCs when the monarch is male).

favourable light by those who had done."

"But in his book, *Law, Justice and Democracy*, Lord McCluskey–"

I did not get a chance to finish my sentence before Bill said, "Yes, difficult judge, and fairly politically-minded. Poor old John McCluskey, I bumped into him just the other day."

"By 'poor old', do you mean he's a tragic figure?"

"No, I mean that he always stepped into the sheogh."

"Accidentally?"

"Accidentally on purpose."

"He says in his book, 'If I were to be asked what temptations a new judge is exposed to I should have to admit that they include arrogance, self-esteem and impatience.' Would you agree with that?"

"No, I doubt if any of our judges are really arrogant. I think, self-esteem: yes, they all think they're jolly clever. Some judges are less patient than others. I think that is exaggerated language, frankly. The sort of thing you'd get from McCluskey, to achieve a readership, to achieve notice. That was his weakness, to project himself. Do we have another drink? I think we might as well. I'm sitting here comfortably with the sun on my back."

On his way over to get the drinks, Bill sat down at the baby-grand piano which sits handsomely in the middle of his large sitting room. He struck a few chords then got up and said, "That is the Russian Imperial March, the anthem before the Revolution. It is scarcely heard these days, though it is a familiar tune. This is my point to you: McCluskey is a little bit 'left' you know."

"But surely there is some justice in his point that judges do not know about conditions in mines and factories and so on?"

"It's in his nature, because he's a socialist, to say there is always a divide between the man who works with his hands and the man who works with his head. I think it's rather a silly remark. The National Union of Mineworkers once said to me, when I was sitting on a Tribunal in Edinburgh, 'You don't know anything about being underground.' I said, 'I certainly do. Not only do I know about being underground, but I know how to do it.' I said, 'I had to dig tunnels when I was a prisoner of war.'

They said to me, 'Would you like to come and see what we do?' They nominated the Victoria pit, outside Edinburgh, where they showed the customers. They took me down. It was an unpleasant experience but I was quite happy to do it. They dropped us about a mile in a rather rickety cage, and when we got to the foot we clambered on to a train and rambled off a mile or two underground. When we got near to where we were going, they said, 'Do you want to crawl to the face?' I said, 'That's what I've come for.' So I got down on my hands and knees and crawled forward. They were digging a three-foot face, which was more than I ever got when I was digging a tunnel. They look upon it as being a tough, hard dangerous job. It is difficult. There are risks. But it's not as dangerous as what I had to do."

"Because you were in sandy soil?"

"Yes. It was very dangerous because at any time it might collapse. And that was not all. We had a very nice officer in the Seaforths—a good-looking man, the same age as me—who was electrocuted in the shaft by amateurish wiring. We worked naked of course, and sweated tremendously. I used to use a candle because if it started to fizzle you knew you were running out of oxygen. They had no means of hauling him out. The shaft was only shoulder width and head high. I got stuck once. I was naked, but I overheated digging and pulling the sand back and shoring up the top and sides. When my stint was over after a couple of hours, I put my head between my knees to turn round to get out and I found that I couldn't get round. I got jammed. I thought this is too bad, but I'll just wait and see what happens. But of course I cooled down and managed to struggle round and got out that way."

The conversation then returned to the courts in Scotland. I asked, "Were you ever accosted by aggrieved litigants, or criminals you had sent to jail?"

"No, not once," Bill said brightly. "I think they regarded me as being strict but fair. I could go round Greenock unarmed, to dinners, occasions on the Bench and so on. I was never abused or pursued."

"Was that because, without a wig on, you were not

recognised?"

"No, I don't think so. My name was in the telephone directory."

"Do think you were unique in not being hassled by the public?"

"No, I think most were like that. There were a few Sheriffs whose manner on the Bench towards the accused could be abusive. But that was unusual."

Bill took a thoughtful sip of his drink as a particularly strong gust of wind whipped the birches over.

"I suppose, to be strictly honest," Bill went on, "there was one occasion when I was abused verbally in court, if that counts as an answer to your question. But only once. Needless to say that was not in Greenock. No man would have treated me like that there. They were polite. This was in Linlithgow Sheriff Court, after I'd come back to Edinburgh. My wife's business— she was much cleverer than me and ran a big travel firm, and was latterly President of the British Tourist Board—she needed to be closer to London so we came back from Greenock, and I was made Sheriff of Linlithgow. It is a strange county, dripping with socialists, including Tam Dalyell."

"Whom I did not realise until recently is married to the first Lord Wheatley's daughter."[64]

"Yes, a nice girl. There was nothing too wrong with Lord Wheatley either, except that he was a Shettleston-imported Roman Irishman. There was nothing too wrong with his views, except that he didn't know much law. But of course he was very useful to the Socialists when they came in, in 1945, because they

[64] John Wheatley was an advocate and Labour MP who became Lord Advocate in the late 1940s, in which role he introduced legal aid to Scotland, in place of the Poor's Roll. As Lord Wheatley, he was one of the very few Catholic judges in mid-century Scotland, and rose to be the Lord Justice Clerk. After he died in 1988, the memorial service for him was attended by the then Lord Chancellor of England, a Scot, Lord Mackay of Clashfern, who was disciplined by his church, the Free Presbyterian Church of Scotland, for attending a service in a Roman Catholic church

could appoint him as Solicitor-General, then Lord Advocate, and put him on the Bench. That was the days when judicial appointments were political. But that's beside the point. This man in Linlithgow had been convicted by the jury of assault with intent to ravish."

"Is ravish equivalent to rape nowadays?"

"Ravish is when you get her knickers down but you don't manage to get your old man up. That's always charged as assault with intent to ravish: when you give the girl a bloody great fright but you don't actually rape her. The maximum sentence I could impose then was two years—silly sentence, but still. Nowadays, it would be five. Then the judges kept themselves strictly apart from the sheriffs in sentencing terms. In a case in which you considered two years hopelessly inadequate, you could send the accused up to the High Court for sentencing. Anyway, in this case I announced the sentence of two years, the maximum, and the man leant forward to me, between his police escort, and said, 'You FUCKING BASTARD!'

"He said it as loudly and strongly as he could, so that the whole of West Lothian overheard him. I was staggered because that had never happened to me in all the fifteen years that I had been sitting on the dickie. So I wondered what the hell I was to say in response to that. Nobody had ever instructed me on how behave when I was given a mouthful. Then I remembered what happened between Mr Justice Darling and F.E. Smith, who became Lord Birkenhead. Darling had said, 'Mr Smith, you're being impertinent in my court today.' F.E. Smith said in answer, 'Well, my Lord, I'm trying to be; you can't help it.' Which was extremely saucy; we'd never dare do that up here. For some reason, in my sub-conscious mind, I dredged this up and said to this chap when he told me I was a fucking bastard, 'I'm trying to be, but you can't help it.'"

We both laughed. Bill went on. "He thought he was being clever because I had given him two years, which was the maximum and that it could therefore not be increased, whatever he said to me. What he had forgotten was that I could sentence him *separately* for contempt of court. So I carried on quite calmly and said, 'I care not what you think of me'—and I didn't; it mattered not—'but I defend the great office that I hold in this county, and you are therefore charged with contempt of court for the words you used. You may say anything in mitigation of the sentence I have now to consider.' He wasn't willing to apologise in any way, so I gave him an extra three months, *consecutive*. That shut him up.

"The police afterwards said to the Sheriff Clerk that while they were warding him to be produced for sentence, he had said to them, 'By Jove, I am going to give that Sheriff a mouthful today if he gives me the maximum.' And they said, 'You just do that!' They knew that I could extend the sentence if there was another charge. The police didn't discourage him; they never do. Amusing, what goes on, isn't it? But that, truthfully, was the only occasion in all my ups and downs I was ever challenged or abused. I could walk in and out through the front door. No man ever jostled me."

As we were on the subject of the police, I asked Bill if he ever saw any evidence of what he thought was inappropriate behaviour towards prisoners.

"I once went to speak to the Chief Constable in Greenock to say to him that I had received from the witness box by accused men complaints of mistreatment on the part of the police and I though he ought to know about them. He must have called in his Inspectors and said, 'The Sheriff's onto you, so you better tell your sergeants and your men to drop this business of giving the man a kick up the arse, because the Sheriff doesn't want that.' And I never had another complaint, so it was effectual. The police on the whole were dependable, but there was the odd one who would step out of line. There always is. They're only a bunch of men, there's nothing special about them, so they have to be well-officered, well-trained and well-watched. They are only human, but they did used to think, in my day, that justice as a whole was a prerogative of the upper classes, and that you would give a not guilty verdict on evidence which they would think worthy of a conviction. They thought that my background would make me more considerate than the average man would be."

"Did that make them resentful?"

"No. I think it made them think that we were a little out of touch with reality."

"They thought you didn't understand the world of the Greenock docker who used to beat up his wife on a Saturday night?"

"Yes, and that happened, regularly. Mostly on pay night."

"Was it as brutal as that?"

"Yes. The Jocks are tough. You don't have to explain to the Highland Light Infantry in Maryhill Barracks in Glasgow how to go into action against the Germans. You just have to hand them a musket and say, 'Get on with it!' They're tough monkeys in the back streets of Glasgow, and Greenock."

"But one Judge said to me there isn't the level of really gross, brutal crime like they have in Birmingham, Manchester and places like that."

"Well, I respect his view. He may have inquired into it. But in Glasgow as a whole, the IRA were never able to make any penetration, although there was mass of Roman sympathetic support for them. When the Krays in London thought of expanding their empire into Glasgow they didn't last a week. The Glaswegians had them out straight away. They ran their own ship."

"How did this manifest itself in Greenock?"

"I had to accept the fact that in the back streets, among the shipyard workers, there was hostility between Romans and Presbyterians, and between Celtic and Rangers. They love that. That's their life. That's what they work for. That's what gives them their whole interest in life, this little sparking game. There is nothing else for them in life. They don't play leisurely games of tennis like you and me. There is quite an emphatic divide between the imported Roman Irish and the native Highland Presbyterian Scots, or Protestants. It's never going to melt because they like it. They enjoy it."

"But occasionally people get killed."

"They do, occasionally. But the people I feel very sorry for are the women. They get themselves murdered up back-streets and side-streets, more really than the men because the women still go in for prostitution as it is called. But my own private view is that it is the man that is the prostitute because the woman can't operate without the man. So I don't like the woman to be rubbed out traditionally as we do by the expression prostitutes, I don't like it at all. They wouldn't be there if it wasn't for the man seeking them out. So what shall we do now? Shall we have another dram before you get on your bicycle? Perhaps we should."

With glasses recharged for the last time, Bill started reminiscing about non-judicial aspects of life as sheriff, one of them being when he acted as the returning officer for the county at elections. He particularly remembered Tam Dalyell "sweating and getting drunk" because he thought "Balkan Billie" might beat him.

"Who on earth was 'Balkan Billie'?" I asked.

"That was Billy Woolf, you know. He stood for the Nationalists, who wanted to Balkanise Britain, so we called him 'Balkan Billie'. He was an excellent man and got a very good turnout. But he could not oust Dalyell, who was not a nice man. He's not convivial; he's awkward. Even his own party have refrained from promoting him to the House of Lords. Lord Dalyell of the Binns, that'd be a hoot! He's a baronet, you know, but he doesn't use that angle because he thinks it's hostile to his image as a socialist in West Lothian—a bit like Michael Ancram, in a way. I gave him his name, you know. He was standing for the Tories and was called Lord Ancram. I said, 'You can't stand for election until you have a name. You must be Michael Ancram.' So he changed. He got 12,000 votes in his first election. He is still Michael Ancram. His father was the Marquis of Lothian. Roman, of course, but a very nice chap."

"Do sheriffs ever get titles?" I asked.

"No, thank goodness. I never wanted a title. I did not even want to be a QC. I was made a QC for the wrong reasons."

"Why?"

"The Lord Justice-General made my appointment as head of a Tribunal conditional on my taking silk because I had to sit with a senior retired physicians and surgeons. He thought the chairman had to be something superior to a mere advocate. So he spoke to the Dean of Faculty and said I was to take silk. I said, 'I don't want that.'"

"Why did you not want it?"

"I had never practised as a QC. It had no appeal for me."

"Surely it's a distinction without a cost?"

"More or less."

"Are you disdainful of honours?"

"I would just like to be one of Jock Tamson's bairns. I would just like to be what I am, and that's an advocate, a proud title in Scotland."

By the time I finally staggered to my feet to start the process of trying to remember where I had left my bicycle, the sun had set and the lights of Fife were glowing through the dark on the other side of the Forth.

As Bill ushered me towards the front door—on which there is a brass plate saying simply 'Mr W.T. Hook, Advocate'—he pointed out his large, luxuriously furnished spare bedroom. "I call it the Michael Davies Room," he said, with a chuckle.

He stood on his step while I fumbled with my keys and fitted the lights to my bicycle.

"I've enjoyed speaking with you," he said. "Don't hesitate to come and speak to me again. I shan't be offended whatever your questions are. My days of experimenting are over now that I'm alone without my beloved wife, who was so clever. I've nothing to console me. I don't find life easy.

"Poor old Michael Davies. I think losing his wife has damaged him. I've just been to a sale at Lyon and Turnbull and I bought him a club which calls itself Calamity Jane. Of course it isn't the original Calamity Jane, which was Bobby Jones's putter, though it is something near it. I thought I'd buy it for him as a gift. It might amuse him. He says he'll stick it on his wall for a short time, then give it to the English Bar golfing society, or whatever they call themselves, in our joint names, and they can have it as a trophy. I composed, in my feeble hand, a letter today to Michael Davies, and am sending it on tomorrow. We haven't a

Post Office here any more so I have to go up to Frederick Street, which is a damn nuisance. Edinburgh is so appallingly mismanaged. Everything has crumbled. It is just the same as Blair and Fatty Falconer's socialist state, which has also crumbled."

Apart from the fact that they both come from a Protestant background in Edinburgh, and went to the same school—George Watson's College—Lord Murray is about as different a person from Bill Hook as could be imagined within the small compass of the senior judicial community in Scotland, not least because he is an Oxford-educated socialist.

As Ronald King Murray, he was a Labour Member of Parliament for Leith from 1970-79. Unlike Bill, he does not play golf, being a keen sailor instead, having kept a boat at Granton until he was 80 years old. Also unlike Bill, he has accepted many honours in his life. He was appointed Lord Advocate and made a Privy Councillor in 1974, and Lord Murray in 1979 after he elevated himself to the Court of Session bench. Finally, he lives in a modern house, a long way from the New Town, and receives visitors with a cup of tea rather than large whiskies. He looks fit and alert, despite the recent death of his wife. What he and Bill do have in common—apart from membership of the controversial Speculative Society—is a welcoming approach to inquirers like me who come bearing lists of questions which cause some of the more timorous judges in Edinburgh to clam up.

Lord Murray is best known to the non-legal community on Scotland for his writings about nuclear weapons, to which he is strongly opposed. This is a big issue in the west of Scotland where Britain's missile-armed Trident submarine fleet, is based. In retirement he has been free to speak his mind—or write it. In 1999 he published a paper, entitled Nuclear Weapons and the Law[65], in which he considered an International Court of Justice advisory opinion, which had been issued in 1996, to the effect that the threat or use of nuclear weapons is generally contrary to

---

[65] *Medicine, Conflict and Survival* vol. 15, pp. 126-37

international law, though there could conceivably be circumstances in which self-defence legitimises their use. He pointed out how the British government had ignored this opinion. He quoted a recent ex-Permanent Under-Secretary for Defence as saying that an "opinion" was not binding on the government, and a Secretary of State for Defence who said that the International Court's view made no difference to British deterrence policy. Murray's concluded that the British defence establishment was wrong in its assessment of the effect of the International Court's ruling. The only difference between international law and ordinary domestic law is that the former is less easily enforceable, though time and custom often eventually gives it as much force as any domestic law.[66]

The context of Lord Murray's paper was arrest and trial of three anti-nuclear protestors after they had boarded and damaged a support vessel used by the Trident nuclear submarine fleet at its Clyde base, on Loch Goil, in June 1999. In a ruling which astonished many people, one of Bill Hook's successors as Sheriff of Greenock, Sheriff Gimblett, acquitted all of the accused after argument was led to the effect that the three protestors committed their openly criminal acts only in order to prevent a much more serious criminal act, as they thought it, namely the threat of the use of weapons of mass destruction. Lord Murray's arguments were quoted at length in court.

By way of appeal, the Crown called upon its principle legal

---

[66] He quoted the example of slavery. The first judicial determination of the illegality of slavery within Britain was made in Scotland in 1757. The practice had never been recognised by the law of Scotland and was inconsistent with its principles. Fifteen years later the famous (Scottish) Lord Chancellor of England, Lord Mansfield, declared slavery unlawful south of the border too. But that did not affect slavery outside Britain, and the slave trade which fed it was not abolished until 1807. It was another sixty years before the principle market which the slave trade was organised to supply, the southern States in America, abolished the practice. A similarly slow process might be at work with nuclear weapons. In democracies, government resistance to humanitarian laws, however resolute, has rarely proved to be sustainable in the longer term.

agent in Scotland, the Lord Advocate, to make an application to the High Court for a judicial determination that, in law, the Sheriff was wrong. The acquittals could not be reversed, but the government wanted a judgement which would prevent such arguments being used successfully by future groups of protestors. The way in which Lords Prosser, Kirkwood and Penrose arrived at their view that the government was right is fascinating. This is not the place to review their arguments in full, but a few examples will serve to convey the flavour of their approach.[67]

Possibly the first point to make is that their Lordships turned on its head the convention that courts do not rule on hypothetical questions. The task for judges is to discover the law and apply it to the facts of a given case. It is not to speculate about what the law might be in general terms. It is for parliament to state the law as a general proposition, and for academic or institutional writers to consider law in the abstract. But not when nuclear weapons are at issue, it would seem.[68] They stated early on: "The questions are general, and not particular." They went on to criticise the protestors for committing acts with general rather than particular significance when they described their protest as "no more than a slightly complicated mechanism for bringing the Crown's

---

[67] Interested readers might care to consult *Nuclear Peace: the Story of the Trident Three* by John Mayer, Edinburgh 2003 (Mayer was the advocate who acted for the protestors). A more academic treatment has been written by the American attorney, Charles Moxley: The Unlawfulness of the United Kingdom's Policy of Nuclear Deterrence—the Invalidity of the Scots High Court's Decision in Zelter, *Juridical Review* (2001), p. 319 (Ms Angie Zelter was one of the protestors). The full opinion is in *Lord Advocate's Reference No. 1 of 2000* (2001), and is available on the Scottish Courts website.

[68] There is a large body of jurisprudence about "standing". The essence of it is that nobody may bring a case into court unless they have a practical interest in its outcome. The officious bystander, for example, or the litigious moralist, may not challenge laws or acts which do not directly affect them. Since in this case the accused had already been acquitted, the government was, effectively, in the position of the officious bystander. But law is usually as flexible as is necessary for the state to maintain what it sees as order and good government, so Lord Advocate's references of this sort are not uncommon.

conduct in relation to Trident indirectly before a court." Of course, that is exactly what the judges themselves were doing.

Their Lordships' argument can be summarised in quotes: "a rule of customary international law is a rule of Scots law"; "the government's actions in relation to Trident must be regarded as entirely lawful unless the breach of international law is established"; "it is thus [essential to] show that the government is in breach of customary international law". So far, so good, but then they said, "the best interests of the state in matters of defence are a matter for the [Crown] prerogative"; and "national security... is *par excellence* a non-justiciable question."[69] This pair of propositions contradicted the first three, which were made on the assumption that law can be applied to war and national defence.

The judges then proceeded to deprecate the International Court's opinion on the pedantic ground that it was "is an advisory opinion, not a judicial determination." This was literally true, but hardly fair since it was "advisory" simply because it was a statement of law in general rather than the resolution of a particular dispute between individual states. But their Lordships were themselves making a statement about law in general. They were using the generality of the International Court's opinion as an excuse for not applying international law in their own, equally generalised, hypothetical judgement about law in Scotland, even though they accepted the fact that "a rule of customary international law is a rule of Scots law".[70]

---

[69] That is what President Nixon wanted to take advantage of when he tried to use the CIA as way of preventing investigation of Watergate (see Chapter 1). That doctrine also explains the attraction of anti-terrorist legislation to governments chafing under the restrictions of the rule of law.

[70] The International Court issues Judgements, Advisory Opinions and Orders. Advisory Opinions tend to be handed down in cases where the relevant parties do not accept the standing of the Court, such as Israel in the matter of the wall it erected between its territory and that of the Palestinian state, or when the issue is a general statement of international law. In the nuclear weapons case, the matter came to court as the result of a United Nations Resolution, so it was not

At the end of this display of logic-chopping their Lordships concluded: "Although the advisory opinion may be regarded as confirmatory of the then rules of customary international law, it is not in itself to be regarded as having changed them... Correspondingly, it is this court's function to reach its own conclusion as to the rules of customary international law, taking full account of, but not being bound by, the conclusions of the International Court of Justice."

There are thirty-two pages of this type of argument, leading to the *ratio decidendi,* which is based on the distinction between the laws of war and the law in peacetime. Weapons of mass destruction—which even they conceded nuclear missiles are—kill indiscriminately, which is contrary to the laws and customs of *war*. But the Trident protestors committed their act in a time of *peace*, when different laws apply to the state whose actions they were opposing. This was their main point. "The rules of international humanitarian law are not concerned with regulating the conduct of States in time of peace. They specifically relate to warfare and times of armed conflict." Therefore "to try to extend the meaning of 'armed conflict' to deployment of forces or weaponry in times of peace" is wrong because "in times of peace, it does not appear to us that these rules are either applicable or capable of application."

This was the key point. Their Lordships held that though the protestors' actions might have been justified during times of conflict, they cannot have been said to have been acting to prevent a possible war crime on 8 June 1999 because a government cannot commit a war crime in peacetime. This

hard for the British state to ignore it. (All this happened before Britain justified its invasion of Iraq by the fact that Saddam Hussein had ignored a United Nations resolution.) Since the Trident case was about the legality of the British deterrent, it is relevant that the book which, to my knowledge, most exhaustively examines the arguments put before the Court, and the resulting Opinion, notes that "the Court effectively delegitimised deterrence as currently practiced." *The (Il)legality of Threat or Use of Nuclear Weapons*, John Burroughs (Berlin 1997) principle, they said, applies "even where a particular State has a policy of deterrence, and deploys nuclear weaponry in execution of that policy. Application of the rules [of war], and the resultant possibility of illegality, will arise only if and when some specific change turns the situation into one of armed conflict."

The proposition that international humanitarian law cannot be used to regulate the conduct of states in peacetime is so highly arguable that a different judge—Lord Murray, say—could quite easily have found differently. This is a clear example of Hamilton's Rule: show me the judge and I'll tell you the law.

It seems that their Lordships understood this because they appear to have wanted to pre-empt a future court, with different judges, taking a different view of international law or the laws of war. They could help to ensure no comparable case came to court at all if they destroyed the protesters other main argument, which was that one crime may be committed in order to prevent a bigger one. They said: "Even on the hypothesis of armed conflict and actual threat, customary international law does not entitle persons such as the respondents to intervene as self-appointed substitute law-enforcers with a right to commit what would otherwise be criminal offences in order to stop, or inhibit, the criminal acts of others."

The irony is that this point is correct when applied against a background of other reasonable arguments. People who destroy genetically-modified crops, for example, or who set fire to animal testing laboratories, however morally justified they may be, are unarguably wrong in law, at least in Scotland where permission to commit one crime in order to prevent another extends only to situations of serious and urgent necessity.

The three judges produced a number of other sound arguments. First, the International Court *did* say that *in extremis*, a nuclear response to mortal national danger could be justified. Clearly, if it can be legitimate to *use* nuclear weapons, a state has the right to *possess* them. Secondly, they drew attention to the distinction, which seems to me entirely valid, between the level of threat posed by routine nuclear-armed submarine patrols and specific, targeted aggression against clearly identified enemies.

Not even the protestors argued that Britain was guilty of that.

Finally, their Lordships eloquently dismissed the idea, which had been aired in court, that the protesters' actions might be justified within the American concept of "citizen interveners", which is what the protesters, one of whom was American, claimed to be. This "busy-body" argument—that personal morality can make public criminality lawful—is regularly deployed by people like bird protection fanatics in Scotland and has been long overdue for the comprehensive dismissal which it got, at least in respect of public property, in this case:

> We were not provided with any definition of "citizen interveners". In objective terms, it appears that they are simply citizens who intervene to damage public property. As such, they are apparently defined by their own decision to intervene, and are thus self-selecting and, it seems to us, self-indulgent. As such, it is not clear to us why they requite any special description such as "citizen interveners". What one is apparently talking about are people who have come to the view that their own opinions should prevail over those of others, for reasons which are not identified. They might of course be people of otherwise blameless character and of indubitable good intentions. But they might not. It is not only the good or the bright or the balanced who for one reason or another may feel unable to accept the ordinary role of a citizen in a democracy. It is one curiosity of the expression "citizen intervener" that citizenship is invoked by persons who apparently claim to be representing some unidentified category or number of "fellow citizens", but who can point to nothing in any generally understood concept of citizenship which would give them any right to act in furtherance of these particular citizens' wishes, and against the wishes of other citizens.[71]

The question arises as to why three intelligent, experienced judges, who had perfectly good arguments for defeating the Trident protestors' legal claims, found it necessary to make the logical excursions they did into such unnecessary legal territory

---

[71] *Lord Advocate's Reference, ibid.*, para 51

as the distinction between the laws of war and of peace. None of that convinced people like Lord Murray, who said that he agreed with most of the judgement, except the crucial part about the laws of war not applying to peacetime acts by sovereign states. "That's ludicrous," he said, laughing. "That would have legitimised Pearl Harbour."

Could it have been because the British state wanted to establish judicial authority for its possession of weapons of mass destruction in a part of the country where it feared direct action protests wee most likely, and the ordinary judges least sympathetic?

Lord Murray's comment prompted me to put to him another example of the arguably partisan use of power over the courts Scotland, one of which I had direct, personal and recent experience. His response was so interesting, and important in a Scottish constitutional sense, that I hope I will be forgiven for sketching in the background at sufficient length that it can be appreciated fully.

On Monday 5 July 2005 perhaps a thousand people marched through central Edinburgh to protest about the G8 summit of the world's leading industrial nations which was taking place at that time at Gleneagles in Perthshire. The media referred to these people as "anarchists", but they called their march a Carnival for Full Employment. About sixty of these people were arrested in the course of the march. The next morning they appeared in the Edinburgh Sheriff Court on a variety of charges, most of them breach of the peace. The police closed the court on that day without, as they now admit, lawful authority. Since justice must not only be done but must also be seen to be done, this was a very grave matter.

As long ago as 1693 the Scottish parliament passed an "Act anent Advising Criminal Processes with Open Doors". As recently as 1998 the British parliament incorporated the European Convention on Human Rights into British Law. Article 6(1) of the Convention states that "in the determination of … any criminal charge against him, everyone is entitled to a fair and *public* hearing." A closed court cannot provide a public hearing.

The principle of open justice is so fundamental to law that it is rarely mentioned in the academic literature, but there has been one occasion in modern times when it was severely tested. In 1971 several hundred Vietnam veterans appeared on the steps of the US Supreme Court building in Washington DC, brandishing toy machine guns and demanding that the court rule on the constitutionality of the war. The veterans' actions were part of a larger campaign against the war and the allegedly corrupt administration of Richard Nixon.

The Chief Justice, Warren Burger, ordered the steps cleared and the huge, thirteen-ton, bronze doors of the Court building closed, for the first time in history. Every other Justice objected to Burger's decision. Thurgood Marshall dictated a memo in which he called this decision an "over-reaction". The demonstrators were entirely peaceful and the Court was in no position to anticipate what they *might* do. Clearing the steps of non-violent demonstrators was unconstitutional, Marshall said: it discredited the whole Court.

When the Lothian and Borders Police closed the Edinburgh Sheriff Court, not only was there no violence outside, but there were not even any demonstrators! I was there myself and saw Chambers Street empty except for a few passers-by, some media reporters and perhaps a dozen uniformed police. I also saw two Special Branch operatives, conspicuous in their attempts to appear inconspicuous, cupping their hands over mobile phones and glancing up and down the street without turning their heads. There was not an anarchist in sight.

Not only was there no violence outside the Court, there had been very little violence the day before which had not, so far as I could see, been provoked *by the police themselves*. Cycling past, I was myself manhandled by an officer in a riot suit who screamed viciously at me. He appeared to have lost all self-control. Press reports at the time suggested that most of the baton-wielding officers were from either the Metropolitan, Manchester or Yorkshire police forces. Many had their numbers concealed, quite unlawfully, to prevent individual identification.

The atmosphere was so aggressive it seemed designed to provoke trouble. It was like an invading army, and I came away sympathising with anyone arrested for opposing this arrogant demonstration of state power. Ugly, noisy, angry and unclean though many of the anarchists were, their behaviour was no more of a threat to public order than that presented by groups of drunk football fans on a Saturday afternoon. I went to court the next day curious to see how the Scottish courts would deal with these people.

But I could not get in. I was told by one of the dozen or so officers standing guard at the gate that "the courts are closed to the public today". I asked another officer the same question and he gave me the same answer. I asked on whose orders had the court been closed. The policeman said, rather uncertainly, "The Senior Clerk of the Edinburgh Sheriff Court."

I subsequently learned that, three hours earlier, a law student called Martin Wallace had, with a group of fellow students, done what I had done, and been given much the same answer. His group was told that they could not get into the court unless they were members of staff, representatives of the media, or legal practitioners. Mr Wallace has used his experience as the point of departure for a full article on the law surrounding this issue for one of the major Scottish law journals.[72] Clearly the police had been ordered to give this answer to everyone.

I cycled back to Leith and phoned the "Senior Clerk of the Edinburgh Sheriff Court", who turned out to be a Mr David Shand. He courteously he explained the position from the point of view of the court authorities, to whom the police are at all times subordinate.

"The position," Shand said, "is that the courts were not closed to the public and if you were told that by a police officer then he was exceeding his authority. Any restrictions that were in place were sanctioned by the Sheriff-Principal. The only restriction I was aware of with the Public Order Unit at the front

---

[72] 'With Open Doors...?' The Police and Public Access to the Courts *Juridical Review* (2006) p. 129

door was identification. If people had identification they were to be allowed into the court and it was business as usual. Justice must be seen to be done."

I asked for the background and Shand said, "Basically the case law on the subject is *Ralston v HMA*[73] which says that the courts can be closed by the Sheriff-Principal. The position today was that the Sheriff-Principal had been contacted by the Chief Constable to say that if any trouble should develop they would want to seal off the court. That is perfectly understandable. But there was no trouble and there were a number of non-G8 courts operating. I apologise that you never had access."

I decided to write to Paddy Tomkins, the then Chief Constable of the Lothian and Borders Police, to ask which of his officers had ordered the court to be closed in contravention of both the Sheriff-Principal's directions and three centuries of Scottish legal tradition. It took me a year to get an answer.

During that year, I asked a senior judge for an opinion on the case.

"The idea that the police would take it upon themselves to say that the court was closed when they haven't got the authority of the court to do that is (a) news to me and (b) quite horrifying," the judge said. "We do close courts sometimes, but only in very exceptional circumstances, like a rape case when we have the complainer in the witness box. Even then, you would hear Counsel on both sides first, and of course you are closing only one court, not the whole building. Judges take the view very strongly that the courts should be open and that the police have got no authority to interfere, none whatsoever."

That is the background to the question I put to Lord Murray after he had given me his views on the Trident case. Did he think, considering all the facts, that the police had acted unlawfully?

"I have no doubt about that," he said. "The officers outside the court were acting outside their authority. The only excuse for closing the court would be something like a near riot near the building, and as soon as that disappeared, they would have no

---

[73] *Ralston v Her Majesty's Advocate* (1987) SCCR 467

ground for it. Therefore the police officer commanding the situation acted outwith his authority, definitely."

I asked in what situation he could envisage the police breaking the law with such evident determination. He explained to me about the role of the Metropolitan Police in Scotland.

"They have no strictly legal right to operate as police constables in Scotland, but of course they get the OK from the local Chief Constable and in effect are seconded into the Scottish police force. But they are a law unto themselves. They come in force with guns and things. There is no doubt that when they arrive, the Metropolitan Police take over, completely."

I said I could understand that for Royal protection duties and so on, but why the G8?

"The Metropolitan police are responsible for diplomatic protection. That would have been their excuse for coming here *en bloc*: all the heads of state at Gleneagles. Technically they can't do that, so their justification would be that the Chief Constable agrees. Without his agreement it couldn't be done. But if he didn't agree, the Chief Constable would disappear for the weekend, or something like that. They would go ahead, all right."

Paddy Tomkins, the Chief Constable, never replied to my letter, but Malcolm Dickson, the then Deputy Chief Constable, wrote several months later saying that the officer who had refused me entry had "acted in good faith" when "under significant pressure", though he did not specify what pressure had been exerted by the sight of a nearly empty Chambers Street.

Dickson said that "members of the public who wished or needed to access the Court Building were allowed to enter." This was completely untrue, as he must have known, having also said that the officer who refused me entry "may not have been fully aware of the arrangements for that day in relation to the court operation."

I replied asking Dickson how he could say that the courts were open to the public and at the same time regret that I, a member of the public, was not allowed access. But my main question was this: "Who was responsible for failing to make the officers at the court gate aware of the arrangements for the day?"

Dickson answered my letter saying, "The officer who refused you entry at that time did so as there had been a specific threat to the court premises." That, I discovered later, was also untrue. There had been two hoax bomb threats early in the morning, but by the time I was there, the courts were operating normally.

Dickson added that after the building had been searched "access to the court for those members of the public who could convince police staff on duty of their need to enter was permitted." But as Martin Wallace had been there at 9 a.m. and I at noon, and the bomb search did not take long, this cannot have been true.

More importantly the Deputy Chief Constable's talk of "need" to enter the court revealed a frightening ignorance of the basic freedom of any well-behaved member of the public to watch any trial he or she chooses in Scotland without the permission of any arm of the state.

Beyond that is the fact that neither Mr Wallace nor myself were ever asked if we "needed" to be in court. We were simply told to go away, in neither case very politely. So Dickson's statement was not only ignorant but untrue.

At this juncture I decided to write to the Sheriff-Principal himself to ask for confirmation that the courts should have been open all day.

Sheriff-Principal Bowen's clerk replied to me saying, "The Sheriff-Principal did not at any point on 5 July give authority to any party to close Edinburgh Sheriff Court to the public. However, having received a report from the police that they had concerns for public safety, he did instruct that security should be heightened and that access should be restricted to court users, persons cited to attend court and members of the public who had proper means of identification."

I wrote to Dickson, quoting the Sheriff-Principal and noting that the public were not being asked for identification, but simply turned away *en masse*, directly contradicting the Sheriff-Principal's instruction. Once again I asked who had been responsible for giving the clearly unlawful order to close the court.

By this stage we were into March 2006 and there was a new Deputy Chief Constable, Ian Dickinson. He adopted a more aggressive approach, implying in his response that I was partly to blame for not having gained access as I had not argued with the policeman on the gate. After being refused entry, "you left the area without making any comment and the officer was not able to explain the circumstances to you," he wrote.

In fact, the officer had turned his back on me refusing to discuss the matter. But, more substantively, Dickinson still had not told me who was responsible for closing the court. I therefore wrote again, repeating my question.

In June a new Deputy Chief Constable, Thomas Halpin, replied saying, "On the date in question agreement was made between the Chief Constable and the Sheriff-Principal that if there was a gathering of protestors or a disturbance within the Court that permission had been given to the Senior Officer on duty to close the Court to members of the public." Halpin then described threats, including "two hoax bomb calls", and said "due to these extreme circumstances the Senior Officer on duty made the decision to close the court."

This was amazing. Was he admitting that all the previous Deputy Chief Constables had been telling untruths when they said the court was *not* closed? Much more serious, though, was the fact that the Sheriff-Principal had never authorised closure of the court as Halpin said he had.

I wrote again repeating my question about responsibility. After completing an internal inquiry, Halpin replied, he had now concluded that the entry in the policy log which he had earlier quoted to the effect that the court may be closed was "with hindsight... [something] that may now be construed as a misunderstanding of the extent to which the Sheriff-Principal had authorised the police to act independently in deciding whether to close the court."

In effect, Halpin had admitted that the police had acted unlawfully. His letter was dated 16 August 2006, over a year after I first wrote asking for information. But I was still no nearer finding out who was behind the order to clear the court. However, Halpin made one helpful concession. He said I could come to Fettes Police HQ to inspect the policy log for 6 July 2005. A month later, I went and read through the log which showed, quite clearly, that the police had not understood the Sheriff-Principal's instruction but instead thought that they had been given "permission to close the Court to the public if there was a gathering or disorder inside the Court."

Since there never was any such gathering or disorder, the officer in charge of the "normal court detail" acted totally outside even his own misunderstanding of the Sheriff-Principal's precautionary instruction when he closed the whole Court building to all members of the public for the day. He logged his decision at 9.40, though Mr Wallace was refused entry at 9.00 a.m. My suspicion is that this officer, whose name I was asked not to reveal and who is now retired, was not wholly to blame.

When, at a later meeting, I had explained all this to Lord Murray, I asked him where he thought responsibility really lay within the police force. His answer was very revealing, especially coming from a person who had once been the senior law officer in Scotland.

"You are looking in the wrong place," he said. "I doubt that the decision-maker was in the police at all. This had all the hallmarks of a Special Branch operation."

Amazed, I asked about the chain of command in that case.

"The Special Branch is nominally under the control of the local Chief Constable," he said, "but they are, in effect, an all-British corps, headquartered in London. Strictly speaking, the Scottish police are separate altogether in a legal sense from England. But they receive what one might call general instructions directly from the Home Office. I am sure the G8 is an example. For the G8, I am certain the Home Office would virtually dictate to the Scottish police what they should do."

If Lord Murray is right, the disturbing conclusion must be that the Sheriff-Principal was a dupe. Without knowing it, he had been put in a position similar to that of Vasily Ulrikh at the Engineers' trial in Moscow when Stalin took all the main decisions. In this case, an unnamed authority in Whitehall, presumably the Home Office, was conspiring to redefine, for immediate practical purposes on 6 July 2005, the law in a Scottish court.[74] The Sheriff-Principal had not been in full control of his court that day. The law had been taken out of his hands by someone in London, speaking silently through the Special Branch. Once again, Hamilton's Rule holds: show me the judge and I'll tell you the law.

---

[74] If it was the Home Office who gave the orders to close the Edinburgh Sheriff Court on 6 July 2005, then it is relevant that the Home Secretary at the time was Charles Clarke. It was he who, echoing Krylenko, proposed earlier that year to put people under house-arrest if "the authorities" suspected they might in the future commit terrorist crimes, and to keep them in ignorance of the crime they were believed to be about to commit (see above Chapter 2).

5

# The Business of Judging

Ian Hamilton wrote a book of memoirs which he called *A Touch of Treason*. The title refers to a famous student prank in 1950, when he and three other Glasgow University undergraduate Scottish nationalists drove down to London and stole the Stone of Destiny from Westminster Abbey. At one stage in his career, Hamilton was made a sheriff, though he found the work so tedious that he resigned after six months, and returned to the Bar. While discussing judges in his book, he describes an important problem for modern Britain which has adopted idea of "accountability" in government so generally that is now frequently argued that it should apply to judges even though they are not, strictly speaking, part of government.

> The public should take a deep breath and decide whether they want people or civil servants as their judges. Civil servants are trained mice. Judges are human. Every now and again one of them lifts a lawless leg and the newspapers go into a great paroxysm of morality. Next month some judge discloses ignorance of the name of the heroine of some soap opera, and the same newspapers say the Bench is detached from life. I prefer an adulterous, fornicating, drunken sort of chap as a judge, who knows his job, to a dweller in a monastery—as most sinners would. I am not saying that there are any like that on the Scottish Bench, but no-one wants saints either. Other societies have had as their judges the utterly pure. They were called eunuchs, and castration for candidates for the

Bench may be the only answer.[75]

The key difference between a person and a civil servant in this context is that a civil servant is accountable to his or her political master, Ulrikh-style or when the British Secret Service are in town, whereas a person in the sense Hamilton means is independent, like the Justices in *Nixon*. In general, a judge can either be accountable—in the sense of reporting on operational matters to a superior—or independent, *but not both*.

In a system in which judges are appointed for life and are accountable to nobody, only their own consciences and the *esprit de corps* of the Bench as a whole, and which has a proper system of appeals to ensure no single will can operate unchecked, the character of the judges is critical. Every jurisdiction is different so international generalisations are not relevant. But comparisons are important, which is why I have tried to establish some benchmarks. How, then, do Scottish judges of the modern era approach the task of judging their fellow citizens? I have discussed this matter with about a dozen judges, some serving and some retired. The conversations below are a composite of their answers, mixed up to give continuity and also so that none can be identified with any particular statement or point of view.

I started most of my interviews by asking what they thought of their own job, as a job. We went on from there inn a variety of directions. What follows is one aspect of these conversations. Others will be dealt with in later chapters.[76]

"Whatever people think of their behaviour, the main thing to understand is that these people are genuinely trying to do their best," was a typical response. "They are highly conscientious people. Most of them are pretty bright, and those that aren't are very bright, and on the whole they do a decent job. But it is hellish, nonetheless. After I come out of court at four o'clock, I

[75] *A Touch of Treason*, Ian Hamilton QC, Moffat 1990, p. 71

[76] Readers should remember that, from the point of view of names, dates etc., these interviews were conducted in 2005-7. But, though faces change, the essence remains remarkably consistent. Where relevant, I have added brief updating footnotes below.

go to my room and fart around a bit, making notes and doing bits and pieces, then I go home about six, have dinner and, for most of my career, after that I have just gone to my study to work. That is the accepted thing, but as I get older, I find it more and more difficult. I am just knackered. It's joyless drudgery. You turn up, judge a case which some low-ranking civil servant has placed in front of you, and you go home again, theoretically to spend your evening in your study writing your opinion. Some of my colleagues really do that."

"Many of them?"

"Oh yes, especially if they're in the commercial court where the cases can be unbelievably complex. If you want to avoid evenings in your study, then you have to be prepared to go to Glasgow to take criminal cases. But that's not to everyone's taste. There are a few who actually prefer the complexity."

"Like whom?"

"Lord Drummond Young is an example. He has an extraordinary mind, which is an incredible repository of general knowledge. If you ask him what the nearest mountain to Lima in Peru is he'll tell you. He's a terrible swotty sort of a bugger. He's a nice guy, a decent guy, don't get me wrong, and a good judge, but he's a serious anorak. He's extraordinarily conscientious. He takes most of the commercial cases, the complicated ones—and they can be incredibly complicated. God knows how many judgements he's got to write.[77] He's under the most appalling pressure. But it would never occur to him to say, 'Fuck this, I'm going out for a pint!' A slightly smarter, more street-wise judge would cut a few corners and get some of the simpler cases settled. He might have to bully Counsel a bit, or take the occasional procedural liberty, but that way the backlog is kept under control. However poor old Drummond Young's only answer is to do more work. It's hard to criticise someone so devoted to his job, but somehow at a human level it's also hard to sympathise."

---

[77] In 2007 Lord Drummond Young was appointed head of the Scots Law Commission.

"From what you say, it would seem that he does not think of his work as 'joyless drudgery'?"

"That's right! And he's not the only one. Look at Alan Rodger, who used to be the Lord President, before he went to the House of Lords.[78] He was a seven-days-a-week man. Literally. His idea of a holiday was to go to Heidelberg for a fortnight and study Roman Law in German. That's his recreation. He is an extraordinary gifted individual, intellectually. His career in the legal profession was glittering, although he didn't make a lot of money because he was in the public service. But he is brilliant. His father was professor of psychiatry, also a very clever man. Alan went to Glasgow University, did an ordinary MA, then got a first in Law, in the LLB. He was one of the brightest students they have ever had. Then he went to Oxford, to Balliol, where he got glittering prizes, and became a Fellow of New College. He has got about three doctorates which he has actually worked for, none of them honorary. He's got a DPhil, an LLD, you know: things that nobody's ever heard of. Then his father became very ill in the late 1960s so he came back to Scotland and went to the Bar. Soon he was Clerk of Faculty, then he allowed himself to be dragged into the Crown office, where he was Solicitor-General then Lord Advocate. Then he appointed himself a judge, as the Lord Advocate used to be able to do, and soon after that he was made Lord President. But by then, he was fed up with public service because he saw all these people who were far less able than he was making significantly more money than him. He was quite resentful. He has enormous intellectual self-confidence, and he saw that he was quite capable of being in the House of Lords. So when he came to be Lord President he spent his whole time ensuring he was going to the House of Lords. The method he adopted was to produce brilliant judgement after brilliant judgement which made people in London say, 'Gosh, this guy's

[78] Since conducting these interviews, the House of Lords, as Britain's highest court of appeal, has been replaced by the Supreme Court of the United Kingdom, whose members are known, American-style, as Justices. Lord Rodger of Earlsferry, as Alan Rodger was from 1992, died in 2011.

hot stuff.' And it worked. He's there to this day, working all the hours God sends. I can't say I envy him."

"But Lord Rodger is a bachelor. That is, surely, a slightly different situation from the married man who can't afford to devote himself so completely to work?"

"Lord Hope could.[79] He was Alan Rodger's predecessor as Lord President, and is now his colleague in the House of Lords."

"But he's interested in bird-watching, I gather. That's an outside interest."

"If you say so. I call it a way of getting out of the house without having to encounter other human beings. But he was another seven-days-a-week man, at least during term time. He'd go to his house in Perthshire and presumably watch a few birds there during the vacation, but the rest of the time it was nothing but work."

"Is he clever too?"

"Well, how do I put this? It is true that he won an open scholarship to Cambridge, but it is also true that he was known amongst his colleagues here as Wee Rettie."

"Wee Rettie? Why?"

"There was a droll fellow called Ian MacDonald who got on the Bench years ago—he's dead now—as Lord Mayfield. He'd won the Military Cross in the war and was a member of the 'club', ex-Army, one of the chaps. A wee smart guy, and everybody gave him great respect because he had an MC. Really he was a chancer, but he did have a witty turn of phrase. It was he who christened David Hope, who's short, Wee Rettie. Rettie is the name of a series of nineteenth century case books which are cited as *21 Rettie, 22 Rettie* and so on. He was known as Wee Rettie because he knew every case in all the books. He'd swotted them up. But for all his knowledge, he is, in my view, a chilling individual. I think his intellectual gifts are limited, but he makes up for that by staggering industry, just appalling. I used to think, this guy is shit-hot because he could present his cases so clearly.

---

[79] Lord Hope of Craighead is Deputy President of the Supreme Court of the United Kingdom

Whereas it would take me about four shots to get the submissions in order, he could get it down first go. To that extent, he was good. But then you discover some limitations: no capacity for wider thought, being one. No originality, absolutely none. If something is brought to his attention he will swallow it and regurgitate it in a beautifully clear way. They all admire him in London, I think, because of the hours he puts in. But his work-life balance is ridiculous."

"Does he have children?"

"Yes, three, though from what I gather they were not allowed to disturb him very much. His work is utterly sacrosanct. I used to think that's how you're supposed to carry on. That was the culture that was around at the Bar, and still is to a certain extent. David Hope is a very decent man, and I am sure loves his children and all the rest of it, but his whole life is utterly and completely dominated by work. He is Chancellor of Strathclyde University, right enough, but he's not what you'd call a people person. But that does not matter in the House of Lords. They are operating at the most sophisticated level of the law. Admittedly most of the advocacy they get is pretty good. That's helpful. A good advocate makes it easy for the judge to understand the case in front of him. But the sheer volume of stuff they have to do is frightening, and there's no let up. They're all competing with each other to show who's the cleverest boy in the class and who's the hardest worker. This is a problem in Edinburgh too. You have to be seen to be working ludicrously hard. You've got to churn it out. It is not an easy number. The workload would make most people ill. But David Hope likes it."

"Does this level of concentration on rules and paperwork, presumably to some extent at the expense of humanity, damage the justice process? Obviously you have to have some rules or there would be no law, but at the same time, you have to have some insight into humanity, otherwise you are judging in effect by a sort of paper-driven computer."

"That's a very interesting point you raise there. There are two sides to the question—as there always is in the law, or we'd all be out of business. David Hope may be rules all the way, and I have just criticised him for that, but there are times when it is right to take that line, and not only in the commercial court, or with administrative law. I'll give you an example. Back in the 1980s, when he was Dean of the Faculty of Advocates, there was this African chap, black guy, who came to devil, to get admitted to the Faculty. In due course, he sat the exams, and passed. For some reason which I now forget, there was an inquiry into this and it turned out that he had gone to a girl in the Faculty office and had offered her something to let him see the papers in advance of the exam. He was found out. He was a nice guy and he immediately admitted what he had done. He was hauled up in front of the Dean's Council, which is a body that does not do much except see that all the rules are obeyed. They gave him a full hearing, to the extent that they had David Edward, later Britain's judge on the European Court, now Sir David Edward, appearing for him to plead in mitigation. David Edward is an interesting guy: a very wide-ranging intellect, a seriously gifted lawyer. He is the best Lord President we have never had. He likes good wine, too!

"Edward is not a criminal advocate at all, but he made this fantastic plea, saying how in the accused's own culture this sort of thing was accepted and how he now realised that it was quite unacceptable in Scotland, and that he would never do it again, he was a reformed character, and so on. It was a brilliant plea. Most people who heard about it seem to have been persuaded that they ought at least to have considered this, to give the guy a chance. But not David Hope. He had not a second's hesitation. Out! Out! Without one minute of discussion. The rest of the Faculty would probably have come to that conclusion in the end, but with him it was: Out right now! Banished forever! Never allowed to come back. The poor guy went the following day. Bang. Never seen or heard of again. And really Hope was right. You can call that cold-blooded but, especially in the legal world, standards have to be taken seriously, or there's no point."

"So where does this complex about work come from?"

"You've read Robert Louis Stevenson's *Weir of Hermiston*?"

"Yes."

"That's a good place to start. Although Lord Weir is thought to be a take-off of Braxfield, the whole scenario, loosely read, has quite a modern ring. It comes partly from a wholly admirable sense of duty and public service, which Stevenson was clear to stress that Weir had alongside his other, less attractive quality, which was the Scottish-Presbyterian, tyrannical-father problem. I gather the famous Lord Cockburn was a bit like that too, which is why he made such a thing of rejecting the Braxfield way of doing things. Most of the guys I am talking about today are both highly conscientious public servants and victims of fathers who told them when they were young that they were no good. Of course, I am generalising, and many of my colleagues are conscientious public servants without the workaholic complex, though they do tend to be the younger ones. The slightly unbalanced craving for work as a form of self-justification before an ever-unsatisfied father was common when I started out in the law."

"Do the ones who do not suffer from that complex make better judges?"

"I wouldn't say that. Perhaps they are less likely to ignore the human dimension in a case—I am speaking here of the criminal courts. Interestingly, all the workaholics are male—none of my female colleagues would be so stupid—and mostly they are over sixty years old. But they are still in the majority. In ten years' time the Scottish Bench will be very different: more sensible, though probably less colourful."

"What is the cause of the *Weir* complex?"

"The requirement that you suppress your emotions and get on in life. Many of my parents' generation did not really have friends, as such. They were too ambitious to relax. So it was quite a solitary life for the children, who accordingly studied, and because they studied they did well, and because they did well, they were pointed in the direction of the law. The thing you have to remember is that in those days Scotland, much more so than today, was a society with its top lopped off and sent to London. Industry was knackered, so about the only thing you could do up here which was well-paid, important, and part of the real world, was to go into the law. Everything else happened in London. It is not the same today. There is much more happening in Edinburgh, and also London has lost a lot of its pre-eminence. Many of the young, ambitious people go to New York, or Paris, or the Gulf, or wherever else the action is. In my day it was London or the law, one or the other. Medicine was an alternative, but that was a different clan, and largely confined to Edinburgh. So my father, who was a fairly senior manager in public service, advised me to take a law degree. I wasn't that fussed. I was just happy to get into University and out of the house. I could get drunk on the weekends and chase girls. Work came second, and I am afraid it showed. I was not one of your Alan Rodgers, or Derry Irvines, or Donald Dewar."[80]

"Why not go into business?"

"That's an interesting one. To be honest, I never thought about it. It was the sort of option that was simply not discussed. I think my father would have regarded it as a blot on the family's honour if I had ended up owning five garages, or a chain of dry-cleaning shops, even if I had managed to sell them for a million quid. If I had gone to London to become a stock broker and driven myself to an early grave commuting into the City every day, that would have been fine because it was respectable. But staying in Scotland and making pots of money in the pub trade, say, would have been seen as almost hedonistic: the sort of thing Catholics did."

"What's wrong with that?"

"That is what I find so hard to explain. I think what I can say is that there was a great deal of emotional meanness within families like mine. They may not all have been officially Presbyterian in the church-going sense, but they were Presbyterian—maybe Calvinist would be a better word—in that

---

[80] Lord Irvine of Lairg was Lord Chancellor of England from 1997-2003. Donald Dewar, who died in 2000, was the Labour Party Secretary of State for Scotland who was instrumental in re-establishing the Scottish parliament in 1999. They and Alan Rodger all studied at Glasgow University where they had a reputation for being clever, hard-working and ambitious.

the display of wealth was a complete anathema. Of course you had to have the right sort of house, but you didn't have a flash car and you were ashamed to be seen spending money, though that was often as much for show as in reality. Many of them didn't actually mind spending money, just so long as the neighbours didn't catch them at it."

"What was the result of these rather strange people becoming judges?"

"There were a lot of them who were really judicial bullies."

"Who? I've heard about Lord Gibson, but who else was like that?"

"Gibson was not so much a bully as a lunatic. In any case, he was never a Session judge, just a Land Court guy with airs and graces. He was part of the long tradition of socialist snobs, like the old Lord Wheatley. He was a dreadful man! I remember years ago every Saturday morning we had the charade of undefended divorces being dealt with. Wheatley, for very good reasons apart from his Catholicism, thought that divorces should not go through on the nod, which they usually did. So, though he was on the Appeal Court, he occasionally used to do some of these. But he refused to be addressed by Counsel without a solicitor present. You may not believe this, but it was true. You had eight or ten of these cases on one day, with all the witnesses milling around. Toward the end of case three, say, a solicitor would nip out to make sure the witnesses in case four were there, because they hadn't been there earlier. He was just trying to keep the thing rolling along. But immediately he left the room, Wheatley would say to Counsel, 'I cannot hear you.' The Macer would disappear and haul the poor solicitor back into Court, at which point Wheatley would permit Counsel to resume."

"Incredible!"

"It was, but that was pomposity rather than bullying. I am talking about something different, a kind of arrogance which mutated into judicial coldness, and which became important because it is one of the main reasons why the courts are in such a mess today. It is quite a long story, but we have had, let me see, seven Lords President since the war, if you exclude Lord

Normand who came to the throne, so to speak, in 1935. Lord
Cooper took over in 1947, when Normand was sent to the Lords.
Cooper was a gifted lawyer, a brilliant Lord President and a man
of an extremely high standards of personal conduct, though he,
too, had emotional problems, I think. He lived with his mother.
I'll say no more. But he was an impeccable judge and a great
Scottish legal patriot, if I may put it like that. It was he who heard
the absurd case about the Royal titles, in 1953. Have you heard of
an advocate called Ian Hamilton—the guy who stole the Stone of
Destiny from Westminster Abbey?"

"Yes, I have."

"A funny little man. He went to court with John
MacCormick, the head of the SNP, after the present Queen came
to the throne and Scotland started to have post boxes with EIIR
on them. Their point, which was quite correct in one sense, was
that Scotland had never had a Queen Elizabeth before so, in this
jurisdiction, she should be known as Queen Elizabeth I, and the
post boxes should say EIR. The case is *MacCormick v Lord
Advocate*[81]. You should look it up. I never knew John
MacCormick, though I knew his son, Neil—everyone did. He is a
genius.[82] He's got a knighthood, though why I have no idea. He's
been a law professor at Edinburgh University since he was 32,
but none of us can understand any of his books. Perhaps the
Queen does. But I did know Ian Hamilton, who was a maverick.
His books are quite amusing to read, but he was not, in my view,
a great pleader."

"What do you think of his rule: show me the judge and I'll
tell you the law?"

"That's nonsensical. Typical of Ian Hamilton: trying to be
funny, which he can be quite good at, I'll admit. But people who
write books aren't usually good Counsel, because good Counsel
need to work too hard. They don't have time to go around

---

[81] *MacCormick v Lord Advocate* (1953) SC 396

[82] Sir Neil MacCormick was Regius Professor of Public Law and the Law of
Nature and Nations at Edinburgh University from 1972 until shortly before his
death in 2009.

making jokes. Anyway, Cooper dealt with the two nationalists beautifully by, on one hand, denying them the judgement they wanted—a judgement which *might* have been justified in theory, but would have been unworkable in practice[83]—while at the same time asserting, for the first time in the Court of Session, Scottish constitutional distinctiveness.[84] That was a judgement whose relevance is still being discovered today, with the new parliament, as we come out of what I think should be called the colonial era of Scots law—but that's another and much bigger subject. The problems we have today arguably started with Lord Clyde, who took over in 1954 when Cooper fell ill. Incidentally, it was he who, as Lord Advocate, presented the case for the Crown against MacCormick and Hamilton in front of Cooper. Clyde is the first one any of us today will remember. He lasted until 1972, and he was a bully. He was a clever, clever man, but he was generally unpopular and difficult, and could be cruel."

"Like Lord Braxfield?"

"Braxfield may have been rough and abrasive, but he was not cruel, and he was not a bully. Being harsh and being a bully

---

[83] I did not want to interrupt the speaker's flow or I would have suggested that to arrive at a judgement on essentially practical grounds and then arrange the theory to fit that was exactly what I understood to be the meaning of Hamilton's Rule.

[84] The case actually concerned the Royal title generally. It was popularly connected with post boxes because some Scottish extremists put bombs in post boxes, presumably because they were the most noticeable examples of the use of the offending title within their everyday experience. Lord Cooper held that the Court of Session was not permitted to review Acts of the United Kingdom parliament and therefore could not say that the title could not be used. It was a very restricted point. However, in the course of making it, he said this: "The principle of the unlimited sovereignty of Parliament is a distinctively English principle which has no counterpart in Scottish constitutional law.... I have difficulty in seeing why it should have been supposed that the new parliament of Great Britain must inherit all the peculiar characteristics of the English Parliament but none of the Scottish Parliament, as if all that happened in 1707 was that Scottish representatives were admitted to the Parliament of England. That is not what was done [in the Acts of Union]."

are two quite different things. Not only was Clyde a bully, but he was not always entirely impartial as a judge. He would take a very active part as chairman of the court, doing a bit of cross-examination himself if he felt like it.[85] In doing so, he would reveal a disposition for one side or the other—not bias, but a disposition. He really made it pretty obvious what he thought."

"How did his bullying manifest itself?"

"I remember as a young greenhorn arguing a case in front of him which had some merit, though not much. Let's say it was 75% negative and 25% plus. But both sides had to be put. Clyde decided that the 25% was worthless too so he started cross-examining me and negating everything I said. He kept going on and I kept saying the same thing. It was an appeal so there were two other judges. They were almost laughing, quietly and unobtrusively of course. But I could see them. Perhaps they did it to give me encouragement; I don't know. But by the end Clyde was shouting at me. It was rude and bad-tempered. But he was like that. He steered things too much. He didn't listen enough. And he wasn't really objective, which was why he was often overturned by the House of Lords."

"Maybe he was just letting a youngster know his place?"

"Not at all; he did it to anyone. I remember a senior Counsel who was at the receiving end of his wrath: a very able man; the son of a House of Lords judge. He was a very nice, gentle sort of person. He'd been at the English bar before the war, then he'd been involved in a motor accident in which somebody had been killed. There was a cloud over him. He went into the forces during the war and afterwards came to the Scottish Bar rather than return to England. He was a good Counsel. He did a lot of complicated land and trust cases and was very successful. He had one problem, which was that he was thought to be homosexual. Whether he was or not, I don't know. He probably was. But Clyde had it in for him because of that. There was a series of

---

[85] As happens in oral argument at the US Supreme Court—see Chapter 1 for the 300 questions the Justices put to Jaworski and St Clair in *Nixon* in the space of two hours.

cases when he was going for this chap, going for him and going for him. Then he died suddenly: probably suicide. I saw this chap being shattered by the treatment that he was getting from Clyde, it was ruthless, remorseless, cruel, unnecessary and, of course, quite unjudicial."

"Did he do this often, or only to the occasional homosexual he took a personal dislike to?"

"No, it could happen to anyone. I remember another very nice chap who was Procurator of the Church of Scotland. He was a very pleasant little man who was a good Counsel too, though nothing like as good as the one I've just mentioned. He was a rather pompous, plump, indoor-ish sort of man, and Clyde had it in for this chap as well, being slightly orotund, as he was, and a bit verbose. I saw him take this man to pieces. He was in his sixties, elderly but not old. He died not long after one of Clyde's classic maulings. Nobody said there was a connection. But I'd been there in the court and seen this man wilting under the savagery he was being exposed to. There could have been a connection. And another time, in a criminal appeal before him I was opposed by a chap who is now a sheriff, but in Clyde's eyes had the double handicap of being (a) a Catholic and (b) a socialist. He hardly let him open his mouth. At one stage, he called him a fool. That was too much. The Dean was brought in. Clyde was forced to apologise."[86]

"What was his background?"

"He had an impeccable background: Edinburgh Academy, Oxford and Edinburgh Universities. His father had been Lord President. He had a son who was a very nice chap, very different from him, and a good judge too: ended up in the House of Lords."

"So why did he behave that way? Was this the *Weir* complex? Did he hate his father too?"

"That I really don't know. I was too young to be privy to that sort of information, but it might be relevant that he was a

---

[86] The Dean is the head of the Faculty of Advocates, which represents all advocates in Scotland.

very political figure before he became a judge, an aggressive Unionist. He had been MP for Edinburgh North, and Conservative Lord Advocate. He appointed himself Lord President. Lords Advocate always used to make judicial appointments and, up to Lord Hardie in 2000, their last appointment was traditionally themselves. But Clyde went a stage further and made himself Lord President without ever having been an ordinary judge, which probably says something about the man and his conceit. But you have to remember that Clyde was born in 1898. There was a bit of the Victorian in him. He had the sort of views that would have endeared him to Mrs Thatcher."

"Was he alone in his approach on the Bench?"

"No, there were several judges who used to bawl in court. Lord Wheatley was one, as was Lord Hunter, and Lord Avonside. Another bad one was Lord Kissen, who was Jewish. He was a very able guy who worked astonishingly hard, but if he felt that a chap wasn't properly up to speed, or was trying to make some daft point, he would slam his pen down, the top would fly off, and he'd say, 'You can't *possibly* say that.' Quite irregular: Counsel can say what they like provided it is relevant and courteous. No judge would get away with that sort of thing today. None of them would even try to behave like that."

"Why has it changed from the bullying judge of the '50s and '60s to the situation today in which, as far as I have observed, the judges are very mannerly?"

"I think life has just got softer generally, less Calvinistic. There is more forgiveness now in Scotland. Even in his day, Clyde was very much in the minority. Also I don't think this was a phenomenon confined to judges. I suspect that in industry, accountancy or whatever there would have been the same proportion of bullies. I think, to a certain extent, it was the times. Maybe the war had had something to do with it. These guys probably killed Germans in unpleasant ways and they came out of the Army and carried on behaving aggressively."

"It was not a class thing, perhaps?"

"Possibly, to a point. I certainly think most of them

considered the working men of Glasgow, particularly those in the shipyards, were liars and chancers by nature. Sometimes they transferred that contempt to the Counsel representing them in things like industrial injury compensation cases, of which there used to be a lot in the days before the health and safety rules became so tight. But I don't see that the class division was always like that. The eighteenth century was rough rather than rude, and in the early nineteenth century life in all professional walks of life in Scotland became more polite. I think the problems with the Scottish class system emerged, in their modern form at any rate, towards the end of the nineteenth century when people who had not grown up accustomed to money started making huge fortunes very quickly in places like Dundee and Glasgow. Some very ordinary families became enormously wealthy and educated their children at English public schools and they took on tremendous airs and graces. The Braxfields and the Cockburns of this world all went to school in Scotland. But the Tennant family, for example, made their money out of bleach in Glasgow at the end of the nineteenth century and sent their sons to Eton. I don't get the impression that the lairds way back before then were quite so snobbish, so anglified and grand. You don't get that sense at all in Cockburn's *Diaries*. By Edwardian times, judges had started aping the newly wealthy industrialists. They all spoke with frightful plums in their mouths. George Emslie, Clyde's successor was a good example. He came originally from Aberdeen, though he grew up in Glasgow. His father was an insurance manager, perfectly respectable, but not grand in any way at all. He joined the Argylls in the war, became a major and came home in 1945 with this astonishing voice. He had turned himself into a sort of Ronald Coleman, *Prisoner of Zenda* figure, with this constructed personality, moustaches and all. Here was a Glasgow boy finding it necessary to re-invent himself as a sort of Piccadilly Englishman in order to be taken seriously."

"Was he the last of that sort, given that he was succeeded as Lord President by Lord Hope who, as far as I can see, is a perfectly normal human being?"

"The last LP, perhaps, but not the last judge and not the last lawyer either. Look at dear old Menzies Campbell, the recent leader of the Liberal Democrats! We all knew him when he was an advocate—he did licensing and valuation—and we got on well with him. He was a nice chap, middle-class, middle-of-the-road, nothing special. Since then, he has become enormously distinguished, dripping with honours, when all he's really done is to state the blindingly obvious in a posh voice from a safe distance. He's never had an original thought in his life. But he's become a sort of pseudo-grandee, at least partly because of the deferential way he has behaved, and that includes his accent. Don't get me wrong, he is a very nice bloke, a gentleman. He would not shit on your head. But he's changed his accent. You should see the television clip of him being spoken to by David Coleman just after he'd given up athletics. You'll remember that he ran in the Tokyo Olympics in 1964. He was there with his law-apprentice's three-piece suit on in the front row of some sportsman of the year awards, and he had a totally different accent from the one he has now. To that extent, he is an inheritor of people like Emslie. You would never have known Emslie was Scottish. And the interesting thing with Menzies is that it is not snobbery. He is not at all stuck up, despite his mannerisms. He does not forget his old muckers. But he speaks to them in a different accent. He modifies his diphthongs. Menzies came from Verona Avenue in Scotstoun, a perfectly ordinary street of terraced houses off the Dumbarton Road, quite respectable, modest, white-collar area. Nothing wrong with that at all, but it's not the sort of place which breeds accents of the sort he has today. You have to ask yourself why he felt the need to disguise himself in that way."

"With people like Emslie, did it go beyond the accent and the moustache?"

"Emslie ended up as a completely manufactured personality, a social cripple who was terrified to let the mask drop. He could never relax because the real George Emslie might slip out: something awful might happen, like a Glasgow accent appearing. So he was completely rigid and very controlled in any company. Because he was the top man, everybody else was paralysed.

Behind that, he was really quite humane. He could see a person who had something to say for himself and would encourage him to say it. He was the best Lord President and Justice-General we have had during my time in the law. He was a brilliant administrator. When he wanted to talk to the civil service, they came to him, not the other way round, as we have today, to our shame. He was also a great protector of the Bar and its traditions. People forget that. But he was also a very arrogant man. He treated solicitors with contempt. He just ignored them. He wasn't rude, he was just cold. He never even had a proper funeral. His funeral was in private. It was the same with Lord Wylie, his contemporary, who could have become Lord President if he hadn't been so lazy. He didn't want a public funeral either. They were not only cold men in themselves, they expected others around them to behave coldly towards the world outside. As a judge, Emslie was fair and, on the face of it, courteous. You couldn't fault him, except that he had this chilling demeanour, in court at any rate. He was not *actually* chilling, like Clyde; he just looked it. But to the outsider—the public, the wee gumshoe court reporter from the *Glasgow Herald*, and the keen little bureaucrats from the rapidly-expanding Justice Department—it amounted to the same thing. And that had tremendous consequences, which are with us to this day."

"What consequences?"

"It is all to do with the problem with the civil service which started developing in the 1960s, but has really accelerated in the last fifteen years. Today we have a Justice Department which does not seem to be entirely clear about the meaning of judicial independence. The civil servants seem to think they are going with the flow in wanting to make judges more 'accountable'. Really that means controllable. It started with the Judicial Appointments Board and is carrying on with recent proposals to have disciplinary sanctions for judges who are thought to be erring. This is the thin end of the wedge of political control and will undoubtedly compromise judicial independence. It is a potential disaster in the making."

"How were Clyde and Emslie part of that?"

"They created a situation in which the judges treated the civil service like minions. I'll tell you a story of a judge, long retired now, who carried separation from the common herd to an extreme. He was a very good judge, and a very pleasant man, but he was known for his aloofness. He had been sitting all week in the High Court in Glasgow and by Friday afternoon everything was finished. The Glasgow Corporation, who still provide food for the judges, had provided drink too, so with nothing better to do the judge and his clerk had a gin-and-tonic together and a wee chat. This had never happened before, so on Monday morning, back in Edinburgh, the clerk, who was a bright guy with a sense of humour, deliberately set out to test this new situation, to see if a few gins had actually softened their relationship which had previously been completely formal. So he met the judge at the beginning of his walk from his chambers to the robing room. He knew that on that walk that he could run around and meet the guy three times before he got to his destination. On the first occasion he said, 'Good morning Your Lordship.' He didn't get any reply, the judge looking straight ahead, as if he wasn't there. So he ran round, got ahead of him and did it again. 'Good morning, Your Lordship.' Nothing. Not a flicker of recognition. Then he did it a third time, and got the same response. Eventually the judge got to the robing room. Immediately he sent for the clerk. 'What was all that about?' the judge said to him. 'Are you *mad?*' This wasn't even in the street; this was in the Parliament House. Clerks do not greet judges. Their relationship has no human dimension. That was his point. Really, it was the judge who was mad."

"Was that attitude unusual?"

"Not thirty years ago. Many of them would have been embarrassed to be greeted by their clerk in the street. It was partly an Edinburgh thing. Remember that in the 1970s nobody wished you a Happy New Year or shook your hand. In Glasgow it was terribly important to shake your hand and say, "Happy New Year to you!" Edinburgh was a great place for ignoring people in the street. There was a general culture of coldness, at least amongst middle-class folk. I suppose it suited a certain sort of judge, Emslie being the perfect example. I said that he was a brilliant administrator, but perhaps I should qualify that: he was a brilliant organiser of the courts. He was in control of everything, possibly too much so. The common saying is that he was the last LP to be in charge of the paperclips. But he treated the officials from the Justice Department or the Scottish Courts Administration the way he treated solicitors: like corporals in the army. Naturally, he made enemies, and the bigger and more self-important the civil service became, the more enemies he made. That was a catastrophic mistake. He refused to adapt to the new 'political' realities of the 1970s and '80s."

"What were those new realities, from the point of view of the courts?"

"Since the War, Britain has become a progressively more and more bureaucratic state. As Lords President, Clyde and Emslie should have tried to accommodate the new taste for rules, committees, 'accountability' and so on. But they didn't. They thought they could run the courts as they had always been run, which was by the LP himself. That may have worked before the War, it may even have been the best system possible, but it was never going to be acceptable in the world of the welfare state.[87] Between the two of them, they occupied the top job for thirty-five years. Clyde became LP when Winston Churchill was still governing the country and Emslie stepped down only a year before John Major took over. In that period, Britain changed out of all recognition. But the Scottish courts did not. When Thatcher came along in the 1980s with proposals to reform the legal profession in England—carried out by a Scotsman, Lord Mackay, after the English refused to do it themselves—the writing was on the wall. Emslie should have realised that in a civil service employed by Whitehall—as it still is, despite devolution—what was sauce of the English goose was one day going to be sauce for the Scottish gander. It is only surprising that it took so long for

---

[87] It is the way the US Supreme Court is run, with total independence from government, subject only to the Presidential prerogative of nominating the Justices and the Congressional confirmation process. Once on the Bench they are accountable to nobody, not even each other.

the winds of change to start blowing up here. But when they did start, in the late 1990s, we were completely unprepared."

"That was surely not the fault of Clyde and Emslie?"

"Not entirely, of course. But they set the tone, and when David Hope took over from Emslie in 1989 he had no tradition of judicial diplomacy towards the civil service to build upon."

"That may have been Emslie's fault, but how was Clyde implicated?"

"The first serious battle actually took place when Clyde was still in charge. When Labour came to power in 1964, Clyde made very clear his dislike of their judicial appointments. So when, under Ted Heath, the Conservatives proposed giving control over shrieval appointments to the civil service, he did not make a fuss about it. Better bad Tory policy than *any* Labour one: I suppose that was his thinking. I'm sure the civil service was offended by Clyde's hostility towards them. In 1974, after the miners' strike, Labour returned to power and Willie Ross became Secretary of State for Scotland. He was effectively the Justice Minister, and he was very anti-lawyer. The Scottish Courts Administration had recently been established and the next proposal was that it would appoint the sheriff-principals, in addition to the sheriffs. Emslie was by now the Lord President and he did say, 'No', helped by wee King Murray, who was Lord Advocate at the time—a Labour man but one who was against civil service interference in the courts. They managed to defeat that, but the wider danger signs should have been obvious. Nonetheless, Emslie seemed to think that he could ignore the civil service, and he did so. Resentment built up. Then, when Emslie retired, Wee Rettie came straight from the Faculty of Advocates, blinking in the sunlight, and was appointed Lord President, never having been a judge before. There was nothing irregular about that, but he really didn't have the weight to deal with the new and increasingly political situation. Also, his breadth of vision was limited by his workaholic tendencies. It is possible that that was what the people who appointed him wanted. I don't think he was interested in court management anyway. I don't blame him: it's a dull subject. But if you take the job you have to do the job, and by the late '80s that job involved court management."

"Does the lack of court management affect the quality of justice?"

"Absolutely! This is what I said right at the start about drudgery. Judges today do not have any control over their own work-load. Some junior civil servant assigns you a case and you have to get on with, it in their time, which leaves no scope for proper consideration of judgements. All they care about is through-put, a 'performance indicator' as they call it.[88] One of my younger colleagues was a keen golfer, and when he went up to Aberdeen on circuit for the first time after being appointed and found his cases had finished by lunch-time on a Friday, he thought he'd go and have a round of golf, much as he might have done as an advocate. But the clerk of the court said, 'Remember, my Lord, I have to report that this court rose at 12 o'clock.' The implication was that had to rush his lunch and leg it down to Edinburgh, which he would reach by about 4.30 or 5, to see if there is any work to do for the last half hour of the day. Ludicrous, a complete waste of time, whose only purpose is to make the judge feel he can never relax and connect with the real world. Judging is not a mechanical task. It requires thought and feel. It is impossible to work properly under that sort of pressure. And also there are the pin-pricks, just to let you know whose boss."

"Like what?"

"Like the fact that we no longer have a vacation."

"Not at all?"

"No, we have a 'recess'. Vacation sounds too much like fun; or maybe it sounds posh, I don't know. Either way, it's pathetic. It's not important, which makes it even more pathetic that they insisted on it."

"How did Hope deal with the encroachments of the civil service?"

"He didn't. That was the problem. He ignored the issue,

---

[88] Contrast this with the US Supreme Court which has full control over its own docket. It can take or refuse to take any case which comes before it.

largely. So did Alan Rodger, who spent his time writing all those brilliant judgements, half of them in German, the other half in Latin, hoping to get into the House of Lords, which he managed. Good luck to him, but hell mend the rest of us. Great guy; outstanding judge; but not a proper Lord President in my view. Hope and he were in office from 1989 to 2001, by which time the pass had been well and truly sold. Except that we deal with law, we might as well be working in a factory. You'd think that someone like a judge would be able to manage his own time, be treated like a grown-up: not in twenty-first century Scotland with the Justice Department in charge. You're a snowflake in the wind."

"In the United States Supreme Court, the judges have three or four law clerks each, plus generous secretarial help. I presume that in Scotland you get less than that?"

"You presume right! Actually we get no help at all. We have to do all the grunt work of writing judgements, locating case references and so on ourselves. Not only that, we do not even have secretaries. There is a typing pool, but that's all. I have to draft all my judgement by hand, after running round the judges' library chasing references. And I get almost no time to do this. I am expected to write judgements on Mondays when the courts do not sit, and in the evenings and at weekends. We get the occasional 'white week', as it is called, when we are allowed a few days off to catch up with our writing. But really you need a day of writing for a day in court. We just don't get that. We're expected to save the state money by working in what other people would call their spare time. It's the same in the criminal court. When I started at the Bar as junior Counsel, I would take notes in long-hand of the case for my senior. The quality of your notes was important, so we learned to take notes properly. It's dead boring. You write down a combination of the question and answer, if you possibly can. I've been doing it for thirty years so it's second nature. It's still boring and hard work. In criminal cases you have to do it in case there is an appeal. Even though the Courts now have digital recording of everything that goes on, virtually never do you say to the clerk of the court, 'Will you go back to so-and-so and play it back for me.' The culture is that we rely on our hand-written notes. We're supposed to be keeping down the cost of litigation by doing that. That is not an intelligent use of a highly-paid person's time."

"You're almost persuading me here that there is a case for a judge's strike."

"Yes, there is. You've no idea. It's just ridiculous. In Edinburgh, we don't even have a proper dining-room any more, just a sort of sandwich bar which we have to finance ourselves."

"The quality of mercy must be a bit strained by all this."

"It is. You can't judge something carefully and subtly when you're flat out all the time. I'm knackered, basically because I have no control over my work-load. The civil service does that. But it's our own fault. If there was any solidarity, if we weren't all individual superstars, as we see it, we might be able to act together. As a group, we are extraordinarily unassertive. We've allowed ourselves to be ridden all over. We've had no leadership from successive Lords President in the face of bureaucratic pressure and a hostile clerking system—though the clerks themselves are usually great."

"You feel that part of the role of the Lord President should be to defend the judges from the civil service?"

"Of course. But they have failed, comprehensively. Since Cooper—in whose day the problem did not exist—we have not had one Lord President who has spent any time at all considering the system as a whole, whether it works, whether it is relevant, how it could be improved, or made more publicly acceptable. Not Clyde, not Emslie, not Hope, not Rodger, not Cullen, who was the last incumbent before the present LP, Lord Hamilton. They've done fuck all. The man I blame most is Alan Rodger. He was the brightest of the lot; and knew perfectly well what the situation was. But he is so conservative, and was so concerned about getting into the House of Lords, that he never bothered his backside. The result is we're in the shit now, and, increasingly, it is becoming hard to get the best people to come forward and apply for Supreme Court judge-ships, so the problem will get even worse as time goes on."

"Presumably exacerbated by having to take a pay cut?"

"Absolutely. Just as in Braxfield's day, a good QC earns much more than a judge. Why would anyone with brains want the aggravation and the tedium of life on the Bench? I went to a dinner the other night for one of my retiring colleagues and I over-heard one advocate saying to another that the only reason people now apply to become judges is because their wives want a title, to be Lady So-and-So. Of course, the guy was wrong in a literal sense. Of the latest batch of promotions, one is unmarried and one is a woman herself. But the point is, or should be, well taken. It won't be though, not amongst the hierarchy today. The most important requirement for a successful legal system, and for general peace and quiet in the country, is public acceptance of the courts. The judges have to be respected. That does not mean being called 'Dave' in court. It means being widely thought of as fair-minded, conscientious and competent. That will be the first casualty of the end of judicial independence, if the civil service gets the upper hand and makes judges 'accountable'. If that happens, and you're looking for someone to blame, look no further than the seven Lords President we have had during the last half century."

6

# Perceptions of Judging

If the first pillar of an independent judiciary is the absence of bureaucratic "accountability" and its related threat, political control—which has recently emerged with regard to sentencing "tariffs" and the end of the prohibition on double jeopardy—then the second pillar is public approval of the courts and judges. Justice must not only be done but must be seen to be done. Perception is vital, not least for the courts themselves. Whenever a judge acts in a way that is seriously and justifiably unpopular, calls for political or bureaucratic control of the judiciary get louder. The price of independence is eternal sensitivity.

In the past, Scotland has taken the public image of its judges seriously. A good example in fairly recent times was the case of the Sheriff in the mid-1980s who pronounced at a party at the Ayr Curling Club that the coal miners then on strike would not receive Legal Aid if they came into his court on breach of the peace charges. It was pure bluster, and probably not meant seriously even when it was said. But some of the people concerned appealed his decision, on quite different grounds, to refuse their Legal Aid applications.

The appeal came before the Court of Session. In his judgement, Lord Ross, the then Lord Justice Clerk, concluded that, though the Sheriff had not in fact brought his declared prejudice into court, and his decisions were quite correct in law, that was not the end of the matter. What was important was not the absence of actual bias but the avoidance of any situation which might gave rise to an *appearance* of bias. In finding for one of those appealing, Lord Ross said:

> There is nothing to suggest that at the trials the Sheriff acted unfairly. What the Sheriff failed to note was that the interests of justice required not merely that he should not display bias but that the circumstances should not be such as to create in the mind of a reasonable man a suspicion of the Sheriff's partiality.[89]

Though this has been the rule in the Scottish courts from time immemorial, there have been exceptions, Lords Gibson and Clyde being examples. But these exceptions have been extremely rare, by any standard. However, the impression has grown up in the public mind that Scottish judges are occasionally happy to bend the rules to favour their own class and kind.

Scotland's most successful modern crime writer, Ian Rankin, has illustrated the common prejudice in several of his books. In *Let It Bleed*, for example, Rankin's fictional detective, John Rebus, admits that judges treat members of the public differently depending on their social background.

> "Aye right," Duggan said dismissively. "And if I was some rich bastard that had been to Fettes, I'd have to pay too, is that right? I'd be treated the same as an Oxgangs drop-out. Come on, Inspector, Kirstie's told me the way it works, the whole system."
> He had a point, one Rebus would happily concede. (p. 308)

I visited Ian Rankin to ask him if he thought this was what actually happened in Scottish courts.

"I think there is a general preconception that people of influence and money will be dealt with more leniently by the courts than people on the wrong side of the tracks," he replied. "Probably it goes all the way back to things like the Guinness guy, Ernest Saunders. He basically got a Get Out of Jail Free card because he had Alzheimer's Disease, which was said to be incurable but from which he recovered as soon as he was released."

"But that's England," I said. "And in any case that was not a

---

[89] *Bradford v Macleod* (1986) SLT 244

judicial decision, it was one made by the Parole Board."

"What you have to remember," Rankin replied, "is that 99.9% of the population couldn't tell you the difference between Scottish law and English law. When I started writing the Rebus books, I had no idea that there were fifteen people on a Scottish jury. My idea of research was to watch Crown Court. It was this cop I met, who became a friend of mine, who said, 'The only point at which Scottish law and English law meet are traffic offences.' So I had to start finding out in what way Scottish law was different from English law, the three verdicts and all the rest of it."[90]

"But is it fair on Scottish judges to present them as class-conscious and prejudiced?"

"My books are fiction, but there *is* a perception in the police that judges are very much of the establishment; they've all gone to fee-paying schools; they all live in big houses in the New Town or whatever. How many QCs and advocates live in council flats? I think part of the problem is that there is no public perception of the judges, except for lurid headlines when people seem to be let off very lightly. You don't get profiles of judges. You don't get to find out what they do behind the scenes, how they get to where they are today, what they are really like."

Leaving aside the point in his first sentence, that he is writing not about a general perception but of a perception within the *police force*, Rankin is surely right when he says that judges do not do enough to make themselves known to the public at

---

[90] The three verdicts are: Guilty, Not Guilty and Not Proven—which means, in some circumstances, that a case can be retried. Scotland is unique in the third verdict, which is why the abolition of the prohibition on double jeopardy in England in 2003 was not relevant to Scotland. But Scotland introduced its own version of the change in 2011 when it allowed cases to be re-tried if the original trial was tainted, if after acquittal the accused admits to the crime, or if significant new evidence is discovered. The principle of the prohibition is outlawed in both the European Convention on Human Rights (from which the UK has negotiated a partial opt-out) and the US Constitution (Fifth Amendment).

large. Perhaps they should not do so if they are to preserve judicial independence, Emslie-style. But if that is their collective view, then they will have to accept that many people will think of them as the tabloid press and the London-based television system portrays them.

I put Rebus's—let's not say Rankin's—point to the judges I interviewed. What did they think of his view of the Bench?

"I think it is utter bullshit," one particularly forthright judge told me. "You are more likely to find the *police* behave differently to people depending on their class background than the judges. You do sometimes get people before the court who have been at public school, but don't think that stops us sending them to jail if they need to be sent to jail. Rankin is ignoring the fact that the courts are subject to public scrutiny. So if there was a pattern of conduct of people turning up in an Old Fettesian tie who should get five years and are only getting five months, I think that would be picked up by the more serious press, not just the *Daily Record*. Not only that, the Lord Advocate now has a right to appeal sentences if they are too lenient, and the Lord Advocate, being a political appointment as head of the Crown Office, is much more influenced by the man in the street and the *Daily Record* than the judges are. So he would not be backward in coming forward to appeal in cases like that."

"It is a popular misconception," another judge said to me, "that judges favour middle-class people. It is actually the opposite. If you are dealing with something like a speeding offence and the offender is an ordinary man who does 50 mph going home from work because he has got a football match to watch, I think he'll get a routine fine, say £50. But if it's a Jaguar chap he might be in for a £500 fine. And there's a certain common sense about that. He's got a lot of money and it's not a problem for him to pay £50, but the same fine is a real punishment for the other chap. What complicates this is the fact that we're far more conscious of press comment than when I started on the Bench. There wasn't any then. The judges could do what they liked. Today we can't. We're looking over our shoulder the whole time to make sure our behaviour is acceptable. You have to reflect what society thinks, even though it is very difficult to find out what society actually does think."

When judges think of "society's view", they tend to think, whether rightly or wrongly, that this is best represented by the tabloid press. But they vary about the extent to which they think they should pay attention to it.

I asked a different judge from the one just quoted whether there was any feeling of being under pressure from the tabloids?

"No, I don't. I personally don't allow myself to be influenced by what the *Daily Record* might say about a sentence of mine. But I do recognise that the public have an interest in what my sentence is. I think there is a balance to be struck in trying to impose a sentence that is going to reflect the wider interests and expectations of society and one which is going to meet the narrow and vengeful interests of certain sections of the tabloid press or the more understandable expectations of the victims. What the tabloids want usually is hanging, drawing and quartering. But who cares about them, really? One week you are the softest judge in the country. Next week you're the opposite. Who gives a shit? I don't see how I could possibly live my life being concerned that when I pass sentence the press are going to say this or that. Comment is their job, and I obviously do not try to interfere with it. Sentencing criminals is my job and I trust they will be mature enough to understand that I couldn't care less what they think about the way I do it."

It is undoubtedly true that there is a delicate balance to be struck between judicial independence and responsiveness to the wider concerns of public opinion. That is a completely different matter from accountability to a civil service structure which means, in a democratic society, to elected politicians. All the judges I spoke to accept that public opinion has a legitimate role to play in their approach to sentencing. Being sensitive to that is not in any way to compromise their independence from the structure of political power. But that is not most delicate of the many issues the Bench has to deal with. Another judge put to me a much more uncomfortable point about sentencing in relation to social class.

"This is a very difficult matter," the judge said. "Most of my colleagues are very conscious of the social class from which the accused comes. It can be a problem if the accused is a middle-class person. You have to be careful not to treat them differently. But what constitutes different treatment? Is giving a poor man a £50 fine for the same offence which a rich man gets a £500 fine for equal treatment? Or does equal mean that they are fined equally? Forget the days when it was quite acceptable to give a middle-class person a more lenient sentence. You cannot do that any more, and quite rightly so. But real justice is a more subtle business than simply treating everyone alike, as if you were a computer. We do not treat mentally-challenged people the same as normal people, so what about financially-challenged people when it comes to fines?

"But the judicial ethics of fining people are simple compared with those relating to imprisonment. Personally—and I may be quite wrong in this—I find it subconsciously far easier to send a guy from a council estate like Pilton to prison than someone from the leafy lanes of Barnton. I know I should not think like this, but I do. I try not to, but it still comes back to me that from the point of view of severity of punishment, prison differs depending on the type of prisoner, just as fines do depending on the wealth of the person being fined. The Pilton guy's Dad will have been in the nick at some point in his life; his brother's probably there already; and his cousin'll be in next week. So it is not such a terrible affliction you are imposing on the individual. But when you get someone whose parents are all sitting in a court for the first time in their lives, looking like the sort of people who still dress up to go on aeroplanes, clearly devastated not only by what their son has done—they're all very respectable and can't understand why he's done it—but also by the thought of the unknown hell that he will be consigned to if he is given a custodial sentence, you'd have to be very insensitive not to feel differently. You see the consequences, writ large, of sending this lad to prison, and they are different from sending the Pilton crack addict to jail. Doubtless there should be no difference. All the sociologists, penal reformers and general wise-guys will tell you that. But you try sitting up there and not feeling sympathy for someone whose whole family, himself included, is in a state of extreme anguish at the prospect of prison: it is impossible."

That view was expressed by one of the younger judges I talked to. I asked one of the most senior ones if he agreed with it.

"Not at all," he said. "You can't let your emotions run riot or we'd have no justice system left. It's like medicine. If you went into hospital, would you want the surgeon to be so worried about causing you pain that he could not operate properly? Of course not. He's got to be detached. It's the same with judges."

"That's an interesting point," I said.

"It's not, really: it's obvious," came the matter-of-fact reply. "An air of detachment is necessary to keep your mind clear for the law. You can't take it too seriously. You've got to be firm but fair. If you get too involved with the case, there's always the possibility that you'll pass far too harsh a sentence. The late Lord Wheatley didn't often do that, but he loved the words 'condign punishment'. Being a high-minded socialist from the east end of Glasgow, he thought the citizens who stood before him would be cowed by that. But they were a pretty hardened lot. It was water off a duck's back to them. They too were detached, in a way. The judge has to match that, or his life would be a misery. You can't let your emotions run away with you. I won't say I am unemotional. Every now and again you feel quite sympathetic, mostly towards women, actually, who have been led into crime, very often by somebody with a stronger personality, a boy-friend or something. But that is unusual. A friend of mine, a QC, was defending a chap once who, he was quite convinced, was being wrongly pursued in the courts. He had a nervous breakdown. That is taking it a bit far. He couldn't carry on with the case, which was not much help to his client. So you must remain detached, or it's hopeless for everybody."

Finally on this point, one judge gave me a good reason for the public perception that treatment varies depending on their position in the Fettes/Oxgangs spectrum.

"If somebody comes into court who is disrespectful of authority," the judge said, "as many young males aged about 16-

21 tend to be, then you are going to treat them in a particular way. But on the whole somebody who has been educated at Fettes is not going to come in unshaven, with his hands in his pockets and looking awful. It is perfectly human to respond to that. When somebody is grunting and sniggering, you can't help but be less sympathetic. The other thing is that the number of Fettes boys a judge will see have to deal with during his judicial career could be counted on the fingers of one badly-mutilated hand. I don't think I have ever seen an accused person who was Fettes-educated. Most crime is committed by people who are not affluent. On the whole if you have been to Fettes the chances are that you are affluent. You might be cleverer at not being caught, I don't know. If you go to the Sheriff Court and look at the addresses of the accused from Glasgow or Edinburgh, you will find they are nearly all from Easterhouse or Drumchapel, or from Pilton or Craigmillar or some other council house area. There's very few from smart addresses like Heriot Row or Moray Place, or whatever their equivalents are in Glasgow. But supposing they catch the man who tried to kill Leslie Cumming–"

"Leslie who?"

"Leslie Cumming. He was the chartered accountant who looks after the Law Society's discipline in relation to the accounts of solicitors' firms. Maybe you didn't hear, but he was stabbed outside his house a year ago. Cumming does his job well and therefore makes enemies. If the guy who was responsible is caught, the chances are he'll have been educated at Edinburgh Academy or somewhere like that, possibly even Fettes, since petty crooks do not tend to have issues with the Law Society. If that turns out to be the case, I can't see a judge taking a favourable view of the accused because of the school he went to. It just doesn't work like that. Attacking a 60-year old man with a knife? He'll get the book thrown at him, wherever he comes from. Believe me!"[91]

---

[91] In fact, that attacker was caught in Australia. He was the Irish-born ex-manager of a tanning salon in Edinburgh, but was only a "hit man". The BBC reported that he had been paid £10,000 "by a guy in a BMW" to carry out the

*

Elsewhere in *Let It Bleed*, Rankin's Rebus gives vent to another common prejudice about judges, namely that they are in cahoots with the police. One of the main characters in the book is "Wee Shug" McAnally, who was given a lenient sentence for raping a neighbour of one of the principal characters. It turned out that he was an informer for the police, and an important aspect of the book's plot revolves around information which the police were given by Wee Shug while he was serving his shorter-than-normal sentence. But how did he get so short a sentence? Rebus mulled this question over and came to the conclusion that the answer was "something he didn't want to think." What was that?

> There was only one good reason he could think of why Wee Shug had been so lucky, one good reason why a judge might be so lenient time and time again. Someone had put in a word. And who was it who usually put in a word with the judge? Answer: policemen. (p. 128)

Inspector Rebus is not alone in this view. In his book *Fallen Gods*, another successful contemporary Scottish crime writer, Quintin Jardine, has his hero, Bob Skinner, enjoying similar influence with the judges, though in this case it is not even for the "noble cause" of police information gathering.

> "[Skinner] wasn't just doing his job when he put in a word to get me a standard lifer's tariff," Lenny said. "Any other copper, you included, would have left me here to rot, doing a minimum of thirty years. So how can I help him?" (p. 204)

I am not aware of any research exploring the Scottish public's attitude towards judges, but I think it is reasonable to assume that such popular writers as Rankin and Jardine reflect widely-held views.

"Do police talk to lawyers and judges about what should

---

attack. He told a friend that he had "done a judge in". He was sentenced in 2011 to 11 years in jail. The identity of the person who paid him the money is, as yet, unknown.

happen to someone?" Rankin said ruminatively, when I asked him about collusion. "Yes, that must go on. If they don't meet formally, they meet informally, at various dinners and what have you. The police do have informers on their books, people who they'd be very keen not to see put inside. So they'd have a word with somebody to try to make sure that the sentence is as lenient as possible. It just makes sense to me rationally that that would happen."

"What evidence do you have for that?" I asked.

"I've no evidence," Rankin replied. "It just seems to me rational that that would happen, that the forces of law and order would trade information, or make sure that information was available, to help out their friends, people who are helping the police."

"In what sort of circumstances do you think policemen and judges might meet?"

"If the case has gone up the ranks to a fairly senior police officer, they would be meeting at Law Society dinners; they'd be meeting at dinners at Police Headquarters; they'd be meeting when Princess Anne comes to town to congratulate Lothian and Borders on their anniversary. There's all kinds of inter-disciplinary places where they could meet. They'd be meeting in the New Club, perhaps. Do you not think the Assistant Chief Constable, the Deputy Chief Constable and the Chief Constable would be in the New Club?"

I asked one judge what he thought of Rankin's view.

"Rubbish," the judge said. "Absolute rubbish. It just doesn't happen. We would be outraged if anything like that happened. Any judge or sheriff I know would be furious if any attempt was made to nobble him like that. I had a case in which a member of the clerking service was, I thought, trying to influence me. I was livid. He was subsequently disciplined for it. He was a very dodgy guy and he should have been fired long before then. His boss said he didn't know he was doing wrong. But this is something we are very strong on. You cannot come to a judgement using any evidence that you have not heard in court, or was not referred to in court. As soon as it became clear to anyone that you were influenced by anything extraneous then the whole judgement would come under attack, not least in the Appeal Court. The Scottish Bar is very vigilant, so we're hot on that sort of thing."

Another senior judge put a more subtle view to me.

"It is the *police*, I think, who are very keen on this notion that someone who has been a useful informer should be in some way dealt with more favourably because of that. That may be helpful to them in their work. I don't know. I am not a policeman. But no-one should believe them, on that subject anyway. I can't see why a person who is only doing what is the duty of any citizen, should get a benefit when it comes to being sentenced for whatever else he has been doing. I cannot see why I should take that into account when sentencing someone, unless it showed a degree of reformed character or something like that. Simply because the accused had been a snitch would not have any affect on sentence."

I asked if there were any circumstances at all in which the police might justifiably "have a word" with a judge?

"Absolutely none. There is no *prospect* of the police having a word with a judge. None whatsoever. If any policeman tried to talk to a judge, that judge would be quite likely to call another policeman to have him removed. It is just not possible. Ian Rankin's understanding of how the legal system works is rudimentary. People do have an impression of the legal system as a whole as being like that, and of course it is perpetuated by this kind of garbage. Really what he is saying is that judges are corrupt. That is what he is saying. There is no two ways about it. It is just not done like that. I cannot even imagine how a police officer would ever get into a situation of having a word with a judge."

"In the New Club, he says."

"The New Club, of course, is crawling with police officers! Bah!"

"Do you think Ian Rankin might have been transferring an English prejudice about whispered words in club-land to the rather different situation in Scotland?" I asked.

"Yes, definitely," the judge replied. "Also, you used to have a more direct role of the police in the prosecution in England than we have ever had here. Years ago you would have the same police officer presenting cases in the lower courts and instructing barristers who went on to become judges. In Scotland there has always been a total separation. The police only appear in court as witnesses. I don't think I have spoken to a police officer, in a professional capacity but outside court, in my entire life."

A retired judge, who had done a great deal of criminal work, had a slightly different point to make.

"Of course it's nonsense to say that the police talk to judges about criminals, and the police know it. That is why they try to do it covertly. I was a judge for twenty years, and I was never approached by a policeman openly, ever. But they did once try to influence my by more subtle means. It was at the trial of the man who was known as the Glasgow intelligent criminal. I was asked to meet them in the company of the prosecutor and the defence. The police informed me that they had information to the effect that the prosecutor and myself were liable to be shot at, therefore they wanted to provide us with protection. I didn't actually believe it, but they said they had information which came from someone who had been in prison with this man's brother, who was also a crook. So both the prosecutor and I permitted them to provide escorts and guards outside our houses and so on. I think they were trying to impress upon me the fact that this guy had to go to prison. Everybody knew the man was a villain. I did too. But in the event he was acquitted. That is the only time as a judge I was ever approached by the police in a way which could possibly have been thought questionable."

Yet another judge made possibly the most telling point of all.

"What you have got to realise," the judge said, "is that judges in Scotland do not trust the police very much, at least not the way they do in England where some of them still think of Dixon of Dock Green."

"Why is that?"

"I cannot speak for my brethren, but I'll tell you about the first time my eyes were opened to their methods. It was a long time ago, when I was still a prosecutor; before I became a judge. There had been a famous robbery in Edinburgh, with a bit of violence, but the people who did it were caught within hours. They also pulled in several other people for questioning. Slightly puzzlingly, the police said they wanted to release one of them almost at once. As a prosecutor I had him on my list of witnesses. The Detective Chief Superintendent in charge of the case came to me and said, 'We would like you not to lead the evidence of this guy.' I said, 'I've not got the slightest intention of leading his evidence. His precognition said nothing. He's no use to me.' I guessed that he was the guy who had sung, who had been the police informer. But I said to the police, 'I have to tell the defence if I am going to take a witness off the list because they have a right to call any Crown witness.' I said to the defence, 'I am dropping a number of witnesses, three, four, seventeen, twenty-six', or whatever. They said, 'We want twenty-six.' That was the informer. So I sent a message to the policeman saying, 'I'm sorry but the defence want him.' An hour later, he escaped from custody. He asked to go to the lavatory. He shut the door and the policeman stood outside for a while. Eventually, as they put it to me later, the officer started wondering what had happened to the witness, so he looked inside. To his alleged surprise he saw the window was open and the bird had flown."

"Were you the only judge who thought like that?"

"I don't think so. It is not a subject we discuss amongst ourselves very much. Maybe we should do, but we don't. It's not as bad now as it used to be. It was much worse before the *English* judiciary finally opened their eyes to what was going on, following the Birmingham Six and the Guildford Four and all the other cases where the police lied through their teeth. Those were the days when the Metropolitan Police Commissioner could talk about 'noble cause perjury'. That meant that if you knew the guy was guilty you made bloody sure the evidence was there. That was in the 1970s. The Metropolitan Police were so corrupt they had to bring in the Chief Constable of Glasgow, David McNee, to sort the mess out. It took a long time for the judiciary to face up to the fact that policemen might tell lies. They all came in clean shaven with their hair properly parted and swore the oath and spoke something vaguely like the Queen's English—but they had all mysteriously seen exactly the same thing. It was only after the Birmingham Six thing that they woke up to what the public already knew, that the police were fixing the evidence all over the place."[92]

"How did they get away with that?"

"Part of the problem was that in England mainly, although also in Scotland to some extent, if you specialised in criminal work, the chances of going on the Bench were zilch. The people promoted were the successful advocates who had made money out of Chancery Division, or Probate or whatever. Criminal barristers were tainted with the criminal. For example, George Carman would never have got on the bench because he was too closely associated with criminals.[93] If you can name me a

---

[92] This is still an issue. The Independent Police Complaints Commission report, published in November 2007, on the shooting of the young Brazilian, Charles de Menenez, by Metropolitan Police officers in July 2005 noted that not one of the seventeen civilian witnesses to the shooting, in an underground train carriage, heard the police shout the traditional warning "Armed police!" But every one of the eight police officers present in the same carriage gave evidence that they heard it.

[93] George Carman QC, who died in 2001, was a noted criminal and libel barrister who came to prominence after defending Jeremy Thorpe, the Liberal Party leader who was tried for conspiracy to murder in 1979. He also acted at various times for Ken Dodd, Richard Branson, Mohamed Al-Fayed and the family of Roberto Calvi ("God's banker"). From the point of view of being appointed to the Bench, Carman's status as a Catholic who had trained for the priesthood before going to Oxford to study jurisprudence (where he got a First), would have been less of a disadvantage in England at the time than in Scotland. Today it would be irrelevant in England and possibly a small advantage in politically correct Scotland. However, since his death, other factors have emerged that might have been known to the authorities at the time. In particular Carman's son has written in the *Guardian* about his father who was bisexual and whose "heavy drinking, ruinous gambling and young prostitutes" were probably caused by sexual abuse at his Catholic boarding school in Blackpool.

criminal lawyer in England who became a judge in the High Court or got into the House of Lords, then I shall be surprised. In Scotland it is not quite so bad because everybody did some criminal work, even if you were just on the Poor's Roll when you were a junior. Even James Mackay did a bit of criminal work before he went on to higher things. In Scotland you have people quite a few people on the Bench who have represented crooks in their younger days, and if you represented crooks you quickly got a nose for who's telling the truth and who isn't. In Scotland people who act for the defence in criminal cases learn about the villainy of the police, and they take that knowledge with them onto the Bench. In England they have no such background. They come with a very bourgeois perspective on policemen."

Another judge, now retired, told me a story which was intended to be representative of a life-time's experience. The judge said most others would have similar stories, because in Scotland all but the few who get closeted in places like the commercial court—Lord Drummond Young is an example—have to do their share of criminal judging. It is a share which is growing all the time. Today it occupies more than half of the time of most of the judges. By contrast, I heard about Lord Scarman, the distinguished English judge who chaired the inquiry into the 1981 Brixton riots, which concluded there was "institutionalised racism" in the Metropolitan Police. He had been a Family Division judge and he told one of my informants that until he was appointed to the Appeal Court he had never been involved in a single criminal case, even as a barrister. That situation is almost impossible with the structure of the Scottish judiciary.

"As an advocate, I was defending a man who was charged with two break-ins," the retired judge said. "They had taken place over two weekends but the *modus operandi* was the same. Explosives had been used. My client had been seen in the street by a policeman off duty on the second occasion, near the premises which were broken into. In both cases they had got into one shop and blown a hole through the wall into the next place and robbed it. In the earlier case they had gone in through a cellar and the police had found a candle with his fingerprint on the wax, so undoubtedly he did that. He admitted that, but he said: the second one, no.

"What happened in that case was that the police, having eventually identified him through the finger-print in the first case, went to his house where they found him in bed. They removed a suit from his wardrobe—in those days criminals wore suits—and they took it to the police station. There they found the turn-ups were full of cordite from the explosions. As my client said to me, 'Can you imagine me going in to blow up a safe with turn-ups in my trousers? Can you imagine me lying in my bed and the police come in and say, "What suit were you wearing at the weekend?" and I say, "That one, over there."'?'

"When I cross-examined the forensic expert who examined the trousers, he admitted he had never seen so much cordite and other safe-cracking material in the turn-ups of a pair of trousers in his life. So the jury acquitted my client. They did not believe the police any more than I did. But getting involved with a case like that, even though you've got a villain with a record as long as your arm, and even though the judge is shouting blue murder at you for challenging the police—that was the late Lord Wheatley—taught me that the police are capable of being villains themselves."

"But framing known villains is not quite so bad as arranging for the conviction of wholly innocent people," I said.

"They can do that too," the judge said. "I remember very well acting for the police in one of my early cases in the Crown Office. A civil action had been brought by a youngster who alleged he had been beaten up by the police. What had happened was that this youngster had been given his first job at the age of fifteen with the Corporation dustcart in Glasgow. The dustmen arrived at a shop premises just as it opened about 9 a.m. They went in and picked up the dustbins. A short time later, the woman in charge of the shop said that money had been stolen from her bag. She had been standing in for her sister who was ill that day. She had gone into the shop with a whole lot of money to give to the traveller. The door opened and in came the dustmen. Next thing: she couldn't find the money. So the police looked at the two guys on the dustcart. The bin-man had been working for thirty years and never a blemish; the boy, however, had previously been alleged to have stolen a 10/- note or something of the kind. It had never been proven but it had been alleged. So he was taken to the police station where he had a few accidents, got bruises and cuts and so on. He confessed to the crime. Not only did he confess to the crime, he took the police to where the money was buried. When they got to the spot, there was no money. They went back to the police station, and they charged him with the theft from the shop. The following morning the woman phoned up and said she was terribly sorry but she had looked at the pocket on the other side of her bag and the money was there. So this poor kid had been beaten up to the point where he not only confessed to the crime but took the police to the scene, yet it was a total fabrication by the police. They had beaten a confession out of him. I had quite a few cases like that."[94]

"I'm surprised you are concentrating this on Scotland," another judge said to me when I mentioned some of more general problems of law, judging and justice.

"Why?" I asked.

"Because the English judicial system is so outstandingly much worse than ours."

"In what way?"

"In almost every way: pomposity, formality, expense, length of trials, inefficiency, self-righteousness."

Expense, length of trials and inefficiency are more managerial problems than human ones, so I asked focussed on the pomposity and self-righteousness. "What is the reason for that?" I asked.

"They have real Tories there," the judge said, "the like of which we don't have up here, or at least not in any significant

---

[94] See Chapter 2 for examples of similar practises in the Soviet Union in the 1930s. The only difference is scale, but it is a principle of both law and justice that you are just as much a murderer if you have murdered one person as you are if you have murdered a hundred. Scale, in other words, is not relevant to guilt.

numbers. The result is that they are deferential. There is not much deference in Scotland. The only defence is formal: to the court. It is not to the judge. In Scotland, for a start, people don't bother much about titles. In England they really do. If somebody is Sir John, he's got to be called Sir John. And if he's Mr Justice X, he's got to be known as that, even in a hotel restaurant. In Scotland, I don't think people care particularly. Our system is far from perfect, but the English system is worse. They've allowed it to be abused. Their trials go on far longer than ours. There is no limit of time. They start off with great long speeches about what the evidence is going to be. We don't have them at all. Forget that! We go into court in a murder trial and we start, 'Witness number 1, right, what've you got to say?' In England you've got Counsel addressing you for a day telling you what he's going to say when he stops speaking and starts saying it. None of that is evidence. It's just filling in. We manage without it. We've had far fewer serious miscarriages of justice, so it can't be absolutely necessary."

"What gave rise to the difference?" I asked.

"The English Bar was populated by the ruling class, and they could effectively do what they liked. Juries in England seem to be more tolerant of upper-class eccentricity than they are in Scotland. So there was no feeling of, 'I might be boring the jury so I'd better keep this short.' Barristers could go on as long as they liked. The judge would be a member of the club as well. They just ran it as they thought gentlemen should run things. As they were being paid by the day, so much the better. And they get paid more than Scottish advocates. There was kind of presumption about the English bar and bench that they were entitled to gentlemanly, leisurely means of procedure which they could always justify by the need for care to be taken before liberty is interfered with, and so on."

"So it is a class thing?"

"Not entirely. I remember from my time in the Crown Office many years ago that the ordinary Customs and Excise officers in England, who mount their own prosecutions, can be just as arrogant. They have a very heavy hand. And of course the

Customs and Excise has powers that the police could only dream of. I remember when I was an Advocate Depute that a bunch of heavies from Ipswich came up and said to me, 'Right, son, we've booked this trial next week and we're going to be prosecuting it.' I said, 'You're not prosecuting it. We're prosecuting it.' 'No, no, no,' they said. 'No, my son. We're the Customs and Excise. We prosecute.' I said, 'Yes, but you're now the Customs and Excise in Scotland. You have no powers of prosecution.' All hell broke loose. 'We'll make sure your superior knows about this,' they said. 'I don't have a superior,' I said. 'Just go home to Ipswich.' They came back, very chastened, as witnesses, the following week for the trial. The whole thing collapsed after about two days because they were so awful. They were as cocky in their own way as barristers in silk tights, just with different accents. By contrast, we Scots were always less confident. As an advocate you were always looking over your shoulder and hoping you were not boring the Court. One result of that is that we are much less long-winded."

"Is it a question of vanity, then?"

"Again, not entirely. But top English barristers do seem to enjoy arguing all day about obscure precedents. There was—it's a lot better these days—a kind of licensed absurdity about the system of precedent because you can find a precedent for anything, especially in a large jurisdiction, like England, where there have been so many cases. It's even worse in America. The end result is almost unlimited complication. And complication is the refuge of the second-rate. The second-rate intellect loves complication because it allows them to baffle the public and to retain its appearance of superiority. Simplicity is the enemy of the second-rate.

"The other point is that it is incredibly expensive, and lack of money can be a serious barrier to justice. To me, the arrogance which pervades the whole English legal system is the arrogance of the untrammelled professional classes. I have no sympathy with Mrs Thatcher, in fact she led me to join the Labour Party for a while. But the presumption as to the entitlement to go on languidly ruining people's lives without limit of time or cost, I think brought Mrs Thatcher down on their heads. I sympathised with her on that one. I suspect that when she was a barrister, she found that as a pushy grammar-school girl she wasn't treated very civilly by these toffs. Probably she remembered that, and that's why she called in James Mackay to sort them out. Really that is what Rankin is writing about when he deals with class in court. It has very little to do with Scottish practice."

"Given all that, does it worry you seeing material in print, and on the television and elsewhere, about the Scottish judiciary which seems to be informed largely by practice in England?"

"Not particularly," the judge said. "That's freedom of speech. Rankin can say what he likes. If I watch a play on television they almost certainly will not know how to dress the judge; they use the English style. They have the Counsel dressed as English Counsel, even in a Scottish case. If you look at the original film of *Greyfriars Bobby*, it was total crap the way they presented the judge. But it's typical. They are so ignorant they don't even know they are ignorant. There is a tremendous lack of observation. Jeffrey Archer wrote a book some years ago which involved the Scottish legal world. Almost everything he said about it was wrong. It doesn't matter if it is Jeffrey Archer or Ian Rankin, there's going to be errors in it. I almost expect it. So, no, it doesn't worry me, though if I were the Lord President, I think I possibly ought to be a bit concerned."

Ironically, the problem of the bad public image of judges seems to worry Ian Rankin almost more than it does most judges. He said to me, "Judges are in a no-win situation. If they appear in the media it is only because they have given someone what others think is an audaciously light sentence. It is never for doing a quiet, good job. That is not news."

He added a rider about his own trade: "The thing about the entertainment industry is that you've got to entertain. You can't entertain if you put across how the law actually works on a daily basis. It is tedious and incredibly convoluted. Nobody would understand it. It just wouldn't be interesting."

Given the problems of the public image of judges in Scotland and the last judge's comment about the Lord President, my own experience in researching this book is relevant.

I started work towards the end of 2004. One of the first things I did was to write to Lord Cullen, through the Principal Clerk of Session, asking for permission to interview judges. He had been Lord President since Lord Rodger was appointed to the House of Lords in 2001, and he served until December 2005, when he retired and was replaced by Lord Hamilton. Thinking that his Lordship would like to know what sort of a person was asking for help, I sent Cullen a copy of my book about law, *The Cost of a Reputation,* which features Sheriff Hook's friend, Sir Michael Davies, as mentioned in Chapter 4. I drew attention to the favourable notices the book received hoping that at least his Lordship would understand that I was a serious inquirer. To my surprise he did not reply. Instead his secretary wrote to me saying:

> Having regard to the considerable workload which is regularly undertaken by judges and those that support them, the Lord President does not consider that it would be reasonable to expect them to give up time, or that this would be of evident utility to the court. For these reasons, I have to inform you that the Lord President is not disposed to afford you the facilities which you seek.

Since I was not asking him to order judges to talk to me, only to permit me to ask them if they would agree to be interviewed, I thought this reply unhelpful, to say the least of it. Of course, I now realise I made a mistake in asking permission. I should simply have gone ahead and tried to interview whoever I felt might be relevant. Several of the judges I did talk to were at pains to point out that they were completely independent and could talk to whoever they wanted to. The Lord President's instructions meant nothing to them.[95]

---

[95] There was a curious sequel to this. Receipt of my book was not acknowledged; neither was it returned. After a year, I wrote to Lord Cullen reminding him about the book. By then it was out of print and I very much

A few months later, in August, after he had retired from the Bench, Lord Cullen chaired a meeting, sponsored by the Saltire Society of which he was President, at the Edinburgh Book Festival in which the future of Scottish literature was debated. I attended the meeting and heard him say that he was concerned to help Scottish writers flourish. I therefore wrote him again asking for an interview. This time I got an immediate reply, and from him personally. This is the full text:

> Thank you for your letter dated 6 September. I am not willing to be interviewed by you. I recall that a similar request was declined some time ago.

I also wrote to Cullen's successor, Lord Hamilton. I would have done so earlier, but he spent most of the first six months of his period as Lord President off work for illness (as will be discussed below). I asked for an interview with him. I did not request permission to interview other judges, as I had done with Lord Cullen, but for some reason he took it that that was what I was asking, and replied saying, not only that he did not give permission, but that he was going to try to prevent any judges talking to me. This is the whole of his letter:

> I refer to your letter of 26 September in which you ask if I might be prepared to be interviewed for your forthcoming book.
>
> I understand that some time ago you approached Lord Cullen of Whitekirk, my predecessor as Lord President, and that he indicated that he was not prepared to afford you the facilities which you then sought, namely, permission to interview a small number of judges and clerks in Parliament House. My response to your request must be to a similar effect. While I have no objection to properly informed literature about the judiciary, I do not believe

---

wanted to retrieve that copy. Once again, Lord Cullen did not reply. Instead his Private Secretary wrote saying that he could "find no trace of [my] book." Since my original letter had been deliberately placed inside the cover of the book, it was impossible that it had not arrived where the letter had. The letter had been replied to, but the book had, allegedly, gone missing. I never got it back.

that the giving of interviews to private authors is in general the best way in which such information is disseminated.

I understand that you have made similar requests to at least some of my fellow judges. While the response of any judge is a matter for him or her personally, I have as head of the court advised my colleagues against co-operating with you.

It is alarming to find the head of the Court of Session apparently unable to understand my letter. My request in 2004 to interview judges generally was quite distinct from my request in 2006 to interview Lord Hamilton personally. He was answering a question I had not asked him, and failing to answer, except by implication, the question I *had* asked.

And why should "private authors" not apparently be able to produce "informed literature about the judiciary"? Which "public" authors did his Lordship have in mind as being better at disseminating the views of the judiciary?

Finally, why did he think that a reasonable response to a request to interview him was to try to prevent others from making a free decision?

If Rankin is right and there is a problem with the public perception of judges in Scotland, Lord Hamilton did not seem to be making much effort to address it.

7

## Judging and the Letter of the Law

One of the most common complaints made about the law generally is that it is uncertain. "Tell me what the law is and I will obey it," the ordinary law-abiding citizen is prone to say, perfectly reasonably. One of the public damaging misconceptions of the law is that it is explicit; that it can be expressed in black and white terms which leave no room for doubt. Of course, in matters like speed limits, littering or the days in the year on which it is lawful to kill common seals, *Phoca vitulina,* as opposed to grey seals, *Halichoerus grypus*, that is true. But almost everything a judge has to deal with does not fall into this category. Cases come to court precisely when they can *not* be determined by simple reference to evidence and explicit regulations. The art of judging is the art of discovering what the law means. When the letter of the law does not cover the situation in question, the spirit of the law is invoked, usually through analogous cases that have been decided in the past. Judging is therefore, centrally, a matter of textual analysis. But different words can mean different things in different contexts.[96]

Take the word "tree", for example. In 1976 Lord Denning,

---

[96] A separate but related problem arises when laws are translated, as European Directives have to be in Britain, and judges need to infer the intent of the legislators from the words used. See "Scots or European Lawyer—Quid Sum?" by Mathew Clarke, in the *Juridical Review,* 1996, p. 361. The author is now Lord Clarke, who sat as an Inner House judge in the Court of Session until 2013.

one of England's most acute and senior judges, sitting in the Court of Appeal, succeeded in turning it into a term of art. Denning was giving judgement in favour of a man who, having been served with a Tree Preservation Order, had allegedly breached it by bulldozing "scrub and pine" on land he owned. The case, *Kent County Council v Batchelor*, was reported only in the *Journal of Planning Law,* so the full extent of Lord Denning's walk on the wild side of language is not recorded. What is known is that he started by questioning what "mixed confers" were, as specified in the preservation order. How can a "conifer" be "mixed", he wanted to know? Why, he went on to ask, was one conifer, the yew, included in the list of deciduous trees? And what is a "tree" anyway? It must be distinct from a sapling, shrub or bush, because they are separately described in the Order. Denning then asserted, without quoting any authority, that "bushes and saplings are certainly *not* trees" because "a tree should be something of 7 or 8 inches in diameter." That was despite the fact that a sapling is a "young tree". And what is "scrub"? Can a single plant be both "scrub" and "a tree"? If so, why are they separately specified?

It was on the basis of such pixellation (if I may use that word in this context) of language that Lord Denning—the champion of plain speaking in law—quashed the month's imprisonment which had been imposed on Mr Batchelor for violating the Order. By "pixellation" I mean that he looked so closely at the words that they ceased to bear their natural and ordinary meanings in the context of the text in question. Denning got so immersed in the detail that he ceased to be able, as it were, to see the legal wood for the textual trees.

Scots law is more willing to tolerate broad categories and the use of words in their "natural and ordinary meaning". In this respect it is more akin to civil law systems. The reason for the difference is important. The concept of liberty under law, on which English jurisprudence is based, was one which evolved in early modern times when individual property-owners started to assert their rights under a "constitutional" monarchy. The power of the sovereign was not limitless, and could be brought to bear on the subject only when he or she broke rules which had been passed into law, usually by an act of parliament. It came to be an accepted principle that the citizen of England was free to do anything that was not specifically prohibited by the law. That law was not always written down, but if not it was generally well known since it was part of the common law which was based on immemorial custom. An example of unwritten law is the prohibition on murder. There is no statute outlawing murder, but it is still a crime in most circumstances to kill someone.

The phrase "English liberty" came to mean that people were free to do whatever was not explicitly outlawed. It was only in the later nineteenth century that it came to be accepted law that a person had to take account of his neighbour's property interest even if that was not explicitly enshrined in law. The "good neighbour" principle, asserting a general duty of care against the public generally, had to wait until 1932 before it was laid down in a landmark case.[97]

The Continental principle, if it may be called that for simplicity, was to promulgate a code of law which was phrased in general terms. It was the judge's task to decide whether a specific act of a citizen contravened the general principles laid down in the code. Arguably, this left a smaller margin for individual initiative which, some scholars say, resulted in the slower development of those societies in early modern times, especially in commercial terms where the freedom to use property in unusual ways permitted innovation. The benefit of the Continental system was its simplicity, which meant that law was more accessible to the ordinary citizen, not least because it was (and is) much cheaper. Bernard Shaw famously said of the courts in England that they were "open to anybody, like the Ritz". The traditional complaint about English-style justice—and this

---

[97] This was *Donoghue v Stevenson* (UKHL 100). Though originally a Scottish case, it was finally settled in the House of Lords as a civil appeal. It set the standard for delict, or tort, law throughout the United Kingdom, and in most common law jurisdictions from that time on. There is a fascinating film about it available at http://www.justiceeducation.ca/resources/Paisley-Snail

applies even more so to the American system—is the expense which inevitably results from the freedom to argue, not least about precedent (as mentioned in Chapter 5), for as long as funds last. Legal Aid is not a full answer to this.

However, there is a larger problem than money, which is that the general idea of "English liberty" is arguably obsolescent as an approach to law. The freedom to do what you like so long as it is not prohibited depends on your ability to know what is prohibited. That may have been reasonable when life and commerce was fairly simple, but with the increasing bureaucratisation and regulation of post-industrial society, and the gathering speed of social change, a concept of freedom based on knowledge of the law is increasingly unrealistic for anyone but a legal specialist.

To understand the change, it is worth recalling how things used to be. A.J.P. Taylor opened the last volume in the Oxford History of England, *English History 1914-1945*, with the following passage:

> Until August 1914 a sensible law-abiding [citizen of this country] could pass through life and hardly notice the existence of the state, beyond the post office and the policeman. He could live where he liked and how he liked... He could travel abroad or leave his country forever without a passport or any sort of permission. He could exchange his money for any other currency without restriction or limit. He could buy goods from any country in the world on the same terms he bought goods at home. For that matter a foreigner could spend his life in this country without permit and without informing the police... Substantial householders were sometimes called on for jury service... [But apart from that] broadly speaking, the state ... left the adult citizen alone.

Today in Britain the situation could hardly be more different. A law-abiding citizen of this country can do very little without encountering some form of state regulation or control, much of which carries criminal sanctions in the event of a breach. Lord Bingham of Cornhill, who had been both the senior Law Lord and Chief Justice, gave a lecture about the rule of law shortly before his death in which he said that one of the threats was what he called "legislative hyper-activity". He observed that it "appears to have become a permanent feature of our governance." He noted that in 2004 parliament passed some 3500 pages of legislation. In 2003 there were nearly 9000 pages of statutory instruments. He commented: "The sheer volume of current legislation raises serious problems of accessibility, despite the internet. And this is compounded by the British tradition of parliamentary draughtsmanship which, for all its technical virtuosity, depends so heavily on cross-reference and incorporation as on occasion to baffle."[98]

Some people ascribe this to the need to transpose European legislation into UK law; others to the trend for imitating America where, they say, the freedom to litigate, especially for public liability, has eclipsed many other public freedoms. One of the judges I spoke to took this view.

"I really think in America they treat people like idiots," the judge said. "I haven't been there very often, and never for more than a few weeks at a time. It has always in a professional capacity and the people I have had to deal with have been polite and interesting. Nice folk, but beyond that, I have to say that I hated every minute of it. There is a constant atmosphere of threat, with big notices up: don't eat in this shop, no shorts, don't cross the street. It is the most regulated society imaginable. They call it the land of the free, but I've never seen so many bloody rules and regulations. There's a standard type of behaviour in every situation, and you ignore it at your peril. I loathed it."

A Scottish example of the problems which an Americanised, common law-based idea of liberty, requiring minute regulation rather than statements of general principle, is the legislation passed a few years ago regulating access to the countryside. I have made a detailed study of this, which is published elsewhere, but the essence of it is illustrated by the difference between the Norwegian and the Scottish approaches.[99] In fact, it is misleading

---

[98] The Rule of Law, *Cambridge Law Journal* (2007), p. 67 (70)

[99] See *Isles of the West op. cit* pp 236-255; *Isles of the North op. cit.* pp. 241-

to talk about the Scottish approach because the Scottish Act was drawn up by Scottish Executive officers who were all employed by Whitehall and working in what Lord Bingham called the British tradition of legislative drafting.

Access to the countryside in Norway is governed by the Outdoor Recreation Act (1957). This runs to eight widely-spaced pages and essentially boils down to this: provided you respect the rights of other users of the countryside, you may go anywhere you like on uncultivated ground as long as you stay more than 150 metres from any dwellings, do not camp more than two nights in one place and do not light fires in forests during the summer.

Compare that with the twenty dense pages of the Land Reform (Scotland) Act (2003) which is devoted to access, and the equally dense sixty pages of the Scottish Outdoor Access Code which expands on the Act's provisions and has persuasive force in court. The Norwegian text has about 3% of the word count of its Scottish equivalent. Indeed the Access Code is misnamed; it is not a code, it is a set of regulations, most of them so detailed that they could be described as "treating people like idiots". For example: "You cannot exercise access rights on any sports pitch or playing field while it is in use"[100]. More bizarrely: "If you need to defecate, do so as far as possible from buildings."

---

242

[100] Part of the problem is the political nature of detailed regulation, as opposed to general principles which the population at large broadly accepts. The rule about access over sports pitches was originally directed at the problem of hikers and golf courses. No-one imagined they could "hike" across the pitch at Ibrox during an Old Firm game and claim immunity under the Access Code. But many hikers see golf as elitist, unlike their own sport. As it was a Labour government which passed this law, hikers had more success in lobbying for their own interests than golfers did. But the civil service, which did the detailed drafting, was more golf-orientated, at least at its senior levels. Executives were confronted by the problem that if they were to descend to the level of specifying different access regulations for different categories of sport, the document would have ended up being massively longer than it already is—hence the apparently patronising language.

The paradox is that an Act designed to promote access, has in fact made it more problematic. The law-abiding citizen who wishes to enjoy an afternoon in the countryside without problems, needs not only to know where to not express faecal matter, but also what it is legal to do on cultivated grass or silage, as opposed to uncultivated but farmed grass, or grass which is neither cultivated nor farmed. Since land is not labelled, it is necessary to have some knowledge of farming terminology and practice. The prudent hiker should also pack a copy of the local land-register, plus information about the management of any farm accessed. Due to the danger of disturbing wildlife, a copy the Birds and Habitats Directives is also recommended because to be convicted of wildlife crime you no longer have to damage wildlife interest maliciously; you only have to do so "recklessly". Transgressions carry fines of up to £40,000 (and a criminal record). The English approach to freedom in the Scottish hills comes at a heavy price.

The fact is that as society becomes increasingly complex, an "English liberty" approach to law becomes increasingly oppressive. There is no answer, even in theory, to Lord Bingham's complaint. But code-based law has its problems too. No system is perfect. However, an argument can be made that hybrid systems, of the sort Scotland has, offer the least worst—if I may put it like that—approach to defining freedom under law in modern conditions.

Scots law, as noted in the Introduction, straddles the Anglo-Saxon and the Continental traditions in many respects. An example which is in use every day of the judicial week is breach of the peace law. This is quite different from the English law of the same name, and is more akin to a code, yet it is also unlike a code it is unwritten and dependent for its daily definition largely on the judge's view of the circumstances of the case.

Breach of the peace in Scotland is usually held to be acts committed in public which are likely to cause serious disturbance, or to occasion fear or alarm. Such an imprecise description—definition would be too strong a word—has occasioned criticism on the ground that it is a catch-all offence for behaviour which the police and sheriffs do not like. But its imprecision is what gives it its flexibility.

The most celebrated recent example is the so-called Naked Rambler, an English hairdresser, who walked in the nude from Land's End to Bilston, south of Edinburgh, where he was arrested and charged with breach of the peace. Sheriff Kenneth MacIver found his conduct such that people were likely to be "upset, alarmed or offended", and drivers distracted, by the sight of him and his female partner walking along busy roads naked from the ankles up. The Rambler intended reaching John O'Groats, but was arrested and charged on eight separate occasions in Scotland. He spent his time in jail naked, but that was not considered a breach of the peace since he was not visible to the general public. However, he was arrested and charged once again when he walked naked out into the prison car park, though, interestingly, he was acquitted of this charge since, as Sheriff Isobel Poole found, there was "no evidence of actual alarm or disturbance".

At the time of writing, the Naked Rambler is in jail again, this time on a charge of contempt because he tried to appear naked in court. It would be almost impossible to frame an Adult Public Nudity (Miscellaneous Provisions) (Scotland) Bill, on the English freedom-based system, which would differentiate between nakedness in places where some cars are travelling fast and others where they are all either stationary or moving at walking pace, as in a prison car park, or between nudity as a prisoner in court or a prisoner in a police cell, and every other imaginable type of situation that an awkward citizen might put him or herself into, without its being either tyrannically simple— criminalizing naturism, for example, and sports club saunas—or so complicated that it would provide endless opportunities for further litigation in the manner complained of by the judge in Chapter 5. The only practical solution, apart from allowing nude walking everywhere, as happened from Land's End to the Scottish border, is to apply reasonable discretion: show the rambler the judge and he or she'll tell him or her the law in the situation concerned.

This principle applies not only to nude hiking but to an immense number of other situations which human beings are likely to find themselves in. Breach of the peace has been "libelled", as the Scottish courts say, for shouting in a public place, for persistent swearing, for hoax telephone calls to the emergency services, for begging, for threatening to commit suicide, for trying to do so, for killing a fox, for kicking a ball in the street, for glue-sniffing, for kerb-crawling (which in England was legislated for as a specific offence), for putting a plastic bag over an elderly woman's head, for threatening to "beat seven shades of shite" out of an unco-operative ex-girlfriend, for staring through the window of a busy off-licence for an hour and forty-five minutes, for spying on a naked woman in a solarium, for hanging fake prostitution adverts with pictures of an ex-girlfriend on the lamppost outside her house in the east end of Glasgow, for cross-dressing near Aberdeen harbour, and for walking over the roofs of parked cars during the early hours of New Year's Day in Lochgilphead—all without a single line of publicly-financed, British-style legislative drafting.

The comprehensiveness of Scottish breach of the peace law has brought it to the attention of the European Court of Human Rights. This Court adjudicates on alleged infringements of the European Convention on Human Rights, one of the most important provisions of which is the right of every citizen to live under laws which are stated clearly enough that the individual has a fair opportunity of complying with them. Many people have argued that the Scottish breach of the peace law does not fit that description. The Scottish courts have taken cognisance of the criticisms relating to the European Convention, and have made changes which, the judges feel, bring domestic law into line with the international standard. Scottish breach of the peace law has survived.

But it still leaves the question unanswered: how does the ordinary citizen know what the law is? Does everything depend on the mood of the judge on the day, on what his wife gave him for breakfast, the state of the weather, or the result of the weekend's Calcutta Cup game? Hopefully not. The judge should not bring his personal prejudices or his private concerns into court. On the Bench, under the wig, he or she is discharging a social duty. But the line can never be clear-cut. No human is perfect. Which is why there is force behind the calls for "computer justice" or "accountability" to bodies other than the Court of Appeal. The most forceful and popular response to Hamilton's Rule is to call for law to be written down more clearly.

I have already described the problem with legislative hyperactivity. But that does not answer the point that it is might be possible, with immense wisdom and gifted drafting, to produce a simple form of words which can act as a basic code, and on which a superstructure of rational action can be based without reference to the character of judges. If so, the Hamilton's Rule could be said to be disproved. The idea that text can give legal certainty where individual judges cannot is a popular one. But I believe it is profoundly mistaken. The clearest demonstration of the failure of words on paper to give legal certainty comes from, the United States, and it concerns the issue of race. It is possibly the most important legal battle ever fought, and certainly the longest, since it lasted two centuries. Anyone tempted to argue that Scotland should move away from its historic reliance on the character of its judges should do so only after careful consideration of the following story.

On 4 July 1776, fifteen months after armed conflict had broken out with the British Crown in New England, the rebel colonists in north America published their Declaration of Independence. "We hold these truths to be self-evident," Thomas Jefferson wrote, "that all men are created equal, that they are endowed by their Creator with certain inalienable rights, that amongst these are Life, Liberty and the Pursuit of Happiness."[101] But Jefferson was

---

[101] From a Scottish constitutional point of view, it is worth noting that Jefferson went on to argue that "to secure these rights, Governments are instituted among men, deriving their just powers from the consent of the governed." This language echoes that of the Declaration of Arbroath, the Scottish "declaration of

a slave-owner, as was John Adams and Benjamin Franklin, the other two authors of that document. So were most of the signatories, and so was the man who successfully defended these shining principles in the War of Independence, George Washington. As with Lord Denning and his trees, the judicious inquirer has to ask what the American colonists meant by the apparently unambiguous phrase "all men".

This was not a question which received much attention in the early years of the new Republic, but by 1860 there were approximately four million slaves in a country with a population just over thirty million.[102] In the north, where slavery was outlawed, their status became something of a *cause célèbre*. In the South it was a part of life. The basic purpose of courts, like parliamentary government and international diplomacy, is to resolve conflicts without recourse to violence. The American

---

independence" which was written in 1320, six years after the battle of Bannockburn. It said that if the King of Scots would not defend the freedom of his subjects from the English then they would "exert [themselves] at once to drive him out as our enemy and a subverter of his own rights and ours, and make some other man who is well able to defend us our King." Francis Hutcheson, Professor of Moral Philosophy at the University of Glasgow in the 1730s, echoed this point, saying "the end of all civil power is acknowledged by all to be the safety and happiness of the whole body" and that "any power not naturally conducive to this end is unjust, which the people, who rashly granted it under error, may justly abolish." This is essentially Jefferson's point. Jefferson credited Professor William Small from Aberdeen, his tutor at William and Mary College in Williamsburg, Virginia, as the person who "fixed the destinies of my life". Small introduced Jefferson to all the Scottish Enlightenment philosophers, including Hutcheson, and also to the Declaration of Arbroath. The other main author of the Declaration was Benjamin Franklin, who spent a long time in Edinburgh, staying with the greatest of all the Enlightenment philosophers, David Hume. At the time of the revolt, Hume said, "I am an American in my principles." Both the Scottish and the American Declarations are based on the concept of the sovereignty of the people, as opposed, since the seventeenth century, to the uniquely English idea of the sovereignty of parliament.

[102] This figure excludes the Native Americans, who were not even given the status of chattels, as slaves were, and counted.

Civil War, therefore, represents one of the greatest failures in Western legal history because it was effectively brought about by a decision of the Supreme Court which was explicitly intended to resolve the problem of slavery. Instead it led directly to war.

The facts of the landmark case were that a slave called Dred Scott had been taken by his master, Dr John Emerson, an Army surgeon who moved around as a result of his work, from Missouri, which was a slave state into Illinois and Wisconsin, which were both free states. In the early nineteenth century, Congress had tried to prevent the spread of slavery by admitting slave states to the Union only with an equivalent number of non-slave states. The convention was that each type of state respected the approach of the other type. But feelings ran high on both sides, not least because of the dawning conviction that, in the long run, a slave economy and a free economy could not exist side-by-side. In the days before rapid communication and widespread commerce, that had not been a practical problem, but by the middle of the nineteenth century it was. Times were changing, and with them morality.

The States' convention of mutual respect was called into question when Dred Scott tried to buy his freedom from Dr Emerson's widow and she refused to sell it to him. For some years, since her husband's death, Mrs Emerson had earned an income from renting out Dred Scott, his wife Harriet, and their two teenage daughters.[103] She was disinclined to part with an asset which generated income at no cost to herself. But after she had, allegedly, beaten and briefly imprisoned Dred Scott, he decided to sue for his freedom. He based his case on the fact that he and his wife had lived for four years while serving Dr Emerson on territory where slavery was outlawed. He had therefore been free while in Illinois and Wisconsin. It was settled law that no-one anywhere in the United States could be re-

---

[103] Dr Emerson must have been a more understanding master than many as slaves could not legally marry. The reason was that each slave was an individually tradable item. Commerce could not tolerate unbreakable unions between items of stock which could be sold independently of any others.

enslaved. Therefore, because of his residence outside Missouri, Dred Scott argued that he was free.

But could Scott sue? Only a citizen can go to court and Scott, being a slave and also, as a separate issue, being black, was arguably not a citizen, and therefore lacked standing. After a complicated series of cases in the courts of Missouri where he was considered a slave, Scott's case came before the Supreme Court, in 1857.[104]

The Chief Justice was Roger Taney from Maryland, an ex-Attorney General and Secretary of the Treasury who, in 1836, had been the first Roman Catholic to be appointed to the Supreme Court Bench. He was a noted liberal who led the way in holding that ownership of private property could, in certain circumstances, carry social responsibilities. Though born a southern "aristocrat", Taney himself appears to have been against slavery. At least he freed his own slaves, at considerable financial cost to himself. But when he gave judgement in *Dred Scott*, at the age of 80, he followed the law rather than his own conscience.[105]

Taney assumed that when the United States Constitution spoke of "we, the people", echoing the Declaration of Independence's phrase "all men", the term was synonymous with the word "citizen". But what precisely did this mean? Was Dred Scott one of these "citizens"? Could he, or could he not, avail himself of the protection of the courts of the United States?

---

[104] *Dred Scott v Sandford* (1857) 60 US 393. Mrs Emerson re-married and moved to Massachusetts, and so assigned both Scott and his litigation to her brother, John Sanford, hence the name of the case. A court clerk misspelled the defendant's name, and the misspelling has stuck. Shortly after conclusion of the case, a well-wisher bought Scott his freedom. Six months later he died of tuberculosis.

[105] It is worth noting that, by 1857, Tsar Alexander II had set in motion the process which was to lead, in 1861, to the abolition of serfdom in Russia. Unlike freed slaves in America, emancipated Russian serfs received land allocations, which ought to have, and up to a point did, contribute to general social stability. Yet American society, in the long run, proved more stable than Russian, principally because an autocratic regime could not, in times of crisis, rely on popular support. It relied on fear more than friendship.

Taney's opinion is worth quoting at length, both in order to answer that question and as an example of carefully-crafted judicial logic based on a written document, the United States Constitution, which is outstanding for its clarity of drafting:

The question is simply this: can a Negro, whose ancestors were imported into this country and sold as slaves, become a member of the political community formed and brought into existence by the Constitution of the United States, and as such become entitled to all the rights, privileges, and immunities, guaranteed by that instrument to its citizens? …

We think they are not, and that they are not included, and were not intended to be included, under the word "citizens" in the Constitution. On the contrary, they were at that time considered as a subordinate and inferior class of beings, who had been subjugated by the dominant race, and whether emancipated or not, yet remained subject to their authority, and had no rights or privileges but such as those who held the power of government might choose to grant them…

It is difficult at this day to realise the state of public opinion in relation to that unfortunate race, which prevailed in the civilised and enlightened portions of the world at the time of the Declaration of Independence and when the Constitution of the United States was framed and adopted. But the public history of every European nation displays it in a manner too plain to be mistaken.

They had, for more than a century before been regarded as beings of an inferior order; and altogether unfit to associate with the white race, either in social or political relations, and so far inferior, that they had no rights which the white man was bound to respect; and that the Negro might justly and lawfully be reduced to slavery for his benefit. He was bought and sold, and treated as an ordinary article of merchandise and traffic, whenever a profit could be made by it…

In no nation was this opinion more firmly fixed or more uniformly acted upon than by the English government and the English people. They not only seized them on the coast of Africa, and sold them or held them in slavery for their own use, but they took them as ordinary articles of merchandise to every country where they could make a profit on them, and were far more extensively engaged in this commerce than any other nation in the world. The opinion thus entertained and acted upon in England was naturally impressed upon the colonies founded on this side of the Atlantic...

We refer to these historical facts for the purpose of showing the fixed opinions concerning that race upon which the statesmen of that day spoke and acted. It is necessary to do this in order to determine whether the general terms used in the Constitution of the United States, as to the rights of man and the rights of the people, was intended to include them, or to give them or their posterity the benefit of any of its provisions.

The language of the Declaration of Independence is equally conclusive. It [says], "We hold these truths to be self evident: that all men are created equal; that they are endowed by their Creator with certain inalienable rights"...

The general words above quoted would seem to embrace the whole human family; and if they were used in a similar instrument at this day, would be so understood. But it is too clear for dispute, that the enslaved African race were not intended to be so included, and formed no part of the people who framed and adopted this Declaration; for if that language, as understood at that day, would embrace them, the conduct of the distinguished men who framed the Declaration of Independence would have been utterly and flagrantly inconsistent with the principles they asserted; and instead of the sympathy of mankind, to which they so confidently appealed, they would have deserved and received universal rebuke and reprobation.

Yet the men who framed this Declaration were great men—high in literary acquirements—high in their sense of honour, and incapable of asserting principles inconsistent with those on which they were acting. They perfectly understood the meaning of the language they used, and how it would be understood by others; and they knew it would not, in any part of the civilised world, be supposed to embrace the Negro race, which, by common consent, had been excluded from civilised government and the family of nations, and doomed to slavery. They spoke and acted according to the then established doctrines and principles, and in the ordinary language of the day, and no-one misunderstood them. The unhappy black race were separated from the white by indelible marks, and laws long before established, and were never thought of or spoken of except as property...

No-one of that race had ever migrated to the United Sates voluntarily; all of them had been brought here as articles of merchandise... The slaveholding States have continued to treat them as an inferior class, and to subject them to strict police regulation, drawing a broad line of distinction between the citizens and the slave races, and legislating in relation to them upon the principle which prevailed at the time of the Declaration of Independence... It would be impossible to enumerate and compress, in the space usually allotted to an opinion of the court, the various laws, marking the condition of the race, which were passed from time to time after the Revolution, and before and since the adoption of the Constitution of the United States...

It cannot be believed that the large slaveholding States regarded them as included in the word "citizens" [for if they were entitled to the immunities of citizens], it would exempt them from the operation of special laws and from the police regulations which they considered to be necessary for their own safety. It would give to persons of the Negro race, who were recognised as citizens in any one State of the Union, the right to enter every other State whenever they pleased, singly or in companies, without pass or passport, and without obstruction, to sojourn there as long as they pleased, to go wherever they pleased and every hour of the day or night without molestation, and it would give them full liberty of speech in public and in private upon all subjects which its own citizens might speak...

It is impossible to believe that the great men of the slaveholding States, who took such a large share in the framing of the Constitution of the United States, and exercised so much influence in procuring its adoption, could have been so forgetful or regardless of their own safety and the safety of those who trusted and confided in them...

No one, we presume, supposes that any change in public opinion or feeling in the civilised nations of Europe or in this country, should induce the court to give to the words of the Constitution a more liberal construction in their favour than they were intended to bear when the instrument was framed and adopted. If any of its provisions are deemed unjust, there is a mode prescribed in the instrument itself by which it may be amended; but while it remains unaltered, it must be construed now as it was understood at the time of its adoption... Any other rule of construction would abrogate the judicial character of this court, and make it the mere reflex of the popular opinion or passion of the day. This court was not created by the Constitution for such purposes. Higher and graver trusts have been confided to it, and it must not falter in the path of duty.

The result of Taney's judgement was the opposite of what he intended. It emboldened the Southern states, and disturbed the hitherto complacent northern idea that slavery was doomed, and could be quietly left to die. Opinion was implacable on both sides, so the case went to the only higher appeal forum than the Supreme Court, namely the battlefield, resulting in the bloodiest war in American history.

After the bloodshed, Congress decided it should take Taney's words at face value and invoke the provisions in the

Constitution "by which it may be amended". In 1865, the Thirteenth Amendment—the first in sixty years—abolished slavery. The following year, the Fourteenth Amendment guaranteed citizenship and full public civil rights to all persons born or naturalised in the United States, except Native Americans. Finally, in 1870, the Fifteenth Amendment ensured that the right to vote could not be denied on the basis of race.

Having amended the Constitution, the mood changed to one of reconciliation. The country wanted to placate the Southern whites, most of whom were bitterly opposed to racial equality. Many Southern states began to apply the doctrine of "separate but equal". This was felt to satisfy the newly enacted rights, while still allowing whites to avoid social contact with blacks. That was the background to the second of the three great Supreme Court examinations of the apparently clear words, "all men" and "we, the people". If blacks were now both "men" and "people" within the meaning of the founding documents, could those categories be split, for practical purposes, into two racial groups at the request of only one of those groups?

The test issue which came to Court resulted from an important non-legal initiative which aimed to help change attitudes in the South. Expansion of the railway network was promoted as a way of ending the isolation and therefore poverty (and, by unspoken extension, ignorance) which was felt to breed racism. The mileage in the southern states more than doubled between 1870 and 1890. In that year, the Louisiana legislature passed the Separate Car Act, which mandated "equal but separate" accommodation for whites and blacks on the state's railroads.[106] Railway companies either had to provide separate coaches for the two races or, if it was a one-carriage train, erect a partition in that carriage.

A group of concerned citizens, of both races, got together

[106] It could do this only for intra-state travel as inter-state travel was a federal matter, under the commerce clause in the Constitution, and segregation was not permitted. Louisiana was not the first state to take action; only the first whose action was challenged in court.

and hired a lawyer called Albion Tourgée to try to resist this measure. Tourgée was a northerner who had been wounded twice in the Civil War, after which he had moved to North Carolina, where he became a judge and was viciously persecuted by the Ku Klux Klan. The group also enlisted an octoroon, as such people were then known—a person who was one-eighth black and seven-eights white—called Homer Adolph Plessy, who was to make the formal challenge to the law. In June 1892 Plessy, who could pass as white, boarded a local train in New Orleans and took a seat in one of the newly-segregated white compartments. When asked to move to the coloured carriage, he refused and was arrested and jailed. The Louisiana court found against Plessy. The Judge had been John Howard Ferguson, who therefore became the defendant when, four years later, Plessy's appeal finally came before the Supreme Court.[107]

Plessy's team had two main arguments. The first was based on the Thirteenth Amendment to the Constitution, which said: "Neither slavery nor involuntary servitude, except as a punishment for crime whereof the party shall have been duly convicted, shall exist within the United States, or any place subject to their jurisdiction." This was irrelevant since there was no link between slavery and the status of octoroons in "white" Louisiana railroad carriages. The opinion of the Supreme Court was delivered by Mr Justice Brown, who said it "too clear for argument" that this law was directed to quite a different set of circumstances from that disclosed by the facts of Homer Plessy's case.

Henry Brown was a mild-mannered, centrist judge who was considered fair-minded, conscientoius and competent. He came from a well-off New England family and had been educated at both Harvard and Yale, though he never acquired a law degree. Unlike Albion Tourgée, he had hired a substitute to perform his military service in the Civil War.

Brown paid much more attention to the second limb of Plessy's argument, which was founded solidly on the Fourteenth

---

[107] *Plessy v Ferguson* (1896) 163 US 537

Amendment. Though much longer than the Thirteenth, the relevant part laid down that: "No State shall make or enforce any law which shall abridge the privileges or immunities of citizens of the United States; nor shall any State deprive any person of life, liberty, or property, without due process of law; nor deny to any person within its jurisdiction the equal protection of the laws."

This was much more to the point: did the separate but equal doctrine, as applied to railway transport, "abridge the privileges or immunities" of Homer Plessy and deny him "equal protection of the laws"? Brown's reasoning on this part of the plaintiff's argument is as interesting as Taney's in *Scott*'s case, and deserves to be quoted at sufficient length to be fairly understood:

> The object of the [Fourteenth] Amendment was undoubtedly to enforce the absolute equality of the two races before the law, but in the nature of things it could not have been intended to abolish distinctions based upon colour, or to enforce social, as distinguished from political, equality, or a commingling of the two races on terms unsatisfactory to either…
>
> Laws forbidding the intermarriage of the two races may be said in a techical sense to interfere with the freedom of contract, and yet have been universally recognised as within the police power of the state.[108]
>
> We think the enforced separation of the races, as applied to the internal commerce of the state, neither abridges the privileges or immunities of the coloured man, deprives him of his property

---

[108] In 1883, the Supreme Court, in *Pace v Alabama* (106 US 583), upheld laws passed by that state punishing interracial marriage on the ground that the Constitution outlawed only race *discrimination*. Prohibitions of mixed marriages could not be discriminatory because "the same punishment [applies] to both offenders, the white and the black. Indeed, the offence cannot be committed without involving persons of both races." The last of the states to abolish prohibitions on inter-racial marriage was Virginia, Jefferson's home state, whose law was declared unconstitutional by the Supreme Court as late as 1967, in *Loving v Virginia* (388 US 1).

without due process of law, nor denies him equal protection of the laws... It is claimed by the plaintiff in error that, in any mixed community, the reputation of belonging to the dominant race, in this instance the white race, is property, in the same sense that a right of action, or of inheritance, is property. Conceding this to be so, for the purpse of this case, we are unable to see how this statue deprives him of, or in any way affects his right to, such property. If he be a white man and assigned to a coloured coach, he may bring an action for being deprived of his so-called property. Upon the other hand, if he be a coloured man and be so assigned, he has been deprived of no proporty, since he is not lawfully entitled to the reptuation of being a white man.

In this connection it is also suggested by the learned counsel for the plaintiff in error that the same argument that will justify the state legislature in requiring railways to provide separate accommodation for the two races will also authorise them to require separate cars to be provided for people whose hair is of a certain colour... or to enact laws requiring coloured people to walk on one side of the street, and white people upon the other, or requiring white men's houses to be painted white, and coloured men's black, or their vehicles or business signs to be of different colours, upon the theory that one side of the street is as good as the other, or that a house or vehicle of one colour is as good as another. The reply to all this is that every exercise of the police power must be reasonable, and extend only to such laws as are enacted in good faith for the promotion of the public good, and not for the annoyance or oppression of a particular class....[109]

So far, then, as a conflict with the Fourteenth Amendment is concerned, the case reduces itself to the question whether the statute of Louisiana is a reasonable regulation, and with respect to

---

[109] Note that this was pure custom. There is no law in the United States which defines the "police power", much less circumscribes it in the way Brown described. His reasoning here is of the same sort as Lord Young's in the Pet Lamb case.

this there must necessarily be a large discretion on the part of the legislature.[110] In determining the question of reasonableness, it is at liberty to act with reference to the established usages, customs, and traditions of the people, and with a view to the promotion of their comfort, and the preservation of peace and good order. Gauged by this standard, we cannot say that a law which authorises or even requires the separation of the two races in public conveyances is unreasonable…

We consider the underlying fallacy of the plaintiff's argument to consist in the assumption that the enforced separation of the two races stamps the coloured race with a badge of inferiority. If this be so, it is not by reason of anything found in the Act, but solely because the coloured race chooses to put that construction upon it. The argument also assumes that social prejudices may be overcome by legislation, and that equal rights cannot be secured to the Negro except by an enforced commingling of the two races. We cannot accept this proposition. If the two races are to meet on terms of social equality, it must be the result of natural affinities, a mutual appreciation of each other's merits and the voluntary consent of individuals… If the civil and political rights of both races be equal, one cannot be inferior to the other civilly or politically. If one race be inferior to the other socially, the Constitution of the United States cannot put them upon the same plane.

Seven Justices concurred with Brown, but one did not. Mr Justice Harlan's dissenting Opinion has been repeatedly quoted since then as one of the great statement of anti-segregationist jurisprudence. It, too, is worth examining to show how carefully crafted words, clearly written legal texts and conscientious judicial reasoning do not necessarily produce an agreed statement

---

[110] This concept of discretion is mirrored in the European Court of Human Rights today when it allows a "margin of appreciation" to individual states in applying the terms of the Convention on Human Rights. This is a political concession to the variety of approaches to law found across the continent.

of what the law is.

John Marshall Harlan was born the son of a lawyer in Kentucky. He attended Transylvania University (in Lexington, Kentucky) and fought for the Union in the Civil War. Despite this, he was a slave-owner himself, and opposed both Abraham Lincoln and the three anti-racist Amendments to the Constitution which were relevant to *Plessy v Ferguson*. Unlike Taney, Harlan did not get rid of his slaves voluntarily, but only when forced to do so by the Thirteenth Amendment. But, also unlike Taney, he believed that his job as a judge was to follow his conscience as well as the law, both of which had evolved between the Civil War and the time he was elevated to the Supreme Court, in 1877.

In the Continental systems of law, judges are professional civil servants and are expected to amass qualifications for judging like any other bureaucrat. In the common law world, the emphasis is more on character and experience of the law as a pleader (though this is changing in Britain). The American Supreme Court is the most extreme example of this, where many of the Justices, including some of the most distinguished, have arrived on the Bench with little or no previous judicial experience. William O. Douglas came from the Securities and Exchange Commission, and Earl Warren, one of the greatest Chief Justices, as will be seen below, came from being Governor of California. Harlan was of the same sort. Though he was a very experienced lawyer, he had sat only for a single year as a county judge in Frankfort, Kentucky, in the 1850s. It is only under such an "amateurish" system that a former slave-owner would be likely find himself in a position to support a black man against the segregationists.

Harlan tried to answer Brown's argument. After describing the legislation which the Court was being called upon to uphold or overrule, the Justice drew attention to the lack of exceptions allowed by the Louisiana law:

> Only "nurses attending children of the other race" are excepted
> from the operation of the statute. No exception is made for
> coloured attendants travelling with adults.... If a coloured maid

insists on riding in the same coach with a white woman whom she has been employed to serve, and who might need her personal attention while travelling, she is subject to be fined or imprisoned for such an exhibition of zeal in the discharge of her duty...

Thus the state regulates the use of a public highway by the citizens of the United States solely on the basis of race. However apparent the injustice of such legislation may be, we have only to consider whether it is consistent with the Constitution of the United States...

In respect of civil rights, common to all citizens, the Constitution of the United States does not, I think, permit any public authority to know the race of those entitled to be protected in the enjoyment of such rights... Such legislation as that here in question is inconsistent, not only with that equality of rights which pertains to citizenship, but with the personal liberty enjoyed by everyone within the United States...

It was said in argument that the statute of Louisiana does not discriminate against either race, but prescribes a rule applicable alike to white and coloured citizens. But this argument does not meet the difficulty. Everyone knows that the statute in question had its origin in the purpose, not so much to exclude white persons from railroad cars occupied by blacks, as to exclude coloured persons from coaches occupied by or assigned to white persons... The fundamental objection, therefore, to the statute, is that it interferes with the personal liberty of citizens...

The white race deems itself to be the dominant one in this country. And so it is, in prestige, in achievements, in education, in wealth, and in power. So I doubt not that it will continue to be so for all time, if it remains true to its great heritage and holds fast to the principles of constitutional liberty. But in the view of the Constitution, in the eye of the law, there is in this country no superior, dominant, ruling class of citizens. There is no caste here. Our Constitution is colour-blind, and neither knows nor tolerates classes amongst citizens. In respect of civil rights, all citizens are equal before the law. The humblest is the peer of the most powerful. The law regards man as man, and takes no account of his surroundings or his colour when his civil rights as guaranteed by the supreme law of the land are involved. It is therefore to be regretted that this high tribunal, the final expositor of the fundamental law of the land, has reached the conclusion that it is competent for a state to regulate the enjoyment by citizens of their civil rights solely upon the basis of their race.

In my opinion, the judgement this day rendered will, in time, prove to be quite as pernicious as the decision made by this tribunal in the *Dred Scott* case. It was adjudged in that case that the descendents of Africans who were imported into this country and sold as slaves were not included, nor were intended to be included, under the word "citizen" in the Constitution... The recent amendments of the Constitution, it is supposed, had eradicated these principles from our institutions. But it seems that we have yet, in some of the states, a dominant race, a superior class of citizens, which assumes to regulate the enjoyment of civil rights, common to all citizens, upon the basis of race...

The destinies of the two races in this country are indissolubly linked together, and the interests of both require that the common government of all shall not permit the seeds of race hate to be planted under the sanction of law. What can more certainly arouse race hate, what more certainly create and perpetuate a feeling of distrust between these races, than state enactments which in fact proceed on the ground that coloured citizens are so inferior and degraded that they cannot be allowed to sit in public coaches occupied by white citizens? That, as all will admit, is the real meaning of such legislation as was enacted in Louisiana....

The question cannot be met by the suggestion that social equality cannot exist between white and the black races in this country. That argument, if it can properly be regarded as one, is scarcely worthy of consideration, for social equality no more exists between two races when travelling in a passenger coach on or a public highway than when member of the same races sit side by each other in a street car or a jury box...

There is a race so different from our own that we do not permit those belonging to it to become citizens of the United States. I allude to the Chinese race. But by the statue in question a Chinaman can ride in the same passenger coach with white citizens of the United States, while citizens of the black race in Louisiana, many of whom, risked their lives for the preservation of the Union, who are entitled by law to participate in political control of the state and nation, who are not excluded, by law or by reason of their race, from public stations of any kind, and who have all the legal rights that belong to white citizens, are yet declared to be criminals, liable to imprisonment, if they ride in a public coach occupied by citizens of the white race...

The result of the whole matter is that while this court has frequently adjudged that a state cannot, consistently with the Constitution of the United States, prevent white and black citizens, having the required qualifications for jury service, from sitting in the same jury box, but it is now solemnly held that a state may prohibit white and black citizens from sitting in the same passenger coach on a public highway, or may require that it be separated by a "partition" when in the same passenger coach. May it not now be reasonably expected that astute men of the dominant race, who affect to be disturbed by the possibility that the integrity of the white race may be corrupted, or that its supremacy will be imperilled, by contact on public highways with black people, will endeavour to procure statutes requiring white and black jurors to be separated in the jury box by a "partition", and that, upon retiring from the court room to consult upon their verdict, such a partition, if it be a movable one, shall be taken to their consultation room and set up in such way as to prevent black jurors from coming too close to their brother jurors of the white race. If the "partition" used in court happens to be stationary, provision could be made for screens with openings through which jurors of the two races could confer as to their verdict without coming into personal contact with each other. I cannot see but that, according to the principles this day announced, such state legislation, although conceived in hostility to, and enacted for the purpose of humiliating, citizens of the United States of a particular race, would be held to be consistent with the Constitution...

I am of the opinion that the statute of Louisiana in inconsistent with the personal liberty of citizens, white and black, in that state, and is hostile to both the spirit and the letter of the Constitution of the United States.

It might almost be said that, just as it took the Civil War to overturn *Dred Scott*, it took the Second World War to overturn *Plessy v Ferguson*. When the Untied States took up arms against Nazism, one of whose most arrogantly flaunted features was racism, the descendents of Homer Plessy were still confined to non-white carriages on the Louisiana railroads.

In the forty-five years between *Plessy* and Pearl Harbor, blacks had not made a great deal of progress in the assertion of the civil rights which were theoretically guaranteed by the words of the post-Civil War amendments to the Constitution. The little headway they had made was mainly a response to the stress of the battlefield. Over 350,000 black Americans served in US forces in the First World War, though most did so in non-combat units. When the Draft was introduced in May 1918, blacks were included, though in both training and service they were segregated from whites to avoid race riots. But the few that saw front-line service—notably the 369th Infantry Regiment, or "Harlem Hellfighters"—fought with distinction. Not only that, all who served in France brought back to America memories of life in a country without segregation. The French government had been so impressed by the Harlem Hellfighters' battlefield prowess that it awarded the whole regiment the *Croix de Guerre*. Despite this, the US government prohibited it from participating in the Bastille Day victory celebration held in Paris.

Nonetheless, the War had emboldened many blacks, which gave strength to the National Association for the Advancement of

Coloured People (NAACP), which campaigned tirelessly in the courts to try to win legal recognition for the civil rights which were theoretically enjoyed by "the people" of the United States. Founded in 1909, the NAACP mounted its first national campaign in 1918—against lynching. The mere statement of this fact speaks volumes for the reality of life in segregationist America.[111] In 1935, it fought for the right of the first black student to enter the University of Maryland, one Thurgood Marshall, later to be the first black judge on the Supreme Court.

But for all the campaigning and legal activism of the NAACP, when America found itself at war with Nazi Germany, the situation of non-whites in the armed forces had not improved. Segregation was still the policy of the US Army. The Navy employed blacks only in the Stewards Branch. The munitions industry regularly discriminated against blacks in terms of employment. One prominent civil rights leader, Philip Randolph, when asked to drop his activism and support the war effort, said, "Rather than volunteer to make the world safe for democracy, I am going to fight to make Georgia safe for the Negro."

A million black Americans served in the armed forces during the Second World War, at first largely in non-combat roles. But in 1942 the first black captain took command of an

---

[111] As part of this campaign, the NAACP proposed an anti-lynching law, which aimed to hold States to account when their failure to curb mob violence had deprived the victims of "equal protection of the laws", as the Fourteenth Amendment mandates. The draft law included the following revealing section: "That any county in which a person is put to death by a mob or riotous assemblage shall, if it is alleged and proven that the officers of the State charged with the duty of prosecuting criminally such offence under the laws of the State have failed, neglected, or refused to proceed with due diligence to apprehend and prosecute the participants in the mob or riotous assemblage, forfeit $10,000, which sum may be recovered by an action therefore in the name of the United States against any such county for the use of the family, if any, of the person so put to death." Between 1882 and 1968 there were 4,782 documented lynchings, the majority of the victims being black. In 2005, the US Senate formally apologised to the victims and their families for never having passed an anti-lynching law.

American merchant ship. In 1944, the US Navy commissioned its first black officers. In November that year, with his armies bogged down in Normandy, General George Patton made his famous appeal to the "Black Panther" Tank Battalion, the first non-white armoured unit to go into battle:

> Men, you are the first Negro tankers ever to fight in the American Army. I would never have asked for you if you were not good. I have nothing but the best in my army. I don't care what colour you are as long as you go up there and kill those Kraut sons-of-bitches.

Two months later, the unit was nominated for a Presidential Unit Citation. The honour was withheld, despite five further nominations, until 1978.

America had gone to war to fight, amongst other things, racism in Europe. After a victory achieved at such cost, it became harder to tolerate it at home. In 1948 President Truman signed Executive Orders which banned segregation in both the Armed Forces and civilian Federal employment. American diplomacy became explicitly anti-racist, especially as it now revolved around international institutions, like the United Nations, which were not segregated. Despite this, life within the southern states went on much as before. *Plessy v Ferguson* was still binding. However, the days of "separate but equal" were numbered: Thurgood Marshall was on the case, literally.

Amongst the many causes which the NAACP took up in the early 1950s was that of a young coloured girl called Linda Brown in Topeka, Kansas. She had to be bussed to the nearest black school, which was some distance from her home, even though there was a whites-only school within easy walking distance. The NAACP went to court to argue that she should be allowed to go to the nearby white school. It argued that segregated schools for blacks were inherently unequal, and therefore in violation of the Fourteenth Amendment. The Board of Education in Kansas was the defendant. It argued for the *status quo*, principally on the ground that life everywhere in the state involved segregation and thus segregated schools were an appropriate preparation for adulthood. The US District Court felt itself bound by *Plessy v*

*Ferguson* and therefore found against Oliver Brown, Linda's father and the plaintiff of record. Taking this case together with a couple of other similar ones from other states, the NAACP went all the way to the Supreme Court, finally getting a hearing in 1953.

By then, the Chief Justice was Earl Warren, a genial ex-Attorney General and Governor of California who had been responsible for implementing the arguably racially-motivated internment of all citizens of Japanese descent living on the western seaboard after Pearl Harbour, irrespective of their loyalty or usefulness to the United States.[112] Without any previous judicial experience, Warren had been appointed to the Supreme Court by the new Republican President, Dwight Eisenhower, who hoped he would hold the line against the Democrat demands for full racial integration, which he did not believe in. At least, he did not want to have to brave the inevitable backlash in the South if it were forced upon reluctant States by the Federal government. According to one author, Eisenhower took Warren aside after a dinner at the White House, while *Brown* was under consideration, and said to him about the Southerners: "These are not bad people. All they are concerned about is that their sweet little girls are not required to sit in school alongside some big, overgrown Negroes."[113]

Warren was deaf to such pleas, which were in any case highly improper given that the case was *sub judice*. Like Marshall Harlan, he was his own man, and prepared to change his mind on the subject of race. By the time *Brown's* case came to Court, he not only thought that "separate but equal" was a violation of the Fourteenth Amendment, but was political enough to realise that a unanimous decision on the matter would be necessary if Eisenhower's fears about Southern resistance were

---

[112] Over 100,000 people were involved, two-thirds of them American citizens. It was not until 1988 that President Reagan signed a formal apology for this act of gross prejudice, the legality of which had been upheld by the Supreme Court in several cases in 1943 and 1944.

[113] *Storm Centre* Daniel O'Brien, New York 1986, p. 87

not to be realised (anticipating Burger's concerns in *Nixon* twenty years later). He was determined to present a united front to the segregationists but, at the same time, to be as unprovocative as he could.

The leader of the legal team which argued for the NAACP against the Kansas Board of Education was Thurgood Marshall. In his brief, he wrote, "Separate but equal is a legal fiction. There never was, and never will be, any separate equality." Marshall had experienced the realities of segregation under law, not just when he fought for the right to be admitted to university, but in the years he traversed the South fighting cases for NAACP on behalf of blacks whose separate status from whites was more obvious than the equality that was supposed to go with it. In later life, Marshall often told the story of an experience he had in a small town in Mississippi in the early 1940s:

> I was waiting for the train to take me to Shreveport. I got hungry and I saw a restaurant, so I decided I would put my civil rights in my back pocket and go to the back door of the kitchen and see if I could buy a sandwich. While I was kibitzing myself to do that, this white man came up beside me in plain clothes with a great big pistol on his hip. He said, "Nigger boy, what are you doing here?" I said, "Well, I'm waiting for the train to Shreveport." And he said, "There's only one more train that comes through here, and that's the 4 o'clock, and you'd better be on it because the sun is never going down on a live nigger in this town." I wasn't hungry anymore.

In a unanimous Opinion perhaps a tenth of the length of Taney's in *Dred Scott*, and less than a quarter of Brown's in *Plessy*, and which was deliberately phrased in dull, uninflammatory language, Earl Warren destroyed the constitutional basis of racial segregation in the United States by producing a third interpretation of the phrases "all men" and "we, the people".[114]

After saying that the Court could not learn anything from the

[114] *Brown v Board of Education of Topeka* (1954) 387 US 483

circumstances in which the Fourteenth Amendment was passed, Justice Warren said on behalf of the whole Court—there was not a single dissent, even though one of the Justices, Hugo Black, had been a member of the Ku Klux Klan in his native Alabama in the 1920s—that the circumstances surrounding public education were so different in the 1860s from the 1950s that no inference could be drawn as to the supposed intent of the framers of the Amendment in this respect. This was especially so as regards the South:

> The movement towards free common schools, supported by general taxation, had not taken place. Education of white children was largely in the hands of private groups. Education of Negroes was almost nonexistent, and practically all of the race were illiterate. In fact, any education of Negroes was forbidden by law in some states... Even in the North, the conditions of public education was usually rudimentary; ungraded schools were common in rural areas; the school term was but three months a year in many states; and compulsory school attendance was virtually unknown. As a consequence, it is not surprising that there should be so little in the history of the Fourteenth Amendment relating to its intended effect on public education...
>
> Today, education is perhaps the most important function of state and local governments... In these days it is doubtful that any child may reasonably be expected to succeed in life if he is denied the opportunity of an education. Such an opportunity, where the state has undertaken to provide it, is a right which must be made available to all on equal terms.
>
> We come to the question presented: does segregation of children in public schools solely on the basis of race, even though the physical and other "tangible" factors may be equal, deprive the children of the minority group of equal educational opportunities? We believe that it does...
>
> To separate children from others of similar age and qualifications solely because of their race generates a feeling of

inferiority as to their status in the community that may affect their hearts and minds in a way unlikely ever to be undone...

Whatever may have been the extent of the psychological knowledge at the time of *Plessy v Ferguson*, this finding is amply supported by modern authority. Any language in *Plessy v Ferguson* contrary to this finding is rejected.

We conclude that in the field of public education the doctrine of "separate but equal" has no place. Separate educational facilities are inherently unequal. Therefore, we hold that the plaintiffs and others similarly situated for whom these actions have been brought are, by reason of the segregation complained of, deprived of equal protection of the laws guaranteed by the Fourteenth Amendment.

That was all. The great deed was done. The practice of nearly two centuries was no longer lawful. Blacks really had to be treated the same as everyone else.

Though this decision concerned education only, it was soon followed by others which made racial equality the general rule. Despite this, it took another two decades to defeat the resistance of the Southern racists, which was often violent. Many critics say that attitudes have not changed in line with the law. But the law does not deal in attitudes, except under Soviet-style regimes. The courts control people's actions, not their thoughts. After *Brown*, the writing was on the blackboard, so to speak, for racial exclusivity in any form.

There are two important comments to make about this decision. First, it was wholly illogical, indeed so illogical that, on almost any other issue, the NAACP argument would most likely have failed. To argue that separate facilities cannot be equal facilities, *per se*, is absurd. Are male public lavatories inherently unequal to female ones because they are separate? Are Jews, as a religious group, rendered inferior to Buddhists, say, or Rastafarians because they worship separately? Is Canada "inherently unequal" to the United States, or the other way round, *because* the two countries are separate? Of course not. The argument is ludicrous. And it was the only argument put in *Brown*. Yet, in that context, it was undoubtedly right. The reason it was right goes to the heart of what courts are and what judges do.

The fact is that segregation, as practiced in the United States in the century following the Civil War, was a device to maintain white supremacy and black inferiority, whatever words were used in the laws. The Warren Court went behind the words to the realities of the situation in a way that only a human being unfettered by bureaucracy and the need for consistent interpretation of words on pieces of paper. No "computer" judge, or publicly accountable Bench, could ever have produced this world-changing judgement.

The judges were criticised at the time for referring to psychological factors about which they had no professional knowledge, and about which, more importantly, the Constitution was silent. It has been pointed out that Linda Brown lived in a mixed neighbourhood; that her school was, as she herself has subsequently emphasised, at least as good as the white school closer to her home. It was also true that only the junior schools in Topeka were segregated; all the higher ones were already integrated. But none of this mattered. A principle was at stake, just as there had been in 1857 and 1896. But that principle was not a legal one, it was a moral one. It went beyond the letter of any law, just as Lord Young had done in the Pet Lamb case. Only free, tenured judges could have arrived at such a decision. An "accountable" Bench in 1953 would have been most unlikely to have been allowed to deliver a judgement so politically explosive.

The best successful judges know when to rely less on law and more on their own convictions and conscience. They therefore achieve broad public acceptance for decisions which stand for generations, as *Brown* has done. The least successful judges are those, like Mr Justice Taney, who sublimate their own personal feelings and convictions to what they see as the indefeasible logic of the law, and achieve results which, in his case, brought misery to millions and death to hundreds of thousands—and which did not last a decade. Law should be a tool of the judge, rather than the judge being a tool of the law. That is why the character of judges is *the* central issue in any successful legal system. That, in turn, is why the only guide to the law is not what is written in statute or case law, but the words spoken by any individual judge on any given day.

The second point about the *Brown* judgement is one which was made by Thurgood Marshall when he spoke to a group of lawyers on the 200th anniversary of the ratification of the American Constitution.[115] He explicitly rejected Mr Justice Taney's view of the law as deriving from the original intent of the Framers.

> I do not believe that the meaning of the Constitution was forever fixed at the Philadelphia Convention. Nor do I find the wisdom, foresight and sense of justice exhibited by the Framers particularly profound. To the contrary, the government they devised was defective from the start, requiring several amendments, a civil war, and momentous social transformation to attain the system of constitutional government, and its respect for individual freedoms and human rights, we hold as fundamental today. When contemporary Americans cite "the Constitution", they invoke a concept that is vastly different from what the Framers barely began to construct two centuries ago.
>
> For a sense of the evolving nature of the Constitution, we need to look no further than the first three words of the document's preamble: "We, the people." When the Founding Fathers used this phrase in 1787, they did not have in mind the majority of America's citizens. On a matter so basic as the right to vote, for example, Negro slaves were excluded. Women did not gain the right to vote for over a hundred and thirty years...
>
> What is striking is the role legal principles have played throughout America's history in determining the condition of

---

[115] Remarks at the Annual Seminar of the San Francisco Patent and Trademark Law Association, in Maul, Hawaii, on 6 May 1987

Negroes. They were enslaved by law, emancipated by law, disenfranchised and segregated by law; and finally they have begun to win equality by law. Along the way new constitutional principles have emerged to meet the challenges of a changing society. The progress has been dramatic. And it will continue...

The true miracle was not the birth of the Constitution, but its life, a life nurtured through two turbulent centuries of our own making... For many Americans, the bicentennial celebration will be little more than a blind pilgrimage to the shrine of the original document now stored in a vault in the National Archives... I plan to celebrate the bicentennial of the Constitution as a living document.

The aim of law is to promote the stability of societies by reconciling conflicts of interest, opinion and desire in a way which enables life to evolve without violence. No law, not even a fundamental law like the American Constitution, must be accorded the status of holy writ, and adhered to rigidly.

Law has to seem to be fixed and impersonal, while in fact being just the opposite. The person who maintains this delicate balance is the judge. As the example of the race cases shows, even in the greatest example in world history of document-based legal organisation, the United States Constitution, which aimed from the outset to secure "a government of laws not men", it is *the people who operate* it that are the most important factor. Hamilton's Rule still holds: show me the judge and I'll tell you the law.

8

# The Future of Judging

If the character of individual judges is the most fundamental factor in a fully independent legal system develops, the most important determinant of the character of the judiciary as a body is how judges are selected. Appointments procedure is controversial world-wide, as most jurisdictions grapple with the problem of reconciling judicial independence with democratic accountability. It is a subject with a vast literature, but it is mostly about principle, rather than personality; analysis rather than anecdote. To start with an anecdote: the story of one of the more controversial episodes in US Supreme Court selection will set Scottish practice in one form of context.

When Lewis Powell retired from the Supreme Court in 1987, Ronald Reagan was President, and the Republican-controlled Justice Department wanted to appoint a conservative to replace him. They nominated Robert Bork, the hastily-recruited Solicitor General who, in October 1973, had carried out the notorious Saturday Massacre mentioned in Chapter 1. Bork had a high reputation as a legal theorist, and had been a successful judge in the Federal Court of Appeals. Predictably for a Nixon supporter, he was a "constructionist", otherwise known as an advocate of Constitutional "originalism" of the sort favoured by Justices Taney and Brown, as opposed to the "judicial activism" of Earl Warren when overturning Brown. While no-one in the 1980s wanted to reverse *Brown v Board of Education*, many felt that the process of taking pragmatic decisions in the Supreme Court had gone too far over the previous thirty years, and ought to be reversed. These were not the only two possibilities. A policy of simple judicial restraint, under which judges would be less ready to look behind the law for the moral issues involved, but would not avoid doing so on a point of principle, would have been equally legitimate, and less controversial. But the increasingly polarised atmosphere created by the opponents of "gay" rights, abortion, religious tolerance and other contentious issues of the time militated against that. The result was the battle about the appointment of Robert Bork.

The lobbying groups opposed to Regan's nominee spent an estimated $20 million on their campaign, even going to the length of publishing a list of the videos which Bork had rented (though without uncovering anything much more controversial than *A Day at the Races*). They left the *Oxford English Dictionary* with the new word "to bork", meaning to use character assassination as a way of preventing a person from attaining important public office. But the candidate contributed to his own downfall. Under questioning in the Senate, Bork proved to be a charmless and unnecessarily aggressive proponent of what were, despite everything, legitimate views. His manner suggested that to be a Constitutional "originalist" meant to be right-wing, rigid and curmudgeonly, which was not necessarily the case, since the Constitution is in many ways a very liberal document. The result was that when Bork was eventually forced to withdraw his nomination some commentators argued that, for all its excesses, the process of public examination of the record and character of Supreme Court judges had once again proved its worth.

There have been other battles of nearly comparable ferocity in America, like the one against the slightly corrupt violin enthusiast, Abe "Fiddlin'" Fortas, in 1968, which left the way open for Warren Burger to become Chief Justice when Earl Warren retired. The public lapped up the details of these controversies, and though there may have been an undignified, occasionally salacious element to them, the amount of publicity they generated ensured that the people at large were informed about the figures who were going to sit on the highest court in their land.

This has not been the British approach. Judges were creatures of the Crown, and their appointment was considered behind closed doors. In Scotland, it was the Lord Advocate, the senior officer of the Crown in the country, who made the choices. Though he did so only after consultation with legal colleagues and senior political figures, he—the first female Lord Advocate was appointed in 2006, after the system had changed—hardly ever attracted criticism for the quality of the appointments.[116] The perceived problems mainly sprang from procedural opacity, though what to one observer was sinisterly "secretive" could seem merely "discrete" to another. But in the 1990s, government style—arguably the substance never changes—favoured the appearance of openness. So when, following devolution, a Scottish Labour administration took office in Edinburgh, few were surprised when it decided to disempower the Lord Advocate and replace him with what is now known as the Judicial Appointments Board. The stated aim was to increase "transparency", in other words to inform the public more about the appointment process. The method has been to select judges by a committee, appointed by the First Minister, which is composed of equal numbers of professional and "lay" members, with one of the latter always in the chair.

---

[116] Though the biggest failure in the twentieth century was Lord Gibson, the best-publicised controversy was the so-called "gay judges" affair in 1992. However, that turned out in the end to be little more than a sordid compost of unfounded press allegations based on a single fact, namely that one Session judge had homosexual proclivities. There was no serious suspicion, and certainly no proof, that he either brought his views into court, or laid himself open to pressure while concealing them. As soon as the allegations were made public the judge in question resigned, and the controversy evaporated. See *Report on an Inquiry into an Allegation of Conspiracy to Pervert the Course of Justice in Scotland*, by WA Nimmo Smith QC and JD Friel (HMSO, House of Commons, 26 January 1993). The problem with aberrant Lords President, like Clyde, is completely different and will be discussed below. There the Lord Advocate had no involvement, ironically until the system was changed, and supposedly de-politicised in 2002 (as will also be discussed below).

Lord Murray, whom I quoted at length in Chapter 4 on the subject of the legality or otherwise of British the nuclear deterrent (and whose uncle made way for Lord Gibson on the Land Court in 1941), not only served as a judge, but, as Lord Advocate before that, had been responsible for appointing no less than ten judges, including two to the House of Lords. He told me how the system worked before the recent changes.

"The actual mechanism was very strict," he said. "The Lord Advocate would nominate somebody, having previously consulted with the Lord President and probably the Lord Justice Clerk, the two senior judges. I certainly consulted Lord Emslie and Lord Wheatley, as well as the Dean of the Faculty of Advocates, and also the President of the Law Society of Scotland, who represented the solicitors. Thinking of my first appointment, there were only about three people who were ripe for judicial promotion and it was a question of who. I consulted in the normal way and said these are the three I have in mind: they are all excellent, and there's another who has recently had a difficult divorce proceeding so he can come later. At the end of the day, two of them were preferred and I said there's nothing between the two of them, but on the whole I prefer A to B. So I put him to the Secretary of State. I cannot remember exactly now, but he might have phoned me up and said I've been thinking of somebody else, so I'd've given the reasons why that person had not been thought particularly appropriate, and then the nomination would go forward to the Queen and that chap would become a judge. It certainly wasn't a public process, but neither was it one open to personal favouritism because there were too many people involved."

"Do you think it is important to have a lay influence on the appointments?" I asked.

"I think as a matter of form it is probably desirable nowadays to have lay representation. But I think the main problem with the old system was quite different. It was that the sitting Lord Advocate very often appointed himself, if he intended leaving politics at around the time a vacancy on the Bench came up. I did that myself. Some time before the 1979 general election, I had decided not to stand for Parliament again—I had been MP for Leith for nine years—and, by chance, one of the judges died six weeks before the election. I went to see the Prime Minister, Jim Callaghan, and said this is the convention, and he said if the Secretary of State agrees—that was Bruce Millan, Labour—then I will. We lost the election, but nonetheless the incoming, Conservative, Secretary of State agreed to my appointment."[117]

"The main criticism has been that appointments were on an old-school-tie sort of system. Did that happen in your day?"

"No, but that was partly because we were Labour! There had been a tendency for a long time for the Conservatives to be the party of law. The first important break-through was Lord Wheatley, who was made Solicitor-General by the incoming Labour government in 1945, and later raised to the Bench. But that was the unusual. Otherwise in the immediate post-war period it was all Conservative. Then the rot, as they would see it, had begun to set in before the War. The Bar became more democratic when a lot of Catholics started coming in from Glasgow, people who wouldn't normally have gone to the Bar previously."

"Why not?"

"Because they were Catholic."

"But they weren't barred because of being Catholic?"

"No they weren't barred, they just never thought of it, and didn't feel they had the backing of the main law firms in

---

[117] After the 2007 General Election in Scotland, the incoming Scottish National Party government decided that the Lord Advocate should no longer sit in the Scottish Cabinet. There had been much criticism under the previous Labour government of the practice, on the ground that it blurred the separation of powers as between the executive and the judiciary—even though the Lord Advocate was not a judge and no longer had any role in selecting judges. In Lord Murray's day, before devolution, the thinking was clearer: the Lord Advocate had to be a Member of Parliament in order that he could be questioned openly in the House of Commons and so be democratically accountable. Now, accountability for the Crown Office is achieved only indirectly, through the Justice Minister.

Scotland, particularly Glasgow where a lot of big Protestant ones were. But Glasgow's economic importance had declined, also an increasing proportion of the working population was Catholic. They were getting better educated, so it was a natural thing to have a flow of Catholics, first as solicitors and then as advocates taking cases on instruction from their Catholic solicitor friends. On the whole they tended to be Labour. Lord Wheatley was a good example of that."

One of the judges whom Ronald King Murray QC, as he then was, appointed told me how he "got the tap", as the saying used to go. "I remember it was a Saturday and I was having a conference with another advocate about a case and wee King Murray, who was then the Lord Advocate, turned up in his gum boots and said, 'Sorry to interrupt you. Can I have a word with you?' Then he said, 'Would you like to go on the Bench?' I said, 'I'd very much like to go on the Bench eventually, but at the moment I feel that I am in reserve as the next Lord Advocate after you.' Lord Wylie had been the Tory Lord Advocate under Heath, and was now a judge. I felt I was under an obligation to remain at the Bar for a bit in case the Tories got back in again and needed me as a Lord Advocate. King Murray said, 'Oh no, you really must think of yourself. You could wait for years.' He was right. McCluskey would have loved being Lord Advocate but he never got the opportunity because King Murray was above him. Life's like that. So I said, 'You're quite right. I'd be delighted.' That was all that happened. I went back to my conference."

There can be no question that the old system lacked transparency, and that a more open procedure for making judicial appointments was desirable. But this is not what has happened. The idea that potential judges might be subjected to the searching public interrogation which is practised in the United States was never seriously discussed when the Judicial Appointment Board's remit was under consideration. Instead, a formal committee whose members are all appointed by the government, and whose Chair has to be a non-lawyer, was to do the work formally done by the informal group consulted by the Lord Advocate. In the name of openness, the previous system, which was half-professional and half-political, has been replaced by one which is half-amateur and half-political. The loss in professionalism has not been compensated for by any gain in openness.

Not only is it still impossible for members of the public to bring pressure to bear on any judicial appointment in Scotland, it is impossible even to take an intelligent interest in the work of the Board. Both the procedure for making appointments, and the work on a case by case basis, are secret. The only information the Board publishes, other than an anodyne, corporate-style Annual Report, is the list of appointments made. Not even the applications refused are revealed. No reasons for any appointment are given, and no list of positive criteria for selection is published. The public is just as comprehensively excluded from the process of judicial appointment after the reforms as it was before. The only group to whom the new system is "open and transparent" is the power elite. The Labour administration which took office after Devolution gave Scotland, despite its long history of judicial competence and independence, a selection procedure for judges which is so bureaucrat-friendly that it bears comparison with the one introduced at about the same time in Russia by President Putin. Few informed critics considered that a step forward.[118]

---

[118] Alexei Trochev describes in his recent essay, "Judicial Selection in Russia: Towards Accountability and Centralisation", (in *Appointing Judges in the Age of Judicial Power*, eds. K. Malleson and P. Russell, Toronto 2006), how Putin has taken control of the judicial appointments process. He has introduced a system whereby appointments are made after an interview (which Trochev calls "a tough, open-book, two-hour oral exam") by a board partially nominated by the government, and half of whose members are non-lawyers (although only one is directly appointed by the President, not all of them as in Scotland). Even though political control of the appointments procedure is less rigid than in Scotland, Trochev comments: "Russia's judicial bureaucracy dominates the process of staffing courts from top to bottom." The bureaucratisation of the appointment process is intended, as in Scotland, to ensure that in long run only those candidates acceptable to the power elite will find themselves sitting on the Bench. The previous system in Scotland was political, and open to criticism on

The Scottish Judicial Appointments Board (originally Committee), which has been operating since 2002, consists of five members of the legal profession and five non-lawyers. Of the latter (at the time of writing), one, the Chairman, had been chief executive of Strathclyde Regional Council, one the personnel manageress of the Post Office in Scotland, one on the managerial staff at the University of Edinburgh, one a chartered accountant, and one a law professor. All of these people were appointed by the government of the day. None is allowed to speak publicly about the appointments they make or decline to make. None was subjected to any public scrutiny of their qualifications, whether professional or political, for the job. They are closer to being faceless individuals than any Lord Advocate ever was, as he always had to be a Member of Parliament for a Scottish constituency and answerable for his appointments to the House of Commons.

Professor Alan Paterson, Professor of Law at Strathclyde University and himself a member of the Board, has written about the aims of the new system. "Lay members," he says, were thought to "bring experience of modern recruitment and selection processes from industry, as well as business experience, performance appraisal skills, and interviewing skills."[119]

But are those the skills required to appoint judges? Can such people really take the proper measure of ambitious, young advocates earning £500,000 a year or more, who have had decades of experience in "persuading" juries composed of just such individuals as occupy the lay seats on the Board?

And why should "industry" be considered relevant to the law, anyway? It is very much a minority activity in Scotland (though admittedly important to the Labour Party electorally).

---

that ground, as the American one is. But at least political parties in government, unlike bureaucracies, change from time to time, and at all times are ultimately accountable to the electorate. No bureaucracy ever is. Our new system was said to have been designed to increase accountability. It has achieved the opposite.

[119] "The Scottish Judicial Appointment Board: New Wine in Old Bottles?" in *Appointing Judges in the Age of Judicial Power, op. cit.* p. 20.

Why are there no representatives from other areas of life, like medical research, financial management, software design, popular literature, the performing arts, sport, or even television comedy? Why should "the lady from the Post Office" as the second in my list of lay members of the Board above is popularly known, be better at selecting judges than the Chief Executive of Standard Life, say, or the person who cloned Dolly the Sheep or, for that matter, Alan Hansen, Sir Cameron Mackintosh, Sir Jackie Stewart (with his penchant for "mind management") or Billy Connolly? Perhaps even Ian Rankin could bring some new thinking to the Board's deliberations?

The main issue in wise judicial selection is the ability to assess character perceptively. There is no evidence that such high-fliers would be any worse and, intuitively, they might be thought to be potentially much better, at selecting people on a "cut of the jib" basis than the lady from the Post Office. And the selection *has* to be done on a cut of the jib basis, as one of the judges I talked to emphasised. There is simply no time to do anything else, because the selection procedure has been trivialised.

"This is a job for life," the judge said. "It is completely inappropriate to introduce commercial methods of selection for judges. If the Board of a brewery or an insurance company makes cock-up and appoints a waster to run their firm for them, they can fire him. But a judge is appointed for life. This Judicial Appointments Board is a totally and utterly superficial basis of selection. If you want to apply for a Court of Session job you simply fill in a form saying what a wonderful human being you are. The only other material that the Board gets, apart from an interview with you, is two references, given by people you, the applicant, chose. They will therefore obviously say what a tremendous fellow you are. You may not believe this, but the Board is *not allowed* to consult beyond that about possible appointments, in case any undue influence is brought to bear. This is political correctness gone mad. The old system had its problems, but this is throwing the baby out with the bath-water. Either they consult widely or they introduce, as they have in

England and Northern Ireland, a much more judge-weighted Board. We need a serious and thorough procedure.

"The people who are noticeably successful in applying for jobs are the Procurator-Fiscals, civil servants, and others who are accustomed to this system of interview for promotion. They know the score. Some of those appointed are good, don't get me wrong. But not all of them. There has been at least one disastrous Court of Session appointment by this Board. I won't say who, but if I did I think you would struggle to find anyone who disagrees with me about it. There is a risk of appointing people who are better interviewees than they are judges. That is obviously not healthy for what is, when all is said and done, one of the most important jobs in a free society."

Another judge said to me, "We have less than forty judges in the Court of Session. It should not be beyond the power of a country like Scotland to devote some serious resources to making sure the right people are appointed. If each judge serves on average just under twenty years, then we are appointing two a year. That is not a crippling workload, even for a group of part-timers. I don't want to be rude about the members of the Board individually. I am sure they try their best. But this is a matter beyond personalities. It has to be taken seriously, and that means much more experience of the real world, and time—lots of it. I know the Board also appoints sheriffs, but that is a different subject, and could well be handled separately. In any case, shrieval judgements are always subject to appeal. I am talking about the judges of last resort, who in many ways shape the law of the land. Appointing the right people is a critical matter, absolutely critical, and should be treated as such by government, not palmed off on a committee, which lacks the skills, the remit and the resources to do the job properly."

An example of the way in which the amateur status of half of the Board combines with political correctness to produce a misjudgement was given to me by a judge who had personal experience of the Board's interviewing technique.

"The lady from the Post Office asked an ultimately unsuccessful applicant how he would deal with party litigants.

Now party litigants, as every judge knows, are a pain in the arse. They are nearly always mad. They don't understand relevance, so they take up huge amounts of time talking about things that are neither here nor there. They have all suffered a terrible injustice, and that is what drives them on. We understand that, and within the limits of our powers we try to help. So the applicant replied by saying, 'I'd just let them talk until they are finished.' That disqualified him. What you are *supposed* to say is that you would assist them in the presentation of their case. That is political correctness, not professional judging, especially when you are under desperate time pressure to get through your cases as quickly as possible, pressure which comes from the same civil service that appointed these people to ask stupid questions like that. There is something depressing, almost childish, about expecting applicants to the Bench to have stock answers for hypothetical procedural questions from retired industrial relations officers when, as every real judge knows, every case and every litigant is completely different. We are dealing with *people*, not multiple-choice sociological categories. But I suppose bureaucracies can only think in categories."

Another argument against the new method of appointing judges is that it does not command the respect of the legal world, and therefore puts off some of the best potential applicants. Some find it demeaning to have to perform in front of a committee half-composed of amateurs. Others do not like the procedure, which is designed to make them feel as if they are applying for a job, rather than being asked to take a drop in salary in order to fulfil a role of profound public trust.

"Think about it like this," an elderly, retired judge said to me, after a dram or two had put him in a loquacious, almost vehement, mood one winter evening. "Malcolm MacEcks—let's call him that—is one of the brightest advocates to force his way through the system here in Parliament House in the last decade. He's nearly fifty, and has been a QC for twelve years; he's served on various Faculty committees; he knows the power structure; he is an amateur historian of Scots law; he is also a hill-walker in his spare time, and a rugby fan; he gets out and about and knows the country; he takes interesting holidays. But most important of all, though he started out prosecuting petty offenders in Dumfries, he is now earning £750,000 a year representing insurance companies, not only in front of the Court of Session in Edinburgh, but also in front of the House of Lords in London, and even, occasionally, in front of the European Court in Luxembourg. Once he went to the Human Rights Court in Strasbourg. For a fortnight every year he runs an advocacy course at a major American law school. He has an interesting life. He is beholden to nobody. He can take time off when he wants to. He's made several million quid over the years and, even after all his enormous expenses and his thumping tax bills, has probably kept at least one of those millions. He has big house at the right end of Bilston Glen. His children are off his hands, so he has enough money to last him the rest of his life, if he's not extravagant, which he is not because he spends so much of his time working. And he does that because he enjoys it.

"What does he want with life on the Bench? All the hassle, the samey routine set by some dreary civil servant who wants to make a toff's life a misery? He'll have to work with an emasculated clerking service courtesy of the penny-pinchers in the Justice Department who want to add petty irritants to the life of people whose motivation they mistrust, and whose standards of duty and conscientiousness they simply don't understand. When he is in the civil courts, he will have to work more hours per year than he has been accustomed to doing lately, or any civil servant has ever done in his entire life. In the Justiciary court, he'll sit day after day judging one sad criminal after another, and getting slyly inaccurate, uninformed, semi-defamatory articles in the tabloid press for his trouble. And he has to do all that for a miserable £160,000 a year plus pension which he doesn't need— why does he want that?

"I'll tell you why. Because he's a Scotsman, and therefore a Calvinist at heart. He feels that, having drawn teeth, financially-speaking, from the insurance world for twenty years, he wants to 'put something back into the game', as his friend Gavin Hastings might say. He has almost got a guilty conscience. Not quite, but enough for him at least to consider making the supreme sacrifice and taking a judge-ship, shackling himself to the Bench for the next and final twenty years of his career. He discusses it with his wife, who's all in favour of a quieter life. His pals think that having a Lord on the committee of the Bilston Glen Rugby Club would add another five pounds a man to the scrum. Millionaire Malky is sorely tempted. Then he hears that he has got to write all this down on a stupid form, and explain it in grovellingly respectful terms to the lady from the Post Office. Nae chance, pal. He's a free man, which is one of the reasons why he is so badly needed as a judge. What does he do? He runs a mile, and the country loses one of the best judicial appointments it could make in the next five years. No, this whole thing is a disaster."

Another retired judge said to me, "The worst of this new system is that it has all been done simply to expand the bureaucracy. The civil service has always wanted to expand. When I started in the Crown Office in the early 1960s there were about a dozen people there: the Crown Agent, the Deputy Crown Agent and an assistant, plus seven or eight extremely competent typists. Now there are 250 people at least, all highly paid. And the so-called Justice Department is also growing exponentially, with very little to show for it, except crack-pot schemes like the this Judicial Appointments Board. The old system did have its defects, but it was simpler and less time-consuming. But the civil service is like that. It is in its nature to expand and expand its empire until it is as vast, incompetent and unmanageable as the Home Office. What most of these bureaucrats do not seem to understand is that judging and committees just do not go together. If you want judicial independence, you have to treat judges as individuals, not as 'human resources'. What would they have made of old Lord Birsay, who used to wear the kilt underneath his robes at all times. What would our great new committee make of that?"

Looking more widely, one wonders what they would have made of Marshall Harlan, Earl Warren, Hugo Black, William O. Douglas and all the other mould-breakers and prediction up-setters—many with few qualifications for the job—who overturned precedent and defended the rights of people outside the mainstream?

The fact that the new approach might not be ideal was spectacularly proved in 2006 when the first appointment by committee to the very top job misfired so badly that the office was vacant for three of the first nine months of the new Lord President's tenure. The incumbent was in hospital with a nervous disorder brought on, it is generally thought and has never been denied, by the demands of the job. If a committee can appoint a person who collapses within five months, it is a serious matter. When that committee is a specially high-powered *ad hoc* one, specifically convened to deal with the highest legal appointment in the country, then it is surely legitimate to question the basis of committee selection *per se*. The only other possible explanation is that the Committee had a political agenda, which would take us back to the old and apparently discredited system. To understand this properly a brief recital of the history is necessary.

In July 2005 Lord Cullen, the Lord President, announced that he wanted to retire. He was 69, and, though he had been a good judge and had an outstanding record as a chairman of public inquiries—Piper Alpha, Dunblane, the Paddington rail crash—he had been a failure as Lord President, being considered by many of his colleagues to have been weak and ineffective. He had done nothing to assert the status of the Scottish judiciary after his ambitious predecessor, Lord Rodger, achieved his goal of getting to the House of Lords.

In conformity with the new orthodoxy, the then First Minister, Jack McConnell, convened a special committee of four to select Lord Cullen's successor. The Judicial Appointments Board was not considered competent to make this appointment, though the requirements of transparency did not extend to explaining why. Two of the members were very distinguished lawyers: Lord Hope, the ex-Lord President who is now Lord Rodger's colleague in the House of Lords; and Sir David Edward (see Chapter 5), who used to be Britain's judge on the European Court of Justice and who now sits part-time in the Court of

Session, and who is Emeritus Professor of Law in the University of Edinburgh. Naturally, the new bureaucratic orthodoxy thought this level of expertise had to be "balanced" by two members without any professional legal experience. They were the Chair of the ordinary Board and his kenspeckle colleague, the lady from the Post Office.[120]

There were five candidates—another supposedly "secret" fact which the fashion for transparency did not extend to revealing. They were Lords Hamilton, Gill, Johnston, Osborne and Hardie. Of these, the two serious contenders were Hamilton and Gill.

Of the three who were not serious contenders, Lord Johnston was the most credible applicant. He was an Inner House judge—he dies in 2008—who was highly thought of by his colleagues, though his reputation for scrupulous fairness was qualified by questions about his reasoning in law, which can sometimes be open to correction.[121] A jovial, red-faced man, Johnston came closest of all five to the caricature picture of the huntin'-shootin', New Club judge, living in the New Town and striding through the city in a Barbour jacket, which readers of Ian Rankin might recognise. In fact, he was typical of a certain sort of Scottish judge in another way: his father had been a judge, his grandfather a Minister, and his great-grandfather a baker in Aberdeen—which perhaps explained his occasional lack of patience with opportunistic logic-chopping in court. I once, myself, witnessed this when he dismissed a plainly ludicrous application by the Royal Society for the Protection of Birds that, on a goose reserve

---

[120] Apart from appointing judges, this person runs a small-holding in Lanarkshire, is a member of the Board of Careers Scotland, is on the Board of Scottish Enterprise, is on the Council of the Institute of Chartered Accountants in Scotland, is a non-executive Director of the Student Loan Company, is a member of the Fitness to Practice Panel of the General Dental Council, is a member of the governing body of Glasgow University and is an Employment Tribunal member. Serious expertise in any one field is clearly precluded by the breadth of her range of responsibilities.

[121] He died, widely lamented, in 2008. He is pictured on the front cover.

on the isle of Islay, the birds should have "absolute priority" over the farmers, who should not be allowed to take any steps to control the size of the flocks descending on their fields to eat their expensively-cultivated grass. "This is getting close to Alfred Hitchcock," his Lordship commented acidly to the flustered advocate below him.[122]

"He's known as Bluff Al, because he used to act a bit like Henry VIII at times," an ex-judge told me. "But he's got a lot of common sense, and that's important, though sometimes he tends to apply his common sense rather than the law. He presents himself like a great toff, but he is a good-hearted, decent man who is innately fair and is recognised as such. He is very popular. If it wasn't for the fact that he has to write judgements, he'd be a great judge. But as soon as he starts writing, it's stream-of-consciousness stuff. He makes John Prescott look like Sir Stafford Cripps. He can't write a postcard. But he is essentially a very decent chap. His only weakness, apart from his incapability of writing, is that he really wants to rule the world. He would, if he was appointed to do so, do it benignly, with the best interests of humanity at heart, just as does his judging."

It has been said of Lord Johnston that his happiest days were when he was Dean of the Faculty of Advocates and out in wine-bars wheeling and dealing, rather than sitting at home in the evenings waiting for the court document service to deliver its

---

[122] Though Johnston rejected the RSPB's application (2000 SLT 22), he did so, perhaps typically, on grounds which were rejected on appeal by Lord Rodger, sitting as Lord President (2000 SLT 1272). However, Rodger, in a judgement of great subtlety, concluded that though Johnston was wrong in law, he was right in effect. Ultimately, the RSPB were totally defeated. Whereas they had gone to court to prevent the shooting of 50 geese (out of an island population of 50,000, increasing at 5% per annum), it would henceforth be lawful, subject to the appropriate Ministerial advice, to shoot up to 750 in order to protect crops. Lord Rodger went straight to the heart of the opaque, vague and questionably translated European conservation Directives. By contrast, I remember seeing Lord Johnston twirling his specs round by their legs, staring at a patch of peeling paint on the ceiling of the court and saying despairingly to nobody in particular, "Who writes this stuff?"

black leather bags full of appeal cases that he would have to peruse before going into court in the morning. It is hard to know quite how seriously he viewed his own candidature for a job that calls for immensely hard work, bloody political battles and lots of patience. Maybe he thought it would involve less judging, which it ought to do if the administrative side is to be handled properly. The Court of Session needs someone to rule it, preferably one who has the best interests of humanity at heart.

Lord Osborne's application was problematical because of his age. He was admitted as an Advocate when Harold Macmillan was still Prime Minister, in the year when the United States Supreme Court ruled that photographs of male nudes were not obscene. He presumably knows who Elvis was, but he might reasonably have been thought to be prone to Lord Hope's problem, which was encapsulated by a remark he is said to have made a couple of years ago when chatting to a Scottish lawyer about his work in London. He mentioned a case he was currently taking which involved a celebrity Briton who was for many years one of the best-known models on the international circuit. "I don't know if you have ever heard of her?" he said.

Osborne is of the generation of judges who used to avoid recognising people in the street in order to preserve their judicial independence. But he is considered a "gentleman" by his colleagues and is said to have accepted "graciously" that he was too old for the job of Lord President, even though he was at the time serving as chairman of the Judges Council, where he is considered to have done an excellent job representing the whole judiciary to the controlling elite. Osborne, it seems, was a viable candidate, but one whose time had passed.

The other applicant was a completely different kettle of fish, Lord Hardie. "He's genial and convivial," a colleague of his told me, "but ruthlessly ambitious." Of all the judges I have discussed with members of the Bar and Bench, only two have come in for widespread criticism. One is a recent political appointment, and the ground there is lack of ability. The other is Lord Hardie. In his case, there were no doubts about ability, but his behaviour both on the Bench and before being appointed to it. He appears to have made a wide range of enemies amongst his colleagues, which cannot be a recommendation for an aspirant Lord President. He is younger than all the others, and still in the Outer House. He was the last Lord Advocate to appoint himself to the Bench, which he did in circumstances that aroused criticism outside Parliament House. As head of the Crown Office, he had the job of organising the prosecution in the Lockerbie trial, which was held in Holland in 2000. Six weeks before the trial started, he resigned his job and, like Lord Murray, took the judge-ship which he advised the first Minster to offer him.

In this case, however, the circumstances were a little different. The *Sunday Herald* described them with its tongue warily in its cheek:

> So, in the People versus Lord Hardie, the charge sheet reads: That the Lord Advocate, having screwed up over the incorporation of the European Convention of Human Rights into Scots law, and having left the Crown Office demoralised and in disarray, and being leery about Lockerbie, and being conscious that time was running out, did in the spirit of naked self-interest, summarily appoint himself to the Bench without paying due care either to his public image or that of his distinguished post... Moreover, the said Lord Hardie did appoint himself to the Bench knowing that it is the express intention of the Scottish Parliament in future to seek to alter the system of judicial appointment, such as to abolish patronage and place the appointment of senior law officers in the hands of an independent appointments board. (20 February 2000)

For abandoning the Lockerbie litigation while it was at such a delicate stage, Hardie was accused in Parliament of "dereliction of duty", "self promotion" and "dishonour". He denied the charges, and said that the Lockerbie case had not been affected by his decision. There was justice in this because to have concluded otherwise would have been to impugn the ability of the judges hearing the case, unless the allegation was that evidence was being withheld due to his own elevation, which it was not.

But he replied to the main charge in terms which were

unwise. "He didn't appoint himself a judge," the paper reported him as having said, "it was [the First Minister] and the Queen [who did]." Since it was he, as Lord Advocate, who made the recommendation on which the First Minister and therefore the Queen acted, this was a cavilling, uncandid response—typical of a lawyer, some would say. Perhaps the new First Minister's *ad hoc* committee saw Hardie in the same light, or were worried that the public might. At any event, they did not put him on their short-list. Of the five applicants, only Lords Hamilton and Gill were recommended for serious consideration at a second interview.

The most controversial—or, to many, risible—part of the process devised by the government for the appointment of the Lord President was the requirement that the judges applying write an essay, on 5 pages of A4, saying what they thought wrong with the administration of the Scottish courts and how it might be improved. It was widely felt to undignified for senior judges to have to make written supplication in this way.

I got a reaction typical of many when I asked a senior court figure, "Was this essay as silly as it sounded?"

"I certainly hope so," he replied emphatically.

"Why?"

"This whole committee business should be exposed for what it is: a complete load of nonsense."

The First Minister together with his Justice Minister, Cathy Jamieson and the Lord Advocate (whose previous role in selecting judges was the reason for bringing in the new committee), interviewed the final two candidates. Since one of the main complaints about the old system was that it was too political, it was absurd that the final selection committee consisted entirely of politicians. Worse than absurd was the fact that they appear to have made a politically-motivated choice in Lord Hamilton, who was felt to be more biddable than Lord Gill.[123]

---

[123] Lord Hamilton retired in 2012, and was succeeded as Lord President by Lord Gill.

The new Lord President's reputation amongst his colleagues is of a man of courtesy and honour, but of being a narrowly-focussed workaholic.

"Arthur Hamilton is a man of complete integrity," one said to me. "He will never do a shabby thing; he will always do what he thinks is right; he will always try to be fair. His problem is the strange, withdrawn persona which he adopted at Oxford, maybe out of shyness. His father was a manger in an insurance company, or something like that. Somebody once said that life for him began when he went to Oxford. He got a scholarship there after one year at Glasgow, and was blown away by the grandeur of the place. He has behaved in the grand manner ever since, changed his accent and that sort of thing. In that respect, he is a bit like George Emslie, except that he hasn't any of Emslie's charisma. He is very conscientious. He's not very bright, but he's grafted away all his life to the total exclusion of everything else. He's quite a limited sort of a guy. He doesn't have any friends. If you pass his house in Heriot Row, you will see him in his study, which overlooks the street, slaving away at ten, eleven o'clock at night. He has worked longer hours than anybody else, with the possible exception of David Hope, but he's not as clever as David Hope. Some years ago, he was put up for a Fellowship of the Royal Society of Edinburgh, but they rejected him because those in the Royal Society looked at his CV and saw there was nothing but law. 'What else has he done?' they asked. Of course the answer was: nothing, not even chairing a conference. About the only thing he has done is to campaign against the introduction of wheelie-bins into the New Town conservation area. He is known as the wheelie-bin man! It is extraordinary that he can be considered appropriate for a job that requires the occupant to be worldly and street-wise. He is a good, decent man, but not a born leader."

The problem Lord Hamilton inherited was that Hope, Rodger and Cullen had all preferred law to administration, so there was a tremendous backlog of organisational work that needed tackling.

"Cullen was a wash-out," one judge said to me, after we had

discussed the problems with Hope and Rodger. "He represents the particularly dead-handed section of Edinburgh society: elder of the kirk, respectable, don't take a chance. He was an able advocate, very hard working, very clear in his exposition of his cases. He was a good Outer House judge, a good Lord Ordinary. But he is completely lacking in any understanding of politics. He paid attention to the court management problem, but he had no ideas about how to solve it. That's no use. What the judiciary in Scotland needs now is a leader with breadth of vision and a lot of gumption. What the civil service wants, on the other hand, is another timorous workaholic without any wider ideas."

Cullen's legacy was not confined to administrative inertia. He fought shy of any legal controversy too. If the law is to develop and adapt, senior judges, led by the Lord President, must sometimes quietly make law, or discreetly adapt existing law to modern conditions when apparently simply re-stating it. Put another way, there has to be a little of the activist Supreme Court Justice, the Earl Warren or the Thurgood Marshall, at the top of the judicial tree in Scotland—though without advertising the fact. Hope and Rodger were both highly competent at that aspect of the job. They did not shirk "politics" in court. Their problem was outside it, on the battlefield between the judiciary and the civil service. Cullen largely avoided political battles even in court, and Hamilton appears to be cut from similar judicial cloth.

"This really should be discussed *sotto voce*," a retired though still active judge told me, "because if the tabloid press got to hear of it there'll be hell to pay. These lay appointers of judges simply don't understand the political—if I may put it like that— aspect of judging, which is, by the way, another reason why I feel more should be written about the courts. To me, it's either totally secret or totally open: witchcraft or Washington DC, if you like; either the Lord Advocate or the rough-and-tumble of a confirmation battle in the Senate. Half-open systems encourage ill-informed speculation. A little knowledge is a dangerous thing, and all that—which is why I am happy to talk to you about all this. The fact is that we sometimes have to use the law in a way which is closer to the American Supreme Court than most people imagine. And there's nothing wrong with that, in my view. In fact it is very important that we do. The senior judge in Scotland should be able to say, in certain circumstances, 'I don't care what the law is, it is wrong, it is out of date', or 'This has never been considered properly in the light of modern conditions', or 'I am going to draw a line here.' The problem in recent years has been that Cullen was quite incapable of doing that, and so, in my opinion, is Hamilton. I'll tell you a story which has been widely discussed amongst the judges, though not outside, and which illustrates that.

"The Appeal court decided in 1999 that what we call temporary sheriffs were contrary to European Convention on Human Rights on the ground that they were not sufficiently independent. They were appointed for five years at a time, and therefore it could be argued that they discharged their duties with one eye on re-appointment. It was in their interests to oblige the bureaucracy. Perhaps some did this, I don't know, but I doubt if that made much difference to anything important. The main case then at issue about temporary sheriffs, *Starrs v Ruxton,* was highly questionable. It could, under the Scotland Act, have been appealed to the Privy Council. Most judges think it should have been. But Hardie, who was Lord Advocate at the time, decided not to. We do not understand why. It would probably have been overturned. At the time, we were getting definite smoke-signals from London to the effect the senior judges there, some of whom are very able people, had begun to say that we are not going to have a coach and horses driven through our legal system by the ECHR. Everything worked pretty well before, and to start dismantling it because of the ECHR is bloody nonsense. So we'll just trim a wee bit here and there, and it'll be fine. Let's be reasonable about this.

"So we come to 2005 and there's three people in the Appeal Court arguing that their trials in 1999 should be invalidated because a temporary sheriff had been sitting. Two of these alleged victims of injustice had actually pled guilty, and the only one who was tried was admonished, that is he was let off with nothing more than a warning. So it was a storm in a teacup, really, except for the fact that there were hundreds of people waiting for the Appeal Court to follow the clear line of previous decisions and declare their own convictions invalid because the court had been presided over by a temporary sheriff. Some would undoubtedly have been serious cases. But the main thing from a 'political' point of view, is that the courts are clogged enough as it is. A review of all temporary sheriff cases would have been catastrophic. From a broad, public policy point of view, enough was enough, whatever the law may or may not have been.

"The issue was considered so important that five judges sat in the Appeal Court. That is very unusual. Normally it is only three. The most grounded of them was Lady Cosgrove, who is a sharp cookie, tough as old boots, quite a formidable person. She, I gather on pretty good authority, was firmly of the view: we're not having this. Lord Philip apparently agreed with her. He's a down-to-earth sort of a guy, a keen piper whose son used to play rugby for Scotland. He's been around and is not interested in legal games. MacFadyen, who's quite an able lawyer, though not much of a personality, soon came round to their view.[124] That left Cullen and Hamilton, who were the other two judges. They could not take a clear policy view. They argued back and forth whether, in law, a conviction by a temporary sheriff was void, or voidable, or null, or invalid, and what the difference was between acquiescence and waiver, and a whole lot of other stuff like that.

"I don't want to go into the details, partly because they are so complicated, and partly because they don't matter.[125] *The real point was that the law was not the point.* You had three judges who said: as a matter of public policy we must not allow this. If we do, the courts are going to be jammed up by clever lawyers operating on Legal Aid who see a good living in the temporary sheriff problem, which was in practical terms solved years ago. All the faulty law had already been appealed. All we were talking

---

[124] He died in 2008.

[125] See *Robertson and O'Dalaigh v Procurator Fiscal, Aberdeen; Ruddy v Procurator Fiscal, Perth* (2005) at www.scotcourts.gov.uk/opinions/xj724-1285.html

about was the technical status of the sheriff. What's the big deal? That sort of question did not seem to weigh with two judges who ought perhaps to have been more mindful than the others of the problems of court administration that would result in allowing every temporary sheriff judgement in history to be challenged and possibly retried. But they wanted to argue the law. Fair play to them, in one sense, but the fact that they eventually came to the same view as the three others makes their attempt to bury the matter in legalisms seem even less wise in retrospect. There had been no serious injustice in this case anyway. The only important issue was the effect on the courts in the future.

"But Cullen couldn't get this. He looked at all the cases he was referred to, conscientiously wrote them all down, and noted what they decided. Hamilton did much the same, just as conscientiously, and just as pointlessly. MacFadyen, by contrast, wrote in uncompromising terms, as did Lady Cosgrove. Both were brief. Philip had the balls to confine himself to a single sentence; nineteen words, I think, was all he wrote. But that did it: three to two. Cullen and Hamilton either had to agree or to dissent. The fact that they then wrote agreeing with a position which they seem to have felt was highly arguable, illustrates the problem. They were corks in the water. That is not what Lord Presidents should be. They need to take a grip. This was a complete failure of senior judges to understand their function. It is a matter of judgement, a matter of political feel. At this level, it's politics we're in, a different kind of politics than what you see on the telly, but politics nonetheless. That fact seems to have passed them by, Hamilton as much as Cullen."

The other candidate for the Lord Presidency in 2005 was Lord Gill, the Lord Justice Clerk, Cullen's second-in-command. Politics most certainly did not pass him by. Indeed that is the source of the general view that as Lord President he would have been less pliable than Lord Hamilton in the face of civil service scheming. I have said that only two judges came in for general criticism during my interviews. I should have said two and a half, because the half, Lord Gill, divided opinion. Some thought him is the best judge in Parliament House, while others could not abide him. Few consider him a bad judge: all the criticism is personal rather than professional. But as Lord President, he would have to be a leader, and therefore acceptable at a human level to those he led, so the point is relevant in this context.

Like Arthur Hamilton, Brian Gill, comes from Glasgow, but from the Catholic community, a fact which appears to have contributed to the situation he finds himself in today. Even his enemies agree that Gill is one of the most able lawyers in Parliament House. He did extremely well at Glasgow University, then obtained a doctorate from Edinburgh University, where he lectured before being admitted as an advocate. He is author of *The Law of Agricultural Holdings in Scotland* (list price £260). In the early 1990s, he was Keeper of the Advocates Library, and later spent seven years as Chairman of the Scottish Law Commission. He is a Fellow of the Royal Society of Edinburgh and a member of the English Bar, being a Bencher at Lincoln's Inn. Unlike Lord Hamilton, he has interests beyond the law: principally music. He is an accomplished organist who is choir-master at St Columba's Roman Catholic Church in Upper Grey Street. For ten years he was Chairman of the Board of Governors of the Royal Scottish Academy of Music and Drama. Billy Connolly was among those awarded honorary doctorates in 2006, when Gill gave his last graduation address.

"I think Brian should have been appointed Lord President," one judge said to me. "I know he has a reputation for being difficult, but I think you have to assess it away from the issue of personality. You can't appoint Arthur just because he is a nice man, which he is. Gill has been the Justice Clerk for seven years, so he has had the experience of the number two job. He's got a proven record. He is undoubtedly very, very clever. He was chairman of the Law Commission and that does not happen to numpties. He writes superbly, which is a very important aspect of the top job. And he's got a vision of where the system should be and how to improve it. Look at the latest civil service white paper, *Strengthening Judicial Independence in a Modern Scotland.* If you read it closely, it is just strengthening the Justice Department. Brian would have stood up for the judges. If the politicians made their choice on who would cause less trouble, Gill or Hamilton, there is a pretty obvious answer to the question of why they chose Arthur."

A retired judge with decades of experience said to me, "Hamilton is a very nice fellow, but he hasn't got the independence of mind or quality of research that Gill has. Intellectually, Gill is streets ahead of Hamilton. But Hamilton is the alleged safe pair of hands. Some people don't like Gill, but you don't have to like him to accept that he has been one of the best Justice Clerks in my lifetime."

A court official who deals daily with the civil service made this point: "I think if Brian Gill had been appointed to succeed Cullen, he would undoubtedly have set about changing the relationship with the civil service. This is something that really has to be said: the senior court officers were—maybe still are— paid a bonus if they reached their targets in terms of number of cases rushed through court per month or whatever. This means that many are not considered as fully as they ideally should be. Either that, or the judges have to spend too many of their evenings working to keep up with the opinions they have to write, the result being that they do not get out and about enough, and so their performance suffers in other ways.

At a meeting of the judges, Gill asked the Principal Clerk of Session, the most senior civil service officer within the courts, if a bonus was paid when more cases are tried. He ducked the question, so Gill asked a second time. Finally, with great reluctance, he was given the answer. Yes, the civil servants are paid bonuses for court through-put—not the judges who do the work, mind you, they don't get the money, but the clerks who schedule it! That is ludicrous. No, it's not; it is more serious than that, it is *scandalous*. Judicial disposals are now a numerical performance target for bureaucrats—incredible! As far as the Justice Department is concerned, the public can go hang. Who's in charge here: the judges or the bureaucrats? Anyway, it was Gill who asked the question everyone in Parliament House wanted answered. It was he who insisted that it be answered without evasion. I can well imagine that that infuriated the high

heid yins at Victoria Quay. Many people around here think that
was one of the reasons why he was not chosen."[126]

"You have to understand," a recently-elevated judge said to
me in less charitable tones, "that Gill is a boy from the other side
of the tracks. He's very clever. He was a very able advocate. He
made a lot of money, had six children and bought a huge house in
one of the smartest parts of south Edinburgh. He's a sharp
dresser, who drives a natty little sports car into court every day.
He's reasonably healthy. He has one of the most interesting jobs
in the Scottish legal world, without a tenth of the responsibility
and worry that the Lord President has. You'd've thought he'd be
pretty chuffed with life. Not Brian! He has got a fish-supper's
worth of chips on both shoulders. He, a Catholic from the east
end of Glasgow, is the victim of a Protestant conspiracy to
deprive him of the Lord Presidency. As far as I can see, he really
believes that. It is all down to his background. He was the only
son of a book interest agent, those guys who went round
collecting insurance premiums. Respectable, sure, but humble,
with the apparent result that he feels pooh-poohed by many of his
colleagues. Added to that is the fact that he is frighteningly
religious; religious in a way that people of my generation simply
are not. He's like a Wee Free, except he has Missals rather than
Bibles lying round his room in Parliament House.[127] To
somebody as far down the pecking order as me, he's really quite
an intimidating individual. He appears socially to be a very nice

[126] It is perhaps an indication of the off-hand way in which the Justice
Department controls the Supreme Court in Scotland that the new Principal Clerk
of Session has no legal background, having previously been Community
Services Director for the Midlothian Council. One of the recurring complaints
of judges is the steady amateurisation, and diminution of status, within the
clerking service, whose morale is vital to any successfully functioning court
system. (These are procedural clerks; this problem is separate from the equally
bizarre one of the lack of legal clerks, as referred to in Chapter 5 above.) This is
entirely the responsibility of the civil service. The stated aim is to save money.
[127] In 2011 he was made a Papal Knight—strictly a Knight of the Order of St
Gregory the Great—at a Red Mass in Edinburgh officiated by Cardinal Keith
O'Brien. The award was made for services to public life.

chap. He doesn't speak posh or anything, which is important in Scotland, but if you deal with him for any length of time, you come to realise you don't have a clue what he's really thinking, which is why some of my colleagues think of him as conspiratorial."

I asked a more senior judge about the allegation that Gill has a sectarian inferiority complex.

"He's a strange guy," the judge said, "because, though some of his attitudes are very close to those of the establishment of yesteryear, they are born of an entirely different cause. They come from a massive negativity and embattlement and result in a sort of half-disguised aloofness with some of his colleagues. He was a clever boy, but was obviously brought up in an environment in which, despite his evident ability, he felt a second-class citizen. You don't get over these things, however successful you become in later life. Catholics aren't like that any more. In Glasgow the Catholic is as confident as the next guy. But not in Gill's generation. In those days you'd never have dreamt of seeing a Catholic in one of the big, powerful blue-nosed solicitors firms, like Maclay, Murray and Spens, or McGrigor Donald. He grew up feeling excluded. The result is that he is not a team player. The old boys—Emslie, Clyde and the like—were aloof, but with outsiders, not with each other. That is important. They believed that if they were seen talking on equal terms to solicitors, clerks or the general public it would undermine their prestige, and therefore the authority of the courts. Gill's chippiness has a similar result, though from a totally different cause. Possibly for that reason, he can seem to be aggressive. People say he might have tackled the civil service. I wonder. The thing is that it needs tackling, but in a co-operative way. We have a fairly new judge, who used to be a civil servant himself before he became an advocate, and he says that the civil servants' main object in life is damage limitation, so if you give them help they are pathetically grateful, as long as you do it the right way. I cannot see Gill being tactful enough."

As Justice Clerk, Gill had a poor relationship with Cullen when the latter was Lord President. Being the two top officers, they should have worked closely together, but they did not. When, at the suggestion of Lord Mackay of Drumadoon, an Inner House judge who had been the last Conservative Lord Advocate, Cullen appointed a small committee to consider judicial reforms in the light of changes being made in England, and other changes proposed by the Justice Department in Scotland, Gill was left out. Not only that, the Chairmanship was given to Lord Hamilton. This was the first time the bookworm of Heriot Row was exposed to civil service and judicial politics. It was probably crucial in the race for the Lord Presidency, which Gill coveted so badly.

"One cannot help wondering if Cullen was trying to marginalize Gill in advance of his own retirement," a senior advocate commented to me. "But if he was, that must have been one of the few times they were pulling in the same direction because Gill, with his prickly attitude, was doing a pretty good job of marginalizing himself. Hamilton, by contrast, would have come across in committee as honest and straight-forward, if dull and cautious. But that is just what the civil service wants—the dull and cautious bit, I mean. The real problem is that it is the civil servants who effectively do the choosing, together with their sponsors in parliament. If it had been left to the judges or the Faculty, I think quite an interesting contest might have developed. Many would have wanted Gill very badly, and for good reason, while many others would be horrified at the thought of the man with the Missal in his room being put in charge—for equally good reason. When Hamilton was proposed, everyone just went back to sleep: Cullen Mk. II."

There is a deeper reason for the view that Lord Gill might not have had quite the probity for a Lord President. This is particularly important as it concerns his behaviour in court.

"Put it this way," another judge said to me, in agonised tones because he is a strong supporter of Gill's, "ten years ago, when Brian was still in the Outer House, he was given, not I think very wisely, a case to decide *vis à vis* failed sterilisation. He produced a judgement, which nobody has ever forgotten, in which he said, 'Children are a joy forever.' I am sure he really thinks that. He has a large and very happy family. And of course, as a human being, he is right. But that, if I may say with all due respect, is nothing to the point. The case should have turned, and ultimately on appeal did turn, on other considerations. That indicated to many of his colleagues a weakness of judgement."

"You think that might have had repercussions this far on?" I asked.

"Yes I do. I know for a fact it was a consideration when it came to appointing him Justice Clerk. Don't ask me how I know that, but take it from me that I do. I wish he had stopped and thought about that statement. It was irrelevant. That was not what the case was about. Arguably, he failed to separate the law from his religious and social views, and you cannot do that. It was not *obiter dicta*, it was the *ratio decidendi*, if you'll pardon my Latin—the reason for deciding the case, rather than a passing observation. It was central to his judgement. That case, which is the only blot on his otherwise spotless records so far as I know, did him untold damage, at least as far as rising to the very top is concerned."

The case in question is worth considering also for its wider illustration of the practice of judicial decision-making. It concerned a Mr and Mrs McFarlane who sued the Tayside Health Board after a supposedly successful sterilisation failed. They were a well-to-do couple who had four children and decided they wanted no more. Mr McFarlane underwent a vasectomy, and was told after subsequent testing that it had worked. But he found that advice to have been wrong when Mrs McFarlane became pregnant for the fifth time in 1991. Though a healthy baby girl was born without complications, the McFarlanes decided to sue the hospital which had given them the incorrect information.

Compensation has been claimed in more heart-breaking circumstances, for example when the sterilisation has been undertaken explicitly because of the known risk of giving birth to a severely handicapped child, which then failed with the result that a handicapped child was born. In the McFarlanes' case, there could be no claim in respect of the child, only in respect of the parents. Mrs McFarlane sued for £10,000 damages in respect of the personal injury which she had suffered, by way of pregnancy, due to the negligent advice about her husband's vasectomy. They both sued jointly for £100,000 damages in respect of the costs of bringing up the child. In 1996, the case came before Lord Gill.[128]

Of the nine judges who heard this case before *McFarlane* was finally laid to rest, the law was stated most clearly by Lord McCluskey sitting in the Appeal Court:

> In Scotland the obligation to make reparation arises when there is a concurrence of iniuria and damnum. 'Iniuria' does not mean injury in the ordinary use of the English word; it means an invasion of a legal right. 'Damnum' in the context of our law of reparation means a loss in the sense of a material prejudice to an interest that the law recognises as a legal interest. When there is a concurrence of iniuria and damnum the person whose legal right has been invaded with resultant loss to him has a right to seek to recover money reparation for that loss from the wrongdoer.[129]

Lord Cullen, preceding McCluskey, correctly but perhaps indelicately, summarised the McFarlane's approach to the law in terms which could have been uttered by a church elder of a different era:

> The concurrence of injuria and damnum took place when [Mrs McFarlane] conceived as a result of the [McFarlanes] acting to their disadvantage in reliance on the allegedly negligent advice... The subject matter of their claims represented the realisation of the damnum that befell them when she conceived.[130]

The allegations of religious bias sprang from the completely different view which Gill had taken a year before the appeal, when he heard the case at first instance. He understood the word "injury" to mean physical injury in "the ordinary use of the English word", as McCluskey later put it. In his judgement, Gill wrote, "I do not consider that a normal pregnancy, even if

---

[128] At first instance: *McFarlane v Tayside Health Board* 1997 SLT 211. On appeal: *Idem* 1998 SLT 307. In the Lords: *Idem* 2000 SLT 154.

[129] *Ibid.* 1998, p. 313

[130] *Ibid.* 1997, p. 310

undesired, and the labour with which it ends can properly be described as a personal injury. In any event, even if pregnancy and labour can be regarded as an injury in a case such as this, I do not consider that that is an injury for which damages are recoverable."

On the separate issue of the costs of bringing up the child, Gill also found for the Health Board. Its argument had been that "the existence of a healthy child is a blessing and a source of countless benefits to the parents... and cannot be regarded as a financial loss." The McFarlanes' argument was that "since the purpose of [the sterilisation] was to avoid the expense of bringing up a further child, the [McFarlanes], in view of their responsibilities under Section 1 of the Children (Scotland) Act 1995, have been put in a position of immediate and continuing loss, none of which would have been incurred but for the alleged negligence."

Since all who claim damages must do everything reasonably possible to mitigate their loss, and can claim only for that which they could not mitigate, the question arose as to whether the McFarlanes should have put the baby out to adoption, or whether Mrs McFarlane should have had an abortion. Mercifully, these issues were not pursued too far. The court also debated what monetary value the existence of a child could be said to have, and whether this should be offset against the claim. If this were not done, it was argued, then the McFarlanes would have a double benefit: the child, with all its blessings, plus a large amount of money with which to bring it up. The costs claimed included for private education. The reason was that all the McFarlanes' other children had been sent to fee-paying schools and it would have been unfair and discriminatory if this child were, by reason of the Health Board's negligence, deprived of equal treatment within the family.

In the course of a thorough review of the law in the subject, including English cases to which counsel drew his attention, Lord Gill noted that in England the damages paid for unwanted children "are greater the more affluent and ambitious are the parents". One wonders how well such a principle would go down in Scotland. Critics of judges in general should stop to think just how difficult such questions are to deal with in principle, especially when every case involves different human beings in different circumstances, and when all the time there is a readership-hungry press looking over your shoulder waiting for you to take a step someone can criticise.

With all due allowance for the difficulty of arriving at a fair decision in this unfortunate case, the criticism of Lord Gill's fundamental reason for rejecting the McFarlane's claim— namely, that he forgot himself as a judge and took a human rather than a legal view of the claim—is substantially borne out by the words he used in his Opinion:

> The primary question is ... does Scots law allow damages to be recovered for the birth of a normal, healthy and loved child? ...
>
> The central problem in every action of this kind is whether, and if so to what extent, the court should mark the fact that whatever pain and distress the mother may suffer in pregnancy and labour, and whatever financial outlays both parents may incur, each has received the gift of a child and all of the actual and prospective benefits, emotional, social and economic, that the child brings to them...
>
> In my view, a pregnancy occurring in the circumstance of this case cannot be equiparated with a physical injury. Pregnancy causes discomfort, pain and sickness. Labour is acutely painful and distressing. But these are natural processes resulting in a happy outcome. They are the natural sequelae of conception and that is an event that in this case can hardly be considered as a physical injury *per se*...
>
> The court should not, for the purposes of damages, dissociate pregnancy and labour from their outcome. To do that is to ignore the existence of the child and the happiness that [Mrs McFarlane] has had and will continue to have from her existence. Since counsel for [the McFarlanes] have accepted that these benefits have come to [Mrs McFarlane], I cannot see how they can either

be disregarded altogether or be held to not to outweigh the natural pain and discomfort inherent in the creation of life...

I am of the opinion that that this case should be decided on the principle that the privilege of being a parent is immeasurable in monetary terms; that the benefits of parenthood transcend any patrimonial [i.e. monetary] loss.[131]

The McFarlanes appealed to the Inner House, where they were upheld. Lord McCluskey answered of Gill's reasoning directly when he said:

I know of no principle of Scots law that entitles the wrongdoer to say to the victims of their wrongdoing that they must look to their gains on the roundabout to balance what they actually lose on the swings...

We were offered the example of a coal miner who, while working in a deep pit, is rendered unfit to work by an accident, caused by his employer's fault, and resulting in the loss of an arm. He leaves the coal industry and becomes a park attendant at a lower wage. Instead of the dust, darkness and dangers of the pit, his environment becomes one of fresh air, birdsong and sweet-smelling flowers. No-one would dream of suggesting that a price has to be put on such non-patrimonial benefits accruing to him as an incident of his working in a park rather than a pit, and that that price should be deducted either from his calculated wage loss or from the money awarded by way of solatium given to mark the pain, suffering and deprivation flowing from the loss of his limb.[132]

The McFarlanes having won in the Inner House in Edinburgh, the Health Board now appealed to the House of Lords in London. Of the five judges who heard the case, only two were Scots, Lord Hope and Lord Clyde—the older Clyde's son, and Lord Rodger's predecessor—yet as a group they undertook the task of stating Scots law in this delicate area. While Lord Gill had

---

[131] *Ibid.* 1997 p. 214, 216
[132] *Ibid.* 1998 p. 316

noted that English and Scots law were not identical on this subject, Lord Slynn of Hadley, who gave the lead judgement, said at the outset:

> Although these judgements refer to the law of Scotland, it is as I understand it accepted that the law of England and that of Scotland should be the same in respect of the matter which arise on this appeal. It would be strange, even absurd, if they were not... Your Lordships [must decide the] principle to be adopted as rule of law of Scotland and England.[133]

Lord Slynn gave no authority for this pronouncement. He did not say how he had come to his understanding about the desirability of the law being the same on both sides of the border, nor who it was that "accepted" that desirability. Neither did he say why it would be absurd if it were not the case.

The Lords dismissed the issues about the Scots law of iniuria and damnum as applied to the McFarlanes' case, and also the controversy over whether the benefits of parenthood were relevant to claims for negligence. Instead, they concentrated on the question of the remoteness of damage from its cause. All claims were relevant but not all should be allowed. Only those incurred due to the birth should be upheld. Those connected with the costs of upbringing should be dismissed.

> The doctor undertakes a duty of care in regard to the prevention of pregnancy [Lord Slynn said]. It does not follow that the duty includes also avoiding the costs of rearing the child if born *and accepted into the family*. Whereas I have no doubt that there should be compensation for the physical effects of the pregnancy and birth... I consider that it is not fair, just or reasonable to impose on the doctor or his employer liability for the consequential responsibilities, imposed or *accepted by the parents*, to bring up the child.... If a client wants to be able to recover such costs he or she must do so by an appropriate contract. (emphasis added)[134]

---

[133] *Ibid.* 2000 p. 158
[134] *Ibid.* p. 162

To most Scottish people, I suspect, and probably to many of their judges too, the idea that patients who are in hospital for vasectomies should make contracts with the doctors performing the operation to provide for the situation when they fail, would be more "absurd" than Lord Slynn's nightmare of Scots law differing from English law in this area.

Another absurdity from a Scottish perspective is implicit in those of Lord Slynn's words which I have italicised in the quotation above. They clearly imply the fact that the parent of an unplanned child must mitigate his or her loss by putting the child out to adoption. This rather nasty assumption may or may not be acceptable in English law, I do not know, but I would be astonished if a Bench comprising every judge I have talked to in Scotland would not find unanimously against Lord Slynn on that point.

The true absurdity in all this is Lord Slynn's assumption, which he did not even bother to justify, that Scotland should be prevented from having its own law, distinct from England, on medical negligence. With a different health system, operating on different principles of public service, it would be absurd if the law governing the details of practical responsibility for mistakes were, for some unstated reason, forced to be the same in the two countries just because Lord Slynn said so. England differs from America, for example, so why should Scotland not differ from England? And since public opinion always has a background role in a healthy legal system—*vide* the American race cases—it is important that Scottish opinion on these matters be reflected ultimately in the way the law develops here. The assumption behind Lord Slynn's arrogant pronouncement is that it would be "absurd" if Scottish public opinion differed on a long-term basis from that in England. Nonetheless, his judgement is binding on all judges in Scotland until such time as parliament intervenes. Show me the judge and I'll tell you the law.

At the heart of the criticism of Lord Gill was the question whether he had brought his views as a practising Catholic into court when considering the McFarlanes' claim. One of the judges, long since retired, who heard the appeal in the Inner

House, gave me his view of the case, unasked, while we were discussing something quite different: namely Hamilton's Rule and the extent to which skilled advocacy depended on understanding the way judges think.

"The basis of advocacy is getting the judge you are trying to impress to understand what the problem is and what the answer is," the judge told me. "Although it may not be immediately obvious to non-lawyers, the same applies to judges who want to write controversial judgements in such a way that they will not be overturned on appeal. I'll give you an example in which I was a judge rather than counsel. This was a decision of Lord Gill who is the Lord Justice Clerk. He's a very ardent Catholic, you know, but nonetheless a very good judge, just as he was a very good advocate. But there was a case which he heard which was quite interesting. This was a chap who had been sterilised by a doctor, in Dundee I think, who did the operation and said to his patient, 'That should be alright. You will not conceive any more children.' But lo and behold, he had another child. He was very annoyed. He sued the Health Board for negligence. To be successful, he not only had to show negligence but also that he had suffered damage. This was the interesting problem that arose because if you are negligent but cause no damage then there is no case. Damages in Scotland are a question of reparation not of retribution.

"This was heard at first instance before Lord Gill, who decided that a child—this is the Catholic approach—was a gift from God. The fact that you had to rearrange your financial life to support five children instead of four was something that couldn't be weighed in the balance against the gift of a child. Of course this chap had worked out what the extra child had cost him and that is what he was trying to recover from the Health Board. We in the Appeal Court held that that was a good point and we overturned Brian Gill. Then the case went to the House of Lords. They overturned us and let the Health Board off the hook again, saying that not all the damages clamed were allowable."

"But that's a different point from Gill's, is it not?" I said. "Gill said that a child is a blessing which outweighs the costs of bringing it up. You said it may be a blessing but the costs are still recoverable if negligence is proved. Then the Lords said that it is not an issue of blessings and costs, but simply of the remoteness of the damage to the negligence complained of. In overturning you, they weren't upholding Gill so much as giving a third view on the case, surely?"

"You're quite right. You should have gone to the Bar. That's just the kind of point that you could make. That is what the art of advocacy is, dealing with a situation like that. It is not just a question of telling the judge what the law is because the law may be uncertain. You have to persuade him that your view of it is the correct one. Some people are very adept at that sort of thing. It is a challenge. It requires thought. It's no good waving your arms about like your friend Ian Hamilton."

"But his point is that the correct view varies depending on who is sitting."

"Nonsense!"

"But you in the Appeal Court appear to have overturned Gill in *McFarlane* on the basis that he had brought his prejudices into court in the Outer House?"

"No, no, I don't say that at all. He is a very deep Catholic. We said to ourselves as judges, I don't mean we discussed it but privately we thought, that a Catholic would naturally be very much against birth control. I met Gill as I was taking somebody round the courts the morning before our decision was announced against him. He just laughed and said, 'I suppose you'll be overturning me on this.' He was quite open about it. But in Scotland—you may not have been told this, but it is well known—religion runs deep. People don't pay so much attention now, but for long enough there has been a more or less unwritten rule that there should be at least two Catholic judges in the Court of Session. I don't think people were appointed for that reason; it may just have been the way it worked out. When Gill was appointed, the Catholic Church was pleased—naturally, because it is like the Supreme Court in America, with the conservatives and the liberals. There was a great row recently about the fact that he wasn't made the Lord President, saying how upset he was, and that he thought it was something to do with his Catholicism. I think that was disgraceful the way that was reported. How did they know that he was so upset, and what he thought? Somebody had told them: a mole in Parliament House. That would never have happened in my day. We spoke to *nobody*. I don't really know why I'm speaking to you now, except that my wife has died, my children live abroad, and I do not have many visitors."

"Do you think, despite *McFarlane*, that Gill would have made a good Lord President? Out of the two of them, who would you have chosen?"

"I think I would have chosen Hamilton, because I know them both. But I would just be adding to the tittle-tattle if I went on about this."

There is a wider point to be taken about the question of having two Catholics on the Scottish Bench at any one time, and which is raised by *McFarlane*. Many members of the public with whom I discussed this case assumed that the outcome would have been different, not only had the judge been non-Catholic—Lord McCluskey, after all, was brought up as a Catholic—but a woman. Would the outcome of cases relating to the entirely female experience of giving birth be different if the judge were, not just a woman, but a mother? All the women judges I have spoken to, in both the Court of Session and the sheriff courts, said they thought that there is no reason why cases concerning childbirth need to be heard by mothers, or ones revolving around birth-control by non-Catholic judges.

Part of the remit of the Judicial Appointments Board is to make the judiciary more representative of society as a whole. There are two possible reasons for this. The first is that even Scottish socialists believe quietly in Hamilton's Rule, the only difference being that, as they think in sociological rather than human terms, they consider that interpretations of the law vary with social classes and categories rather than from person to person. Show me the judge's socio-economic background and I'll tell you the law, they presumably say, forgetting Earl Warren and Marshall Harlan and others whose opinions evolved with time. This approach does not disregard the professional qualification of the judge, but merely sets it within a class structure, rather as Presidential nominations for the American Supreme Court sets judges within a political structure.

The other possibility is similar to the one above, except that it downgrades professional competence in a way which used to seem modern and forward-looking, but now looks very dated. Wanting judges to be "representative of society" is in some respects a pale, post-Marxist version of the Lenin-Krylenko argument that anybody can be a judge so long as they have the correct revolutionary consciousness. Only a victim can try another victim, if what the Bolsheviks called patrimonial justice is to be avoided. Thus in modern Scotland, only women can properly interpret the law on women's issues, Catholics the law on Catholic-related issues and so on. Without exception, every judge I spoke to regarded such ideas with total scorn. Not one thought that Lord Gill should have recused himself, either because of being male or Catholic, from *McFarlane*. In fact, simply asking the question tended to rally support for his Opinion, which some said was at least honest and clearly argued.

"If you want to have only women taking women's cases, lesbians hearing lesbian-related cases and so on, then where do you stop?" a female sheriff commented acidly. "Do you have drunks hearing trials arising from alcohol abuse? Do we want dope-smokers on the Drugs Court Bench? Is the problem with the Lockerbie trial the fact that Lord Maclean and his colleagues were not Muslims?"

"And dead people taking murder trials," I said.

"We have fewer than forty judges in the Supreme Court," she said through tight lips, ignoring my joke. "Does each one have to represent a class of victim in society? And how many types of victim are there? More than forty, I'll bet. In any case, there is a much more important problem than having teetotallers hearing drunk-driving cases."

"What is that?"

"Politics—at least if you think one of the roles of the law is to defend the citizen from the power of the state. The line of argument that says you need to know about the particular circumstances of a case from personal experience beyond the evidence led in court—which is what they are really saying when they suggest that only a woman can try a woman, or a Sikh a Sikh—is a highly, highly dangerous one. Ultimately, it means that, to take an example you seem to be interested in, only Nixon could have tried Nixon because only Nixon really understood the full background to Nixon's allegedly criminal acts. That's the end of the rule of law, of course. It is what the English call self-regulation. It is what a sovereign parliament delivers in constitutional terms to politicians: freedom to take their own view of the law when they want to. That is why we need a proper constitution in Scotland. It is also why we need a serious defence of the profession of judging, which all our workaholic Lords President over the last twenty years have avoided doing. That is why *McFarlane* is unimportant and Gill should have been made Lord President."

Lord Hamilton was sworn in as Lord President on 2 December 2005.[135] He marked the occasion with a speech in the course of which he said, "The courts are no mere service industry. They are the protectors of our rights and liberties in a free democracy.... The independence of the judiciary from the other organs of government is a prerequisite of the upholding of the rule of law. The rule can and should be upheld without the need for conflict with the executive and the legislature. Respect for the courts and what they do will be maintained only if the institutions which the judges head are strong and are capable of resisting inappropriate

---

[135] Just as the Judicial Appointments Board only makes recommendations to the First Minister who, technically, is free to reject them, so the second committee of politicians, which interviewed Gill and Hamilton for the Lord President's job, did not actually appoint Hamilton, but merely recommended him to the Prime Minister, Tony Blair. Both the Lord President and the Lord Justice Clerk are still, despite devolution, appointed by the British Prime Minister of the day. In 2013, Lord Hamilton retired and was succeeded as Lord President by Lord Gill. Broadly speaking, this seems to have been a popular appointment, except perhaps amongst some of the civil servants he will have to deal with.

pressure from whatever quarter."

This was a clear statement of the underlying problem. Unfortunately, the Lord President collapsed soon after making it and was not able to do as much resisting as many people would have liked. He started feeling unwell within a month of being appointed, and by the spring was in the Priory Clinic in Glasgow where he stayed until the early autumn. He was not shirking: he was very ill.

"The strain was absolutely awful for him," a judge who knows him well told me. "It just broke him. He had quite a few outstanding judgements to write at the time he was appointed. Then he had all the work associated with the Lord Presidency, which is huge. He has never been able to delegate, because he has a habit of almost obsessive attention to detail. He just hit the wall. He had worked so hard all his life that he had nothing in reserve. He couldn't cope. It's like a Greek tragedy. He has been undone by his virtues. He has my deepest sympathy. The people I blame are those who appointed him. They chose the wrong man. They chose someone who is a good judge and a very nice person, but not up to that very demanding job. If they are such clever interviewers they ought to have known that Arthur was working at his limit already. You don't appoint someone who, four weeks in, just cracks up. Quite why they made that decision, I don't know. The obvious choice was Gill. The obvious conclusion was that they wanted to avoid him at all costs."

"The problem is that Brian Gill and David Hope never got on," another, very senior, judge told me. "They were Faculty officers together and they clashed. Brian said to a colleague of mine, 'When I heard Hope was on the selection Board, I knew I was toast.' He will think it is anti-Catholic, even though it probably isn't. I think Brian should have got the job. He would have had his problems. He would probably have run it for himself, organising it so that he had a reasonable amount of time off. He is not a workaholic like some of the others. He resents the way the law eats into his time. But so long as that filtered down to the other judges, which it probably would, that would be an entirely good thing. Really he *ought* to have got it. He is very disappointed. I gather that he will not speak to David Edward now, because he was on the Board which rejected him. If Edward walks into a room, Brian gets up and goes out."

Other judges think differently.

"My own view is that he is as close to not being up to the job as poor old Arthur," one said to me. "Brian Gill is very able, but unlike David Hope, say, he doesn't have a public service ethic. That is very important. If you are in that game you have got to understand what it means to be a public servant. He operates entirely on his own agenda. But I think his main problem is that far from everybody trusts him. To an extent, I think that is because he is a Catholic. If so, it's not entirely fair. All the fuss that was raised about that vasectomy case was not because of anything Gill wrote in his judgement. I stand to be corrected, because it was a long time ago, but I don't think you'll find anything explicitly religious in his Opinion. It was more that *other* people found Catholicism where a Martian who had never heard of the Pope might have found simply humanitarianism. The thing is, we judges are still a pretty blue-nosed lot, even if very few of us are religious. You could argue that the opposition to Gill on *McFarlane* was actually more sectarian than his Opinion was.

"His problem is not so much his Catholicism as his character. At the meeting of the Court to say goodbye to Cullen, for example, he got very shirty and made a fool of himself. He'd been phoning round everybody, howling about how ridiculous the appointment of Hamilton was, that it was anti-Catholic and so on. You're dealing with a very strange guy, but you aren't necessarily Catholic just because you are strange. McCluskey's a Catholic, or was, and he's alright. He rather likes the sound of his own keyboard, I'll admit, but his judgements were usually pretty sound, and he doesn't go round making enemies because he thinks everyone is anti-him. Like many people with chips on their shoulders, Gill has, to a point, made his own reality. He's ghettoised himself, if you like. I don't think he would have been any good as Lord President, for a start because he loathes some of the senior civil servants. I think he's absolutely right. One in particular, who is very influential, is a complete shit, and knows nothing about the law. But a public servant must learn to disguise such feelings. If you want serious reform of the relationship between the judiciary and the civil service, it's not going to work if you have the Lord President sending out rays of hatred over the conference table."

"So Lord Hamilton got the job."

"So he did. But in my opinion it would have been better if someone else altogether had been appointed."

"Johnston, Hardie or Osborne?"

"None of those, nice people though two of them are."

"Which two?"

"I'll leave you to guess that," the judge said with a grin. "The problem, as I'm sure you know, is that many of the right people will not debase themselves in front of the lady from Post Office by applying. It's nothing personal; purely professional. One of the people I would consider appointing if the position were in my gift has a double first from Cambridge, a quarter of a century of extremely high-powered law behind him, and is one of the best judges we have on the Bench today. The idea that Post Office interviewing techniques—superb though they may be for ParcelForce marketing executive recruitment—are appropriate for the likes of him is not just silly, it is contemptuous. This is not a popularity contest, like the election for sheriff of a small town in Louisiana.

"The other person I would consider appointing—I am not going to name her but you should be able to guess—would not apply because she thinks she's done enough judging for one lifetime. But in my opinion she would have been ideal. She had the independence of character which is the main requisite for the top job. As a judge she was very hard-working, very smart, very Jewish, very single-minded, sod the rest of you. She was highly competent, but was socially-speaking outside the blue-nosed, old boy network, which would have been important politically. And she was clever too. She could write opinions much quicker than me. I dither about and fart around, thinking is this right, or that? But she could get them done really quickly. She would have wanted to reduce the general judicial workload. She never wanted to work all the time, which is quite a reasonable life-style decision, having regard to the fact that her husband is a dentist and they have had two incomes all these years. Their children are both away, and they've got houses in London, Tel Aviv and Edinburgh. That alone says something about her suitability. We want somebody whose horizons are a bit wider than Parliament House, Abercromby Place and the pavement between the two. But can you imagine a civil service which is paying bonuses to clerks to get judges to try more cases welcoming a Lord President who wants to *reduce* the judicial workload? To his credit, Gill would probably have taken the same view.

"And there's a third possibility that I would consider, whose identity I am not even going to hint at because this person is actually gay, and in these liberated times that is the kiss of death. Many of my colleagues consider this person one of the brightest judges we've got, and certainly one of the most professional in the sense of getting business through the courts quickly and being utterly ruthless with all those fee-grasping solicitors and advocates who make a meal of nothing at the expense of their clients—which is one of the main things that gives the courts a bad name. We desperately need judges who can reassert the authority of the Bench over these parasites. George Emslie would have had them out before breakfast. Many of us want to do something about it, but we need a lead from the top because otherwise we are out on a limb, and risk having the press come down on us like a ton of bricks for prejudicing the interests of so-called deserving litigants. Each of the three I have mentioned would take this point. But would any of them be prepared to go and get their hair cut, put a clean hankie in their pocket and line up outside the door to see our couthie little committee? I hae ma doots.

"Under the old system, you were approached by those who thought you right for the job. You did not have to put yourself forward like some kid on Opportunity Knocks. Many of the better judges we have actually refused appointment at first, but allowed themselves to be persuaded. None of those would have applied, obviously. The system we have now was designed by numpties for people of their own sort. I won't say that it is operated by numpties, that would be harsh. And I am sure they mean well, but that is not good enough.

"This is real life, especially as regards the committee to recommend the next Lord President. They need to be tough, independent people who have the breadth of experience and depth of insight into character that you find in an Alex Ferguson or a Jock Stein—there: I'm showing my age! Those guys could pick a team! That's the sort of skill we need when selecting leaders of the Scottish Supreme Court Bench, not, with all due respect, Wee Rettie and the lady from the Post Office."

"But are they the ones who are really doing the choosing?" I asked. "What about the committee of politicians?"

The judge looked out of the window for a long minute, then said thoughtfully, "I'll tell you a story which is very worrying. A colleague of mine—I won't name him either, but he's one of our more political judges—came back from a trip to London a year or so ago saying that A, B and C were about to join us. This was long before the Board had met to consider the applications of these people. One of them was a former government person whom none of us either like or respect. Sure enough, they were three of the next four appointments.

"The point we all took from that was that there were people in high places who were identifying potential judges before the Judicial Appointments Board had met. The implication was that the Board was being more or less told who to appoint. I don't know if that is true, but the mere fact that such rumours circulate is very concerning. To have this charmless, graceless individual, who is not particularly bright, on the Bench is going to do none of us any good. One of the others who was appointed at the same time was pretty feather-weight.

"Right enough, we have some oddballs from the older generation of judges, who were appointed before the new system came in, but they were mostly pretty good lawyers and they were all human beings. This new draft of politically-acceptable judges seems to me to be chosen from a different sort of person. I have to say I don't like it, though maybe that is just another sign of my advancing years. But I still think the older ones were more fun and, despite their appearance and manner, actually more down-to-earth, and more human.

"Without humanity in judges, you can't have a humane legal system. If you appoint politically-correct functionaries to the Bench you are on the high-road to computer justice. That would be the end of our tradition, one which has lasted, for better or for worse, since the middle ages. I hope I am not around to see it."

9

Passing Sentence

In the course of my research for this book, Lord McCluskey told me a story which, from my other researches, I think has general significance for the criminal justice system in Scotland. In retirement, he was involved with the society run by Lady Smith—the widow of John Smith, the Labour Party leader before Tony Blair—which promotes contact between Scotland and Russia. On one occasion, McCluskey was taking a group of young Russian lawyers round various Scottish places likely to be of professional interest to them. One was Barlinnie Prison.

McCluskey was keen to show these heirs of Ulrikh and Vyshinksy how we in Scotland manage things. There was no condescension in this. Russia has a population 28 times that of Scotland, but 140 times as many people in jail, and the conditions in Russian jails are notorious for their brutality, disease and emphasis on retribution rather than rehabilitation.[136] Having looked round the prison, McCluskey asked if he and his party might talk to some of the inmates. The Governor said that so long as the prisoners concerned agreed, he would have no objection. Accordingly half a dozen of them were presented in a meeting

---

[136] My own limited experience confirms that, having seen inside a small part of Butyrka Prison in Moscow and been shown round Shotts Prison in Lanarkshire. They are both purpose-built, maximum security establishments, though the Scottish one dates from 1978 while the Russian one from 1879 and appears to have been largely unmodernised since.

room to the half dozen Russians, who duly introduced themselves. Then McCluskey, sitting at the head of the table, asked the prisoners to give their names and state the length of their sentences. All did so, until he came to the last, sitting on him immediate right, who sat silently, looking at him quizzically.

"So, tell me, what is your name, and how long are you in for?" McCluskey asked.

"You ought to know," the prisoner said, in not unfriendly tones. "It was you who put me here!"

"We cannot have a really oppressive justice system," McCluskey commented to me, "if that kind of exchange is possible between a judge and the man he sentenced. Try to imagine the situation in Russia—or America, even!"

In the long run, any successful criminal justice system needs to reconcile the individuals it punishes to the punishment they receive. Beyond McCluskey's example, how successful is it at doing that?

I asked an ex-colleague of his, Lord Coulsfield, about sentencing policy. In retirement, Lord Coulsfield—who was one of the Lockerbie judges—led a group inquiring into the efficacy of various forms of punishment for criminals (published as *Crime, Courts and Confidence*, London 2004). He told me about how small the evidence is that sending people to jail makes any difference to society at large. Crime rates have risen over the last century—before which no reliable statistics exist—but arguably at a rate which reflects the increasing number of acts which parliament has defined as criminal. In other words, human behaviour has changed remarkably little. The re-offending rate has stayed almost unchanged over the whole period, at about 55%, a fact which argues that the policy towards criminals makes very little difference statistically. Does that mean it is pointless?

"When I was introducing our report," Lord Coulsfield told me, "I coined the phrase 'constructive pessimism'. Politicians do things like saying we are going to set ourselves a target of reducing the re-offending rate by 10% in five years: that is absolute rubbish. The rate may or may not go down, but if it does it is a pure matter of luck. But although the overall statistical picture is flat, there are plenty of success stories. There are projects which for shorter or longer periods do a lot better than the average. What we regarded as important was not to try any new forms of community penalties, or airy-fairy schemes, but just to do the simple things well. You can make a difference to individuals. That may not be important to politicians, or the tabloid press, but it is to the individuals concerned. What I am saying is pessimistic in one sense, but there is a lot that can be done for actual human beings, even if that is not going to change the world from a sociological point of view."

If Lords McCluskey and Coulsfield are right, in their different ways, the overwhelming need is not to devise different forms of punishment, or to rearrange the justice system in general, it is to increase public knowledge of how it operates, and how justice is best done in practice. The best person to talk about that is Clive Fairweather, Scotland's longest-serving Inspector of Prisons.[137]

"The vast majority of people in prison are not serious and persistent criminals," Fairweather told me, echoing many of the judges I talked to. "But those who are, you should have in prison for as long as it takes to change them. If necessary they die in there. I don't have any difficulty with that. But I have a great deal of difficulty seeing a large number of people wasting their time, their lives and yours and my resources in prison. Personally, I have nothing against the idea of chain-gangs, or youths with signs on their back saying Offender while they are clearing up the streets. I see nothing wrong with humiliation if that is necessary for rehabilitation. What I am dead against is waste, waste of time, of life, of resources, even of talent in a few cases. Our prison system is bad at preventing waste. A prisoner once said to me, 'I

---

[137] Clive Fairweather CBE grew up in Edinburgh and made his career in the Army, most dramatically when, as a member of the SAS, he was second-in-command of the team that stormed the Iranian Embassy in London in 1980. He retired as Colonel of the Scottish Division in 1994, soon after which he was appointed Chief Inspector of Prisons for Scotland in which role he was known for his efforts to make prison conditions more humane. He died in 2012.

feel as if I am sleeping my life away.' He had absolutely nothing constructive to do in prison. That is tragic. Worse than tragic, it's unnecessary."

I asked about the popular image that prisons have become humanised at the price of their deterrent value.

"Certainly prisons are less brutal than they used to be in a physical sense," Fairweather said. "But in a psychological sense, jail is still a terrible punishment. Over the eight years I was in the job, I talked to a very large number of prisoners, asking them, how are things in here? There was one feature that was absolutely common to every one that I ever spoke to. They were all to a man or a woman outraged at the fact of being locked up. It has a far more profound effect than you see on the television. There is a deep, deep resentment about their loss of liberty, no matter what they have done, no matter how much they think they deserve their sentence, and in that sense accept the way their case has been disposed of in court. No matter how much they can say, 'I killed someone and I deserve to be locked up', they resent very, very fiercely that they have no more control over their lives. I have not found, in all my time, one prisoner—not *one*—whom I could sit with who would not eventually get distorted. They are no longer capable of taking a rational view of their situation. They are prisoners, and they are not the person they were before they went into jail. Being made a prisoner lasts for an awful lot longer than they think, and long after they are released. Some are more vociferous than others. But they all have a great big stamp on their forehead. It really does mark them. Most people are marked for life."

"So why," I asked, "do you think there is such a clamour for even harsher treatment of criminals?"

"Overall, we are a very retributive society," he said. "The great question when I talk to Rotary Clubs and the like—I can see it coming from an old gent at the back with a regimental blazer on—is this: 'Don't you think it's time we brought back hanging, Mr Fairweather?' I always say to them that in 63 years, from 1900 to 1963, we hanged 35 people. In my eight years as Inspector of Prisons for Scotland 137 people killed themselves in our jails, D.I.Y! We don't need to bring back hanging. They are doing it for themselves! What more do you want?"

Fairweather's point implied that an accountable judiciary would probably be a more retributive one that we currently have, quite aside from the problem of being less responsive to the facts and circumstances of each individual case.

"There was a great trumpeting some years ago," one of the judges I talked to said to me, "when Lord Ross, who used to be the Lord Justice Clerk, organised with Strathclyde University a computer programme with all the High Court sentences in so you could look them up. You could key in rape, no previous convictions, and out would come the sentences that had been given. All my colleagues say the same, namely that when you start at the beginning you use it for a wee while, then you get the feel of it and you never look at it again. It has more or less fallen into disuse. The intention was that it would provide consistency in sentencing, but in fact we all develop our own scale."

"So judges all have an individual approach?" I asked.

"Some are severe and some are extremely lenient, and both ends are bloody-minded about it," the judge said. "The lenient ones tend to be very senior, or of the public school variety."

"The Nimmo Smiths of this world?" I asked, naming the only Old Etonian on the Scottish Bench.

"No, he's pretty mainstream. Nimmo Smith's alright.[138] He is a very conscientious judge, which is possibly why he has absolutely no sense of humour. He takes himself and his work very seriously, but he does try to do a good job, as do most of my colleagues. I have no problem with Nimmo Smith. Some of these senior chaps, like Kenny John, who is now retired, Lord Cameron of Lochbroom: he was unbelievably lenient, though an extremely nice bloke. But there is no doubt about it, sentences are now more severe than they used to be. It is partly to do with newspaper coverage, and with politicians leaping on the bandwagon. In the last ten to fifteen years, my perception is that the cry for harsher sentences has been louder than government pressure not to send

---

[138] Lord Nimmo Smith retired in 2009.

people to prison in order to save money. Governments tend to want to keep sentences up, but keep the prison population down. Every politician is completely two-faced about this. But since Mrs Thatcher—and Labour has leapt on this bandwagon too—there has been no touchy-feely, green lobby in sentencing policy. The result is longer sentences across the board. But then we are supposed to reflect what society thinks, up to a point."

I asked another judge, now retired, whether he was ever worried that he might have been accused by the press of being soft on crime.

"Personally I never had any feelings about possibly being thought to be soft," he replied. "I have no idea what people thought of my sentences. I never had any feedback at all, except for the Appeal Court. I certainly imposed long prison sentences without a qualm on people who had committed serious crimes. Equally, I put people on probation or community service, aware that I might be criticised for being too soft, also without a qualm. In Scots law there are no tariffs. You can sentence somebody for life for assault if it is bad enough, and you can equally give an absolute discharge in which there is no conviction recorded."

"Does that ever happen, in real life?" I asked.

"Oh yes! I once gave man accused of culpable homicide an absolute discharge, even though he had pled guilty. It was a very unusual case. It was a pub situation. A noisy drunk tried to provoke a perfectly decent, innocent man, but he declined to be provoked, and just moved away. When the innocent man left the pub, the obstreperous drunk followed him and started to attack him. The innocent man pushed him away forcibly and the drunk fell and hit his head on the kerb and was killed. It was charged as culpable homicide. When I heard the whole story, that it was accepted by the Crown that he had shown no ill-will to this man, and that all he had done was to give him a hard push, which wasn't unreasonable in the circumstances, I said, 'It's an absolute discharge.' That was despite his guilty plea, which was the result of thoroughly bad advice. As far as I know nobody criticised me for that."

The most extravagant exponent of the Scottish freedom in

sentencing was Sheriff Nigel Thompson, now retired, who wrote a book about his experiences on the Bench, called *In and Out of Court.* I asked another judge about Thompson's unconventional sentences.

"There is a distinction between the Sheriff Court and the High Court," the judge pointed out. "It is much easier in the High Court because we deal with rape, murder and things like that. There are very few cases in which prison is not the obvious outcome in the event of conviction. Nigel Thompson, whom I knew, was a son of the Manse, and very conscientious, but also a great showman. He used to give the most remarkable sentences, in fairly minor cases it is true, where he'd tell a chap accused of possession of a small quantity of soft drugs to go and write and essay on the harmful effects of cannabis. The chap, who'd probably never put pen to paper in his life, would be rather taken aback. But if he came back for his sentencing diet [hearing] with a half-decent essay, he'd get off with just a talking-to."

"Do you think that is a bad thing or a good thing?" I asked.

"It was an eccentric thing, and he was an eccentric. When I say 'eccentric', I mean that he was out of step with his colleagues in the sentences he passed. But he was true unto his own lights. It was a Christian upbringing he'd had. He caused amusement more than anything else. There is no reason in law why you shouldn't do what he did. But if all the sheriffs were like that the place would be full of criminals running around looking for dictionaries."

Convicted people can be surprised by conventional sentences as much as by unconventional ones, as another judge, who had been sitting in the High Court in Paisley, told me one evening over a gin and tonic during the last formal interview I conducted for this book.

"You've probably got an awful lot of serious stuff filed away," the judge said with a smile, "so, to lighten your load, I'll tell you a true story about something that happened in my court this morning. Every day this week I have had to deal, first thing, with deferred sentences for matters I have heard previously. Today I had a two-man drugs case in which both pled guilty to the being concerned with supplying. One of the men had a one-ounce bar of cannabis resin in his possession. That was all. I accepted that it was for supply to his friends, not for gain or anything like that, and I let him off with a biggish fine and a stiff warning. The second chap had a mixture of Classes A, B and C drugs, including £10,500-worth of cannabis resin, £2,500-worth of cocaine, and £3,000-worth of ecstasy. That was clearly going to be a custodial sentence. He turned up by taxi from Greenock for the sentencing diet, dead on time, which doesn't always happen. He told the driver to wait because he was only going to be in the building for a few minutes. After half an hour, the driver chap came in looking for his passenger. By then the next case was in progress and the Court was closed because there was a sexual element to it. The doors should have been guarded, but for some reason they were not. So when this guy entered the Court, the Macer immediately rushed over to put him out. The chap said to him, 'I'm looking for this man, Murdo. He was here a few minutes ago and I'm his taxi-driver. He told me to wait.' The Macer said, 'I'm afraid you're going to have to wait for three years.'"

A few weeks later, while taking tea with Ian Hamilton where he lives now in retirement by the side of a loch in north Argyll, I happened to mention this story.

"Who told you that?" he asked.

I explained that I was not at liberty to identify any of my sources, and asked, "What difference does it make, anyway?"

"I was just wondering whether to accept that interpretation of the facts rather than the more obvious one," he said.

"Which is?"

"That it was a smart way for your man to get a free ride up from Greenock."

He ignored my laughter and went on, "That is my fundamental point to you, Ian. The first rule of successful pleading is to know your judge."

6849160R00164

Printed in Great Britain
by Amazon.co.uk, Ltd.,
Marston Gate.